THE
Antigua
AND BARBUDA COMPANION

Melanie Etherington

First American edition published 2003 by

INTERLINK BOOKS
An imprint of Interlink Publishing Group, Inc.
99 Seventh Avenue, Brooklyn, New York
11215 and 46 Crosby Street, Northampton,
Massachusetts 01060
www.interlinkbooks.com

All photography by Melanie Etherington except
for page xi Jennifer Meranto; 102-3 Nathalie
Ward; 104, 106, 114, 115 EAG; 138-9
NeilKeeling.

**Library of Congress Cataloging-in Publication
Data**
Etherington, Melanie.
The Antigua and Barbuda companion / by
Melanie Etherington.
    p. cm.
ISBN 1-56656-477-8 (pbk.)
1. Antigua and Barbuda—Guidebooks. I. Title.
F2035.E84 2002
917.297404—dc21
                                          2002008863

Design by Mick Keates
Typesetting by Lisa Garth
Illustrations by IP Design
Cover photos by Melanie Etherington

Colour separation by
Tenon & Polert Colour Scanning Ltd

Printed and bound in Malaysia

To request our complete 40-page full-color
catalog, please call us toll-free at **1-800-238-LINK**,
visit our website at **www.interlinkbooks.com**,
or write to:
Interlink Publishing
46 Crosby Street, Northampton, MA 01060
e-mail: info@interlinkbooks.com

Contents

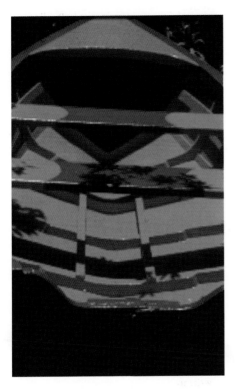

Scire ubi aliquid invenire possis,
ea demum maxima pars eruditionis est.

Knowing where you can find anything
is the largest part of knowledge.

ANONYMOUS, ROME

List of Maps

Foreword
by Sir Vivian Richards

I am very pleased to be associated with this comprehensive guide to my home country, Antigua and Barbuda. It is no secret that the twin islands enjoy an international reputation as one of the most exotic and romantic pieces of real estate on the planet. For this reason, I must congratulate the writer for her in-depth research into every aspect of the islands' past, and present, which invokes such a sweet memory of national pride.

I wish to extend my very personal invitation, not only to my fellow countrymen to use this guide as an aid to further increase their knowledge of the country's history and to discover its ever changing spots of interest, but also to all our foreign guests, who are welcomed visitors.

It is my sincere hope that the guide will prove to be a useful social and historical road map to our island and help to create a lasting, memorable taste of our side of paradise.

Welcome to Antigua
and Barbuda

– Islands of superlatives

Yes, welcome indeed to Antigua, the 'Heart of the Caribbean', and to its sister island of Barbuda.

One of the leaders of tourism in the Caribbean, these twin islands today stand out proudly, uniquely unspoilt in a world of cloned resort destinations crowded with high-rise hotels and contrived entertainments, all but destroying any trace of their culture and history.

Antigua and Barbuda jealously, zealously, protects its heritage, its natural charm and serenity, its traditional architecture, yet does not shirk from a programme of progress and evolution which includes protection of its environment. Thus these jewels of islands, sparkling on their bed of turquoise sea, can offer the visitor a rare symbiosis: the ambience of a peaceful and tranquil isle with just that gentle touch of modern amenity and sophistication.

Time seems to stand still in Antigua and Barbuda. Warmed by the tropical sun, cooled by the trade winds that whisper through the palms and the casuarinas, the islands drift along unhurriedly from day to day. The wise visitor floats along, lies back and enjoys refining the art of doing absolutely nothing, shedding the stresses and strains of life back home.

One of the special delights of a holiday in Antigua and Barbuda is that the visitor is not 'packaged'. These are not islands conducive to coach parties. Tours of the island are available, of course, and you are certainly recommended to spend some time sightseeing, but chances are you will do it yourself by rental car or with a small group of other visitors by taxi or with one of the several very professional tour companies here. In Antigua and Barbuda you are encouraged to do your own thing, at your own pace, and if that means nothing more energetic than rising from your sun lounger to avail yourself of something tall and cool in a glass from the bar – well so be it. Relax; savour and enjoy a hedonist's dream.

Antigua is world famous for its beaches – a necklace of 365 of them, one for every day of the year as is often quoted. Nobody has ever stopped to count them, but you are welcome to use as many as you like (and count them if you have the notion). All beaches, you should know, are public beaches, including hotel beaches. The beaches of Barbuda are equally famous. It's almost as if it is a beach with an island in the middle and this idyllic, timeless outpost of an isle is unquestionably well worth a visit to reveal its secluded, little known secrets.

However, it would be a shame to spend all your time imitating one of the native lizard species. As one would expect, Antigua has a wealth of water sports to offer. The scalloped shoreline guarantees beaches that are safe, secluded, and ideal not only for swimming and snorkelling, but for scuba diving, sailing, windsurfing, water skiing, paddle boats and hobie cats. Most beaches are caressed gently by the Caribbean Sea; a few, on the east coast, are pounded spectacularly by the Atlantic.

These same benevolent waters, that provide so much enjoyable sport, also provide abundant catches of fish and shellfish, all of which find their way daily to the dining room tables of hotels and restaurants: fresh, clean and deliciously prepared in a variety of styles.

There is much to do and see. Explore, and get to know the spacious, open countryside, picturesque villages and the charming and dignified people; play golf or a set of tennis, go horse riding and try a whole host of other land sports, whether as a participant or spectator. Famed for its world-class cricketers as much as for its beaches, naturally sport is high on the local agenda.

A stroll around St John's, Antigua's capital is an absolute must and a scene of amiable contrasts. Here you will find the old and the traditional often side by side with the new, yet without a clash of cultures. This is where you will find the local markets and the most stylish of modern shops and duty-free facilities, street vendors of delicious fruit, drinks and snacks, and a variety of watering holes for refreshments, breakfasts, lunches, dinners and all stops in between.

The fascinating, historic area of English Harbour is a major attraction and on most visitors' sightseeing lists. Used as a safe haven by the Royal Navy three centuries ago, Nelson's Dockyard stands testimony to the importance of this era and has been faithfully and lovingly restored, remaining as one of the Caribbean's most highly rated yacht basins. It is part of the National Parks area, all of it an environmentalist's and historian's dream.

The vibration of distinctive West Indian music can be heard virtually everywhere and you can feel the rhythm of the islands through the soles of your feet as the sounds seem to resonate from the hilltops to the valleys and deep into the earth. Street talk, heckling and laughter create street theatre and highlight the truly joyful, positive character and spirit of the people, who love nothing more than a party, illustrated by the plenitude of annual festivities and events.

So … once again, welcome to Antigua and Barbuda. The people extend their hands in greeting.

The author

Having worked, lived and travelled throughout the Caribbean for many years, Melanie Etherington chose to settle in Antigua, above all other islands. Although producing and publishing many visitor-related magazines for the island, her passion for the people and the land could not be satisfied by mere articles. Her desire to bring previously little known information and many fascinating aspects of these special islands to the widest possible audience, was the inspiration for this book.

Jennifer Meranto

Personal note

It has been my sole aim in writing this book to be able not only to make your visit here as effortless and special as possible but for you to be able to feel, see and savour just a bit of the magic to be found in these fascinating islands. It has always given me the greatest pleasure to discover unusual facts and aspects sure to bring a smile or extra excitement to a visitor's day.

It is difficult enough to enter into the spirit of an island, to appreciate its history, culture, sights and sounds on your first visit, especially when all you may well want to do is to get to your accommodation, shower and hit the beach or bar!

So, I sincerely trust that my research and experiences will help you not only to get here as stress free as possible, but to also gain an insight into these charming islands and the people you have chosen to visit. I also hope that in reading any small extract from this publication, you will be further inspired to venture out to discover these twin islands' many intriguing aspects.

The Antigua and Barbuda Companion is the culmination of many years' research and curiosity and would not have been possible without the assistance of those who guided me. It is of immense satisfaction and pleasure to have the privilege of living and working alongside the people of Antigua and Barbuda, and I shall continue to delve, question, photograph and devote time to show even more of what these beautiful and spiritually uplifting islands have to offer.

About this guide

The *Antigua and Barbuda Companion* is your guide to these islands; some of the information relates to both, some specifically to Antigua, some to Barbuda and with a mention given to Redonda.

At the front of the book are two major sections. Section 1 is designed to help you prepare for your trip and gives essential travel planning and travel tips which should be able to answer any questions you may have before leaving home. Section 2 gives essential easy reference information to familiarise you with various and useful aspects of these twin islands, allowing you to get here, settle in and get the maximum from your stay with the minimum of difficulty.

Sections 3 to 16 encompass just about every facet of Antigua and Barbuda, past and present. These cover all the major sights, attractions, flora and fauna, calendar of events and festivals, sailing, sport and recreation, island exploration, ecology, shopping, eating out, local cuisine, nightlife, buying and renting property,

investment and more, including lesser known qualities, facts and interesting snippets. Even a quick glance through the pages will enlighten you as to the abundance of fascinating, readable and tempting information contained within.

At the end of the book is a comprehensive Appendix, which lists all names, organisations, agencies, companies and their contact information which you may require both before departure and during your stay. This is followed by an Index, so finding any subject matter is made easier.

The Antigua and Barbuda Companion is more than just a basic guide book. It is intended to reflect the character of the people and islands, and to be as absorbing whilst being read in an armchair at home as when you are here on your holiday. It is packed with information to point both the first time or regular visitor, and even Antiguans and Barbudans, in the direction of the unusual as well as the more obvious, and to enable readers to glean facts not generally known about these remarkable islands.

Reader input request

Some of the information within this book is subject to constant change and so by no means can this be a definitive work. Whilst absolutely every effort has been taken to ensure factual and correct descriptive information, times, people and management change.

Therefore, I have chosen specifically not to include personal opinions of establishments

in this guide, and sincerely welcome from visitors any information, comments, experiences about Antigua and Barbuda which may aid others and help future visitors to further their enjoyment. Your letters will be considered seriously to help update future editions and will be greatly appreciated. The best ones will be awarded a free copy of the next edition.

Acknowledgements

I extend my heartfelt appreciation to the following people for their support, help and cooperation in the compilation and research for this book – and with separate and special thanks to Neil Keeling:

Sir Vivian Richards, Mrs Grathel Richards, Desmond Nicholson, Michelle Henry, E. T. Henry, Gillian Cooper, Dr Rodney Williams, Keva Margetson, David Stubbs, John Fuller, Karen Corbin, Jenny Meston, Todd Challenger, Nova Alexander, Kelcina Burton, Blanche Frank, Gillian Noel, Gerald R. Price, Warren Woodberry, Kathleen Sharpe, Madeleine Blackman, Irma Tomlinson, Louise John, Trevor Simon, Yolanda Woodberry, Noval Lindsay, Nzinga Pelle, Geoffrey Pidduck, Don Ward, Brian Stuart-Young, Ian Fraser, Stephen McGarrie, Anne-Marie Martin, Al James, Lawrence Gonsalves, John Martin, Ras Franki Tafari, Norma Prudhon, Annette Michael, Vernon Harrigan, Michael Rose – and all those friends who gave me encouragement to continue in this lengthy quest!

Thanks also to those individuals who helped me whilst working on the ever increasing and evolving information required for this guide book and on the subsequent checking, verification and accuracy: Alison Archer, Marie Diedrick, Agnes Meeker, Valerie Hodge and Milton Shapiro.

The author and publisher wish to thank the following for permission to use copyright material:

Edward Kamau Brathwaite: from 'Rites' from *The Arrivants: A New World Trilogy* (Oxford University Press, 1973). Reprinted by permission of the publisher.

Paul Keens-Douglas: 'Pan Rap' from *Tanti at de Oval. Selected works of Paul Keens-Douglas, Volume 1* (Keensdee Productions, 1982), 1981 Paul Keens-Douglas. Reprinted by permission of the author.

National Anthem of Antigua and Barbuda. (Words by Novelle H. Richards; Music by Walter P. Chambers). Reprinted by kind permission of the Antigua and Barbuda High Commission of London.

Every effort has been made to trace all copyright holders, but if any have been inadvertently overlooked, the author and publisher will be pleased to make the necessary arrangement at the first opportunity.

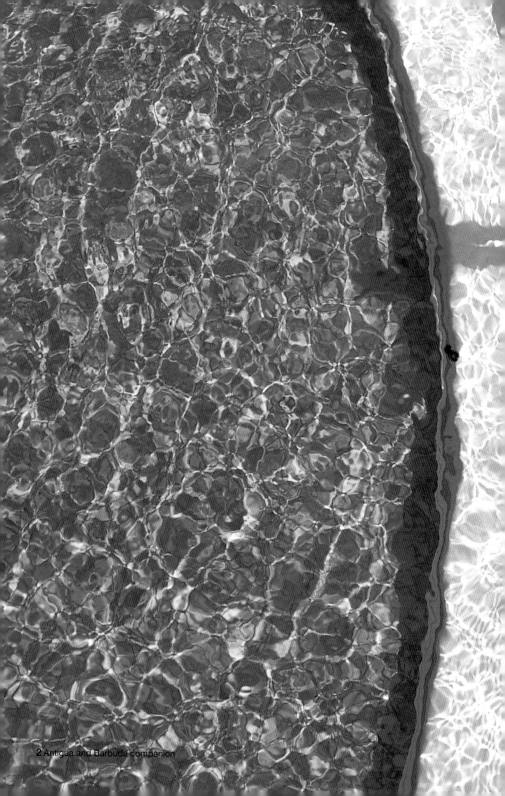

Pre-departure travel tips

and essential information for travel planning
– making dreams into reality –
preparations for booking and departure

TOURIST OFFICES

Considerable media exposure about Antigua and Barbuda, through travel articles in newspapers, magazines and television programmes, expound the virtues and facts about these islands but, should you wish for further information, you may like to contact the tourist office in your home country. All of these offices should also have a CD-ROM available.

Canada: tel: (1) 416 961 3085
fax: (1) 416 961 7218
e-mail: info@antigua-barbuda-ca.com
France: tel: (33) 1 53 75 1571
fax: (33) 1 53 75 1569
Germany: tel: (49) 61 72 21504
fax: (49) 61 72 21513
e-mail: antigua-barbuda@karibik.org
web site:
www/antigua-barbuda.karibik.org
Italy: tel/fax: (39) 02 877983
USA
Miami: tel: (1) 305 381 6762
fax: (1) 305 381 7908
e-mail: embantbar@aol.com
New York: tel: (1) 212 541 4117
fax: (1) 212 757 1607
Toll Free: 888 268 4227
e-mail: info@antigua-barbuda.org
web site: www.antigua-barbuda.org
Washington DC: tel: (1) 202 362 5122
fax: (1) 202 362 5225
Toll Free: (0) 888 268 4227
United Kingdom: tel: (44) 207 486 7073 fax: (44) 207 486 1466
e-mail: antbar@msn.com

The local tourist office in St John's, Antigua will help you once you are here.
Antigua and Barbuda: Lower Nevis Street, PO Box 363, St John's
tel: (268) 462 0480/462 0029
fax: (268) 462 2483/462 6093
e-mail: deptourism@candw.ag
Antigua Hotels and Tourist Association: Island House, Newgate Street, St John's
tel: (268) 462 0374 fax: (268) 462 3702
e-mail: ahta@candw.ag
Antigua Independent web sites:
www.antiguanice.com
www.AntiguaToday.com
www.AntiguaToday.com/Island Arts
www.Cinesecrets.com

CLIMATE

Antigua has an impeccably benign climate, balmy tropical weather and steady year-round temperatures, hovering around 80°–85°F (27°–30°C) during the day. Even more attractive, the island is also blessed with wonderful northeasterly trade-wind breezes to cool and refresh.

Traditionally, the cooler winter months from November to April have little or no daily rainfall, with around nine hours of daily sunshine, and refreshing evenings. Only varying slightly, the sporadically cloudy and rainier summer season is between May and October, but still offering up to seven hours of daily sunshine. Antigua has a notably low annual rainfall, but tropical showers are nothing to fear anyway, as they typically fall hard and fast and then stop abruptly, when everything dries out rapidly. They are surprisingly localised, with rain often seen falling at one end of a street or beach – and not at the other!

Whilst the weather vagaries of today and intermittent years subject to the El Niño phenomenon have, as elsewhere in the world, affected the islands' normal climatic patterns and rainfall, you can, nevertheless, still be sure of plenty of that healing Antiguan sun to warm you.

Very occasionally, the Caribbean can experience tropical storms or hurricanes, which may occur between July and October. However, the island in general is always well prepared with sophisticated early warning systems (as are the airlines and airports), and hotels and villas are built to withstand such unlikely events. It has to be said, though, that due to such atmospheric pressures, August and September can sometimes witness more downpours and be more humid, although this never detracts families from flocking to Antigua during this time when the children are off school.

TIME ZONE

Antigua is in the Atlantic time zone, four hours behind Greenwich Mean Time (thus, not accounting for daylight-saving variations, when it is 8am in Antigua, it is noon in the UK).

It is one hour ahead of Eastern Standard Time in the United States (i.e. 8am in Antigua would be 9am in New York). However, during daylight-saving time, the time in the eastern United States is identical to Antigua.

With respect to time and time keeping, it is interesting to note that whilst the island can tend to run on 'Antigua time', with a fairly relaxed attitude to promptness of business appointments (or even maintaining them), restaurant bookings and social engagements, the taxi drivers are sticklers for arriving on the very dot of the time booked. Just relax into this island way and as we say here, 'relax and go with the flow!'

LANGUAGE

English is the official language. Whilst generally perfectly understandable, when asking locals for directions or if out in the countryside, you may well hear English spoken with the local musical lilt, and not necessarily grasp what is being said (see also Antiguan Sayings and Proverbs, page 248).

MONEY

CURRENCY

Antigua and Barbuda's official currency is the Eastern Caribbean (EC) dollar, issued by the Eastern Caribbean Central Bank (ECCB) and is the common currency of the Organisation of Eastern Caribbean States (OECS). This is linked to the US dollar, which is also widely accepted, at the fixed rate of US$ 1 to EC$ 2.67 (shops and restaurants may only give you EC$ 2.60). As currencies can fluctuate, it is probably advisable to travel with US dollar cash or traveller's cheques for the best rate of exchange (when buying foreign currency in Antigua there is a 1 per cent government levy).

There is no restriction on the amount of money brought in, or taken out, and most hotels can change currency. Money can also be changed at the many banks in the capital, St John's, with various branches at English Harbour, Jolly Harbour, the airport and Friar's Hill Road, just north of St John's (see Appendix for individual banking hours and services, page 312).

When booking a taxi, charter, guide or any other service, always confirm whether the currency quoted is the local EC dollar or the US dollar.

COSTS

If you are on an all-inclusive holiday, you are only likely to need money for souvenirs, gifts and personal items, all of which are reasonably priced, and for any additional island or off-island tours (and not forgetting the departure tax of EC$ 50).

Bars and restaurants vary in price range, as anywhere else in the world, and in the main are quoted in EC dollars. There are plenty of 'happy hours' for drink bargains, and eating out varies from the local rum shop to the finest gourmet cuisine imaginable (see pages 282 and 259).

For those self-catering visitors, there are plenty of well-stocked supermarkets (the larger ones may accept credit cards) for fresh, dried and tinned provisions, some huge and air conditioned and others resembling a corner shop. Certain items may be more costly than you are used to simply because of the shipping and high import costs; however, in general, there is no great difference. Local fruit and vegetables are not only very reasonably priced, they are wonderfully fresh and wholesome, compared with the sometimes questionable produce arriving in huge containers from the US.

Certainly, the greatest bargains are the ranges of top-name alcoholic spirits and tobacco at unbelievably low prices.

CREDIT CARDS/TRAVELLER'S CHEQUES
Most shops, restaurants, hotels, car hire, yacht charter and sightseeing companies accept major credit cards and the universally accepted traveller's cheques (eurocheques are not accepted anywhere on the island). American Express is the official card of Antigua, offering various services to cardholders through its local representative, Antours.

Remember though, you will still need cash for some small hotels, guesthouses, local restaurants, bars, petrol, markets, vendors, and for tipping.

American Express
c/o Antours, St John's
tel: (268) 462 4788 fax: (268) 462 4799
web site: www.americanexpress.com

WHEN TO GO
Anytime is a good time. Much will depend on your own schedule and the schedules of those travelling with you and Antigua remains a sublime place to visit from one end of the year to the other. Since it is, fortunately, not an over-commercialised island, as are many others, you will not have to suffer from crowds of tourists at any time of the year. Naturally, the inclement North American and European winter weather conditions encourage many thousands to seek refuge on Antigua and Barbuda's shores and therefore these months are very busy. Flight bookings should be made well in advance, and due to such demand flights and accommodation are likely to be more costly. But for many, the lure of warm hedonistic days are more than compensation; it's all a question of balance.

The summer months offer better deals and easier availability of flights, cruises, charter yacht bookings, and accommodation (although Easter and August can see more family bookings and be busier), and Antigua is more relaxed after the main winter 'season'. Consequently, it is during these months that there are more festivals, international events, local exhibitions and, of course, the celebrations of Carnival. All involve locals and visitors, presenting great opportunities to sample local food, drinks, music, heritage and culture, and to view or partake in island traditions.

So you may like to consider planning your trip around the world famous Classic Yacht Regatta, Antigua Sailing Week, International Test Cricket, Carnival and International Hot Air Balloon Festival events, amongst others, or the Sportsfishing Tournament, Powerboat Race, Model Boat Race Competition, Mountain Bike Race, varied music festivals, and more (see Calendar of Events page 70). The choice is yours and you will be more than welcome at any time.

PUBLIC HOLIDAYS
(see Calendar of Events, page 70)
New Year's Day 1 January
Good Friday late March/early April
Easter Monday ditto
Labour Day first Monday in May
Whit Monday eighth Monday after Easter
Caricom Day first Monday in July
Carnival Monday first Monday in August
Carnival Tuesday first Tuesday in August
Independence Day 1 November
Christmas Day 25 December
Boxing Day 26 December

GETTING THERE AND TRAVELLING TO AND FROM ANTIGUA AND BARBUDA

BY AIR
International services
Most international and inter-island visitors will arrive by air. Antigua has long been regarded as the international travel hub of the eastern Caribbean and as such enjoys frequent international, charter and regional carriers from North and South America, Canada, the UK and continental Europe.

Among the major scheduled and chartered airlines with a direct service to Antigua are: Air 2000, Air Canada, Air Europe, American Airlines, Balair, British Airways, Britannia, BWIA, Canada 3000, Condor, Continental, Miami Air, Royal Air, Skyservice, TWA, Virgin Atlantic. Other airlines which link Antigua, via other islands in the Caribbean, with Europe, Canada, United States or South America are: Air France, American Eagle, Delta, Guyana Airways, Iberia, KLM, North West, TWA, United Airlines and US Air.

Approximate flying times: New York – 4 hrs; Washington DC – 4 hrs; Miami – 3 hrs; Baltimore – 5 hrs; Toronto – 4¹/₂ hrs; Puerto Rico – 1 hr; Caracas – 2¹/₂ hrs; London 8 hrs; Paris – 8 hrs; Frankfurt – 9¹/₂ hrs; Zurich – 9¹/₂ hrs.

Inter-island services
Barbuda
If you decide to arrange a visit to Antigua's idyllic sister isle of Barbuda (see page 297), whether before you leave home or whilst you are in Antigua, it is easily done, directly or through your travel agent. Either privately charter a small plane (see Appendix page 312) or book a scheduled flight with Carib Aviation for this short hop from Antigua. Day trips are also available (see Travel Agents in the Appendix, page 320).

Regional
As Antigua is so favourably positioned within the Caribbean chain of islands, it is well worth taking advantage of its easy access to other islands in the region. Island hoppers are well catered for with both private charter and scheduled local and regional airlines (see Appendix, page 312).

Established and based in Antigua for over 40 years is LIAT (from the original name of Leeward Islands Air Transport), serving around 19 destinations regularly, as far as Trinidad, South America and Puerto Rico. With many day-trip options to neighbouring islands, they can even get you back in time for dinner in Antigua, if you wish (see later in this section, Purchasing Air Tickets and Airfares and check Travel Agents in the Appendix, page 320). They offer a range of small aircraft from the 37-seater sleek DHC 8-100 (Dash 8), to the DHC 8-300 aircraft with a 50-seat capacity.

The newly formed airline, Caribbean Star, has a fleet of De Havilland Dash 8 aircraft, both the 100 and 300 series. Commencing operations in the summer of 2000 they service 12 islands.

BWIA (pronounced 'Beewee'), the national airline of Trinidad and Tobago, with international routes, also flies to most of the larger Caribbean islands and South America, for those wishing to go further afield. Exceptionally easy to arrange, it need not be expensive to take a day out to see more of the region (see also Ferry/Local boat runs, page 14).

PURCHASING AIR TICKETS AND AIRFARES
To Antigua
For those who choose to book a tour operator package holiday, naturally, the air fare would be included, unless otherwise stated. Similarly, a package trip including Barbuda would include the onward connection and short flight.

For the independent traveller, international airfares to Antigua fluctuate tremendously depending upon time of year, class of travel, whether charter airline or scheduled, and many last-minute bargains are available all year round. Modern computer and television technology can access most of these special offers, but be sure to check the details carefully as some may have minimum and maximum stays and advance purchase conditions to take into account. Alternatively, check with a reliable travel agency for the latest fares, purchase requirements and conditions to suit your itinerary and budget.

Regional inter-island
To book regional inter-island travel, there are several options. Booking a private air charter is straightforward enough, whereupon you will be quoted a price dependent upon your destination and whether you wish for a totally private charter or could share a charter (number of people being booked). This serves as cost effective for personal service, to suit your schedule and requirements and ensure reliable time-keeping (see Appendix page 312).

With a scheduled inter-island airline such as LIAT (see also Regional under Inter-island services on this page), the 'Airpass', for instance, which allows travellers from Europe to stop over at between three and six destinations anywhere within the LIAT network (from Puerto Rico in the north to Port of Spain, Trinidad and Georgetown, Guyana, in the south), is valid for 21 days, but must be purchased in Europe in conjunction with an international ticket to the Caribbean, with firm reservations being made at the time of booking.

Their 'Explorer' offers three stopovers, also to be purchased outside of the Caribbean, with no change in itinerary allowed. It is valid for 21 days, returning to the point of origin to connect with your international flight.

Once here, you can still book their 'Super Explorer', which offers unlimited travel for 30 days throughout the entire LIAT network covering all destinations. Enquire about their thrift fares, group fares and special offers through a travel agent or local LIAT office.

Whether private or shared charter, LIAT, BWIA or any other airline serving the region, discuss the island of your choice with your travel agent at home, or once here, with your tour representative, or through the many reputable travel agencies on the island (see Appendix for listings, page 320). The advantage of not booking independently is that the flight, arrival arrangements, lunch, extensive sightseeing and accommodation options, if desired, can all be arranged and tailor-made for you.

However, you can, of course, also organise your trip in true explorer fashion by booking directly with the airline of your choice. Do check for any special deals, combination trips and discounts for senior citizens, which may be available (see Appendix for full airline listings, page 312).

AIRPORT
Antigua
The island's sole airport, V. C. Bird International Airport (named in 1985, in recognition of the then Prime Minister, the Rt. Hon. Vere Cornwall Bird Sr, also First Chief Minister and First Premier, affectionately called 'father of the nation') is located in the northeastern part of the island, just five miles east of the capital, St John's. The 9000-foot runway accommodates all types of aircraft from the smallest single-engine to large commercial jets and Concorde and its well-designed, modern terminal features the latest in air-traffic control technology.

The ground floor hosts APUA and Cable & Wireless coin and card phones, a 24-hour phone card machine, car rental booths, taxi rank, post office, bank, ATM and a snack and liquor shop; the first floor has an observation deck, security, administration, airline and meteorological offices, an excellent full service air-conditioned restaurant and bar (so good, people from St John's lunch there), plus the 17°61° Executive Lounge.

The many facilities of this VIP lounge are available to first-class passengers of BWIA, British Airways, Air Canada and Condor; American Express also offers access to this comprehensively equipped, private lounge for its gold and platinum cardholders. It can also be made available to other guests at a charge.

V. C. Bird International Airport
tel: (local calls) 462 3084/4672
fax: 462 0642
17°61° Executive Lounge
tel: (268) 480 6981/6976
fax: (268) 480 6999

Barbuda

The Codrington airport building houses a ticketing and check-in desk, but with all flights going to and from Antigua and being under the same jurisdiction, immigration and customs are not required here.

Codrington Airport
tel: local calls 480 5849
fax: local calls 480 5849

ARRIVING BY AIR
To Antigua
Visitors by plane will fly into V. C. Bird International Airport, a modern international terminal where straight-forward arrival procedures follow the norm.

After passing through immigration (see also Entry Requirements, Immigration and Customs, page 9), you will inevitably be met by a neat row of smartly dressed 'Red Cap' porters vying for your custom. Brightly dressed in red and yellow uniforms, they are often found standing behind their trolleys and

are very helpful and polite. Their take home pay largely relies on carrying your baggage, so they whisk you through the obligatory customs desks, keen to get back to the next awaiting visitor. There is a standard charge of US$ 1 per bag, but many visitors pay more for the privilege of what is normally an excellent service.

There is a large Antigua and Barbuda Department of Tourism counter, accessible whilst waiting for your luggage to come through, where all manner of questions and bookings can be dealt with, along with the availability of various tourist literature and flyers. It is also here where you would be met by your holiday tour representative, should you have booked an all-inclusive package.

Once outside the airport arrival hall, there is a branch of the Antigua Commercial Bank where you can change money (see Appendix, Banking Hours and Services, page 312), plus a Royal Bank of Canada

ATM which accepts most major credit cards.

Those on pre-booked holiday packages are escorted to pre-booked taxis for transfer to their hotels, and independent travellers will find taxis immediately as they exit. The government have authorised an EC dollar (and US dollar) based list of standard taxi fares island-wide, and this is on display for your verification.

Should you wish to hire a car immediately upon arrival, you will find agents for many internationally recognised and local rental com-panies, to your right just outside the arrivals exit (see also Public Trans-port, page 40).

To Barbuda
Upon arrival at the small Codrington airport, if you have not made previ-ous arrangements, there is often someone there willing to help you with transport to the beach, who can arrange an island tour, or help with accommodation (see Appendix, page 320).

LEAVING ANTIGUA
DEPARTURE TAX – IMPORTANT!
There is a departure tax for all visitors staying for more than 24 hours, leaving on domestic or international flights. It is EC$ 50 or US$ 20 (children under 16 years are exempt); citizens from CARICOM (Caribbean) countries pay EC$ 35 or US$ 14. All are payable at the check-in counter at the airport when you present your copy of the immigration form, retained from when you first arrived. So be sure to put this fee aside from the start of your holiday, before you spend it! (It may be included in pre-booked package tours.)

General advice
Remember to ensure that you, the hotel receptionist or your tour representative reconfirm your flight at least 72 hours before departure (see Appendix for local contact details of all airlines).

It is advisable to check in at least two hours before your departure time (don't forget you need to hand back the copy of the immigration form you completed upon arrival), firstly to avoid being a casualty on an over-booked flight or where, in high season, people are on stand-by and secondly to secure a seat of your choice.

There is a good shop landside for a variety of last minute purchases, the post office for last minute sending (there is no facility inside the departure lounge, and neither is there one for changing money); upstairs, there is a highly-recommended air-conditioned bar and restaurant, with a First and Business class travellers lounge (see Airport earlier in this section). APUA and Cable & Wireless coin and card telephone boxes are available on both floors.

Once in the departure lounge, there is an excellent choice of duty-free shops, more telephone call boxes, and a cafeteria bar available.

Photographic film and computer disks
Upon going through to the departure lounge, it is strongly recommended for those travelling with fast or professional photographic film in hand luggage (or even normal speed film) and floppy disks that you remove these from your bag or briefcase and place them in the basket provided at the side of the X-ray machine.

Experience has shown most X-ray machines which screen hand luggage in these parts can fog camera film and corrupt disks – and of course as it is even stronger, don't put such items in your pocket and then walk through the X-ray arch! Despite any possible assurances to the contrary, it's simply not worth taking any unnecessary risks and losing out on the time and trouble taken to produce such precious holiday memories, or those important business documents on disk.

**ENTRY REQUIREMENTS/
IMMIGRATION/CUSTOMS**
British, US, Canadian, South American (most countries), the Commonwealth and most West European citizens do not need a visa, but others do. These are Haiti, China, Iraq, India, Pakistan, North Korea, South Africa, Bulgaria, the Czech Republic, and countries of the former USSR, to name some. Contact the Antigua and Barbuda High Commission for further information.

US and Canadian residents need only proof of identity (with a photograph); a birth certificate or voter's registration card (not just a driving licence) will suffice, although a passport is preferable.

Citizens of the United Kingdom, other European Union countries, British Commonwealth countries, Australia, New Zealand, South America (Argentina, Brazil, Colombia, Mexico, Peru, Venezuela), Japan and CARICOM countries require a passport.

Therefore, all other citizens will need both a passport and a visa (unless in transit for no longer than 24 hours). All passports require at least six months' validity at the time of arrival. Bring a current driving licence if you plan to hire a car.

The first Antiguans you will meet will be the immigration officials who, contrary to the traditional approach often received elsewhere, make an effort to be pleasant and friendly. They will need to see your onward ticket and date of departure, without which you are likely to be refused entry (obviously with the exception of nationals and those with Antiguan citizenship).

The airline you arrived on should give you a carbonised immigration form to complete. You will need to hand this over as a matter of formality, having completed your personal and home details, and your address whilst on the islands. Immigration will retain the original and give your passport back with the stamped carbon copy, which must be kept and surrendered at the time of checking-in to depart (see previous page, Leaving Antigua). Immigration will only stamp you for up to three weeks' duration on the island; if you wish to stay longer, you will have to pre-arrange an extension at Police Headquarters on American Road, St John's.

Canada: Antigua and Barbuda Department of Tourism and Trade
tel: (1) 416 961 3085
fax: (1) 416 961 7218
e-mail: info@antigua–barduda–ca.com
UK: Antigua and Barbuda High Commission
tel: (44) 207 486 7073/5
fax: (44) 207 486 9970
e-mail: antbar@msn.com

US: Embassy of Antigua and Barbuda
tel: (1) 202 362 5122
fax: (1) 202 362 5225
e-mail:embantbar@aol.com

Customs

Having collected your luggage, you will pass through customs and officials will offer no departures from the norm in asking how long you are staying on the island, where you are staying and what is in your bags. Assuming you are an innocent visitor, customs clearance is immediate and you simply proceed outside. (Each adult is allowed 200 cigarettes or 50 cigars or half a pound of pipe tobacco, together with two 26 oz bottles of wine or spirits and five ounces of perfume.)

However, all luggage is subject to inspection as naturally it is the customs' job to decide if you are carrying goods to sell on the island, or duty-able goods, and to charge duty accordingly, and whether you are carrying anything strictly forbidden from the usual list of illegal imports, such as drugs or firearms. However relaxed you may think island life is, it certainly isn't when it comes to the last items – don't even think about bringing either in; the consequences are far too dire.

Plants, flowers and fruit are unwelcome on most Caribbean islands, and Antigua is no exception in order to protect crops from foreign pests and diseases. If you do wish to bring such items into the country, you must first obtain a phytosanitary certificate from the originating country's ministry of agriculture to present to customs in Antigua.

Vaccinations

No specific immunisation or vaccination certificates are required for Antigua, and the vast majority of visitors do not require any vaccination treatment, particularly as most will have had immunisation against the major diseases during childhood. Nevertheless, there are the over-cautious Western medical practitioners who, strictly speaking, could advise the full range against polio, typhoid, tetanus and hepatitis A. For quite a few visitors, previous visits to other countries such as India, to name one, would have required these inoculations anyway. Antigua and Barbuda are classed as low-risk areas, having no modern record of malaria, typhoid, dysentery or other common tropical diseases, but clearly, if you would feel happier, ask your family doctor's advice at least four weeks prior to leaving.

BY SEA
Cruise ships
Cruise ship lines
Not surprisingly, Antigua is included in most schedules of the main cruise lines visiting the Caribbean. However, they normally only stay for the day or for a few hours, allowing just enough time for a quick abridged island tour. Some cruise-ship companies offer a fly-and-cruise option, affording up to a week's stay in Antigua.

Some of the major cruise lines calling at Antigua are: Arcalia Shipping, Carnival Cruise Lines, Celebrity, Club Med, Costa Cruises, Cunard, Deutsche Seetouristik, US Festival Cruises, Holland America, Louis Cruise Line, Majestic Cruise Lines, Norwegian Cruises, P & O Lines, Princess Cruises, Royal Caribbean, Royal Olympic, Seabourn, s/c Keruzfahrten, GmbH, Star Clipper, Sun Cruises, Windjammer.

The gracious schooner *Sea Cloud* makes its home port in Antigua during the winter season, offering one- or two-week Caribbean cruises; the stunning *Star Clipper* is also based here during the winter, with one- or two-week holidays available. Contact the cruise lines direct, or see your travel agent and pick up a brochure for sailing dates to Antigua and their respective package-cruise deals.

Cruise ship ports
The major cruise lines dock at either St John's Deepwater Harbour, or at the super-dredged Heritage Quay facility in St John's, which means that cruise-ship passengers are actually delivered to the door of the island's superb duty-free shopping complex and casino. To stand even only a short distance away on one of the streets facing the waterfront stimulates the imagination, as one of today's huge, modern cruise liners towers above the tiny, colourful local buildings, as if parked at the very end of the road!

Yacht/cargo ships

Many from the yachting fraternities of the UK, Europe and America make their annual pilgrimage to the Caribbean, especially to Antigua and Barbuda, famed for their abundance of excellent anchorages, uninhabited isles, cays (small archipelagos) and bays. It is often possible to pick up a yacht sailing here, following the traditional summer season in the Mediterranean, which will generally return after Antigua Sailing Week in May.

Unless on a yacht, options for travelling across the Atlantic independently to the Caribbean are very limited. There are cargo ships available, such as the four director-class ships of the Geest Line, which depart from Southampton, UK. Taking anything up to 14 days one-way, it is a grand way to travel on a working cargo ship, enabling six passengers on each trip to sample the ship's busy schedule, whilst enjoying the langurous journey. Passengers are free to take off and sample local delights from a range of ten islands. Albeit with limited berths and facilities, the demand for sailing in the old traditional way can create long waiting lists for their weekly passages (fortnightly to Antigua), so booking ahead is advisable.

Cargo Ship Voyages
tel: (44) 1473 736265

Yacht chartering

Whether crewed or bareboat, yacht chartering's popularity in general has increased immensely, and Antigua's ideal weather conditions continue to make it a first choice.

The exotic image of sailing around warm, blue tropical waters, drink in hand, feeling and looking a million dollars is further enhanced by comparatively reasonable rates, and the more of you, the cheaper per person. Whilst winter is the 'high season', early summer charters are very popular due to the perfect sailing conditions created after the northerly swells and before any tropical storms and the 'hurricane' season.

A popular landfall since Nelson's days, situated directly on the trade-wind path from Europe to the West Indies, Antigua provides a safe and perfect cruising base, nestled as it is, in the heart of the Caribbean.

The incredible rise in ocean-going yachts and sailing vessels from the region to Antigua's various anchorages and full-service marinas has resulted in a substantial increase in facilities and Antigua boasts a fabulous combination of services for yachtsmen and women (see Marinas, Appendix, page 319).

Varying with the season, size, type, berths and so on, you can charter a yacht or motor cruiser in Antigua, with either a travel agent or chartering company in your home country, or with one of the specialist charter companies in Antigua.

Day chartering
Should you wish to privately charter

a yacht for day sailing around Antigua, to the many special outer islands or to neighbouring sister isle Barbuda, there are yacht charter companies which can arrange such a trip to suit all your requirements. For pre-organised, regular day tours on other types of sailing vessels and boats, see Day Cruising Tours, page 162.

Local yacht charter companies
Antigua Yacht Charters
tel: (268) 463 7101 fax: (268) 463 8744
e-mail: marlowl@candw.ag
web sites: www.caribbeansail.com
and www.classiccharters.com
and antiguayachtcharters.com

Nicholson Yacht Charters
tel: (268) 460 1530/1523/1059
fax: (268) 460 1531
e-mail: nicholson@candw.ag
web site: www.finestyachts.com

Sun Yacht Charters and Stardust Charters
tel: (268) 460 2615 fax: (268) 460 2616

e-mail: charterservices@candw.ag
web site: www.sunyachts.com

Sunsail Club Colonna
tel: (268) 462 6263 fax: (268) 462 6430
e-mail: colonna@candw.ag
web site: www.sunsail.com

Ports of entry
There are four main customs stations or ports of entry for sailors to Antigua: St John's Deepwater Harbour, Heritage Quay, Jolly Harbour, and English Harbour.

The skipper of any yacht entering Antigua and Barbuda must produce clearance papers from the last port of call. On arrival at the chosen port of entry, the skipper (only) must clear customs and immigration. Once cleared and entry fees paid, the skipper will obtain a cruising permit, enabling the boat to sail in Antiguan and Barbudan waters for up to a month, and which is renewable.

All crew members must have a valid passport or relevant iden-

tification (see Entry Requirements, page 9). plus a valid airline ticket to their next destination if not sailing out on the same yacht. Crew members are not allowed to transfer to a different vessel, unless it is just leaving or, if it is remaining in Antigua, without prior approval from customs and immigration.

After harbour dues have been paid, outward clearance of the yacht is granted on the day of departure.

Barbuda has one small customs station, but cruising permits are not available, so yachts must clear customs in Antigua first.

Barbuda
Customs, Codrington
tel: (268) 460 0085
Immigration, Codrington
tel: (268) 460 0074/0354

English Harbour
Port authority tel: (268) 460 9824
VHF channel 16
Customs and immigration
tel: (268) 460 1397 VHF channel 16

Heritage Quay, St John's
Customs and immigration
tel: (268) 462 6403 VHF channel 16

Jolly Harbour
Port authority tel: (268) 462 7931
VHF channel 16
Customs and immigration
tel: (268) 462 7929/32
VHF channel 16

St John's Deepwater Harbour:
Port authority tel: (268) 462 0050/51
VHF channel 16

Port manager tel: (268) 462 2239
Customs and immigration
tel: (268) 462 0814
VHF channel 16

Antigua and Barbuda coastguard
tel: (268) 462 0671 VHF channel 16

Ferry/local boat runs
Although slow and basic, it is possible to catch a very inexpensive ride to **Barbuda** on one of the cargo boats out of the Point Wharf dock at the end of Newgate Street, St John's, which makes its four-hour run from Antigua to River Wharf, Barbuda with stocks and provisions. The three boats: *Lady Mary*, *Concorde* and *Enterprise*, don't operate to a strict timetable but tend to leave the wharf once fully loaded. Do note that as these vessels are traditional working boats: there are no facilities on board, so prepare for the trip with at least some drinks, a hat and vital sunscreen. However, it is an adventurous form of travel and a pleasant way to meet local people whilst sitting on deck. The River

Wharf dock in Barbuda is three miles from Codrington, so a lift or onward transport would ideally have to be arranged.

For those interested in visiting the small remaining safe area of the volcano devastated island of **Montserrat**, a daily ferry, the *Opale Express*, a first-class high speed catamaran capable of carrying 200 persons with luggage, operates six days per week, Monday to Saturday. Journey time is one hour, leaving Heritage Quay, St John's, daily at 6.30am and 4pm (check in one hour before at the office at the rear of the Heritage Quay Hotel).

The return journey from Montserrat to Antigua, departs Little Bay Jetty at 8am and 5.30pm, Monday to Saturday. This vital link provides a regular crossing to and from Antigua for the still somewhat beleaguered Montserratian residents to purchase extra foodstuffs and supplies. Tickets need not be purchased in advance, but passengers should report one hour before departure each way.

The Montserrat Ferry Service
Carib World tel: (268) 480 2990
fax: (268) 480 2995
e-mail: arthurtonp@candw.ag
web site: www.carib-world.com

BOOKING A HOLIDAY

PACKAGE TOURS
For many wishing to visit Antigua and Barbuda, the convenience of purchasing a package tour from the plethora of general and specialist tour operators available can be very

attractive and alleviates all holiday worries and concerns. In many cases, as tour operators have such strong bargaining power, both with airlines and hotels, they are able to offer a package tour holiday for less than it would cost the independent traveller.

INDEPENDENT TRAVEL
Travelling independently allows for greater freedom, flexibility and non-conformity. Not everyone wishes to stay at a tourist hotel, possibly bumping into people they saw on the plane, or who oft times coincidentally even live nearby them at home – accessible travel makes the world a surprisingly small one these days. Naturally, staying at small inns and guest houses and travelling off-season is the most economical option for the non-package visitor. Travellers who usually frequent the middle or top end of the market will be used to negotiating their own rates.

All hotel rates are subject to a 10 per cent service charge and 8.5 per cent government tax. Many visitors take advantage of the 'modified American plan' (MAP), which is breakfast with dinner, whilst those wishing the option of dining elsewhere can choose the breakfast plan (CP) or room only (EP). There is also the 'full American plan' (FAP) which offers three meals per day.

It is always advisable to book accommodation in advance, particularly during the high season (winter). Of course, as travel agents obtain their livelihood from the fees gained from airline, cruise and hotel companies they book on behalf of their customers, you could find them a convenient, time and cost efficient method. When booking flights, remember to ask for a computer print out of all the check-in details and so on to be sent with your tickets and when booking accommodation, remember to ask for confirmation by fax or post, so that you have it to present upon arrival. Try to notify wherever you are staying if you are going to be delayed, as, in common with elsewhere in the world, reservations may not always be held after 6pm, unless otherwise notified.

ACCOMMODATION GUIDELINES

Antigua and Barbuda have such a wonderful balance of accommodation that even the most fastidious will find the perfect place to stay. Whether absolutely first class and luxurious to small, intimate or local, all-inclusive or not, there are resorts, hotels, inns, guest houses, self catering villas, apartments and cottages awaiting. Some have every internationally accepted facility available; others have none. Whereas some are very modern, others have an old world Caribbean charm. Most are situated on or near one of the renowned beaches, though some are in town or in the country. You could literally describe your choice and find it here.

One aspect you won't find is wall-to-wall blocks of apartment houses and hotels; or vast impersonal resorts rambling over huge, bland areas. This delightful twin-island state is well known for exceedingly well-spaced accommodation, often amongst lovingly tended, landscaped gardens,

with room to breathe and savour your tropical surroundings.

Barbuda has two extremely exclusive hotels, but caters to other visitors with a mid-range hotel and several small, informal guest houses.

There are no youth hostels or official camping sites on either island. However, for those who have the equipment and wish to camp, enquiries can be made with Mr Hugh Piggott at Orange Valley (see page 190), although facilities there are limited and this unspoilt area is about a mile from the main road.

To gain as much information as possible, regularly check travel sections of newspapers, the many travel journals which abound, browse through travel agent brochures and tour operator magazines, 'surf' the Internet, or contact your local tourist office with your requirements.

Further detailed information can also be obtained from the Antigua Hotels and Tourist Association in Antigua (see page 315 for full hotel listings).

Antigua and Barbuda Hotels and Tourist Association
tel: (268) 462 0374
fax: (268) 462 3702
e-mail: ahta@candw.ag
web site: www.antol.ag

GETTING MARRIED

Antigua and Barbuda have regularly been named amongst the world's top ten tourism destinations for weddings and honeymoons. Small and large hotels offer a variety of very attractive wedding and honeymoon packages, increasingly popular when the entire package including air fares can be substantially cheaper than the cost of a wedding at home – and so much more romantic.

Such packages can include complete administration of the service, together with the cake, champagne, flowers and photographs, even a best man and bridesmaids if necessary! Amazing value for money, this is often all part of the tour package price, but at most would be a modest extra cost.

LEGAL REQUIREMENTS FOR OBTAINING A MARRIAGE LICENCE WITHIN ANTIGUA AND BARBUDA

SPECIAL LICENCE

1 Valid passport, or birth certificate *and* valid identification papers with photograph: e.g. driving licence or state issued identification (UK/European residents beware. The latter refers to US citizens; lose your passport and you cannot marry!)

2 Proof of status:
Single: a declaration is signed within Antigua and Barbuda.
Divorced: original decree absolute which includes the seal of the court issuing the decree *or* a certified copy of the decree which includes the seal of the court where the decree was issued.
Widow/widower:
a marriage certificate
b death certificate of late husband/wife

3 Application form is filled out and signed at the Ministry of Justice and Legal Affairs in St John's.

4 All applicants must be over the age of 18. If under, then written parental consent must be obtained.

5 There is no waiting time in the country in order to obtain a special licence.

6 The petition for a special licence shall be accompanied by a fee of US$ 150.00.

7 Both parties *must* be present at the time of the application.

ORDINARY LICENCE

1 Valid passport, or birth certificate *and* valid identification with photograph e.g. driving licence or state issued identification (UK/European residents beware. The latter refers to US citizens; lose your passport and you cannot marry!)

2 Proof of status:
Single: a declaration is signed within Antigua and Barbuda *or* a letter stating status by some person well known in the community.
Divorced: original decree absolute which includes the seal of the court issuing the decree *or* certified copy of the decree which includes the seal of the court where the decree was issued.
Widow/widower:
a marriage certificate
b death certificate of late husband/wife

3 Application form is filled out and signed at the Ministry of Justice and Legal Affairs in St John's.

4 All applicants must be over the age of 18. If under, then written parental consent must be obtained.

5 One of the parties must be resident in Antigua and Barbuda for a period of 15 days immediately preceding the date of the application for a licence.

6 The petition for an ordinary licence shall be accompanied by a fee of EC$ 100.00.

7 Both parties *must* be present at the time of the application.

CEREMONY

1 The wedding is performed by the Registrar, Deputy Registrar, Assistant Registrar or any of the Marriage officers.

2 The day selected for the ceremony depends upon the parties.

3 There is a registration fee of EC$ 100.00 to be paid at the Registrar's office.

4 If the wedding ceremony is to be performed outside the Court House in St John's, please note that there is a Marriage officer's fee of EC$ 135.00 or US$ 50.00.

5 Ceremonies can be performed between the hours of 6.00am and 8.00pm.

6 Every marriage must be solemnised or celebrated in the presence of two or more credible witnesses.

Change of name

If a change of name has taken place in the case of any applicant, then the deed poll under which this was done must be produced.

Alternatively, you may wish for additional or completely different requirements for which there could possibly be additional or separate charges. Tailor-made ceremonies can be as lavish or simple as you choose, formal or barefoot. As with everything else, low season prices are more economical than at peak periods.

Some visitors celebrating are not even newlyweds but have chosen to renew their vows here, or celebrate a wedding anniversary.

Discuss your needs with your travel agent and be sure to consider all aspects: the setting desired (for example, a tropical garden with flower arch, on the beach, on a yacht), flowers, photography, video, champagne, wedding cake, music, reception and any personal preferences. Larger hotels invariably have full time wedding co-ordinators who meet you after arrival, discuss all your needs

and generally arrange and oversee all details, thereby further alleviating those pre-wedding nerves!

Such is the demand that as well as including weddings and honeymoons in their main brochures, some tour operators produce special supplements and brochures specifically catering to this ever-increasing market.

Many have been carried away with the romance of Antigua and decided to get married whilst on holiday, and certainly there are many high-class jewellers in Antigua who can provide the ring. Amendments to legislation now make it possible to marry immediately (see Legal Requirements, above), as there is now no waiting time in Antigua in order to obtain the special licence required. So, even cruise ship passengers can get married here on their short visit.

BUSINESS TRIPS

Most hotels offer the usual telecommunication facilities, but do enquire about in-room telephones. This is, after all, essentially a holiday island and the smaller or mid-range hotels do not always offer a phone and direct-dialling facilities in the room.

Business people wishing to stay in contact with office and family can have the accessibility and convenience of a rental cellular phone. Available through APUA (using GSM technology, see page 35) or Cable & Wireless Caribbean Cellular, AMPS-compatible (North American analogue) phones can be used via their network. Some of the other facilities offered by Cable & Wireless of interest to business people are Internet connections and e-mail, via your laptop or their desktop PCs (for their full services, see also Telecommunications, page 34).

More extensive business needs are more likely to be met at the larger resorts and higher bracket hotels, where conference rooms and the like would be available. With enviable natural settings, first-class hotel and resort accommodation and facilities, the island hosts many incentive groups, meetings, conventions and corporate events of varying sizes, including smaller, more intimate rooms for seminars and workshops (see Appendix for listings, page 313).

Conference room sizes vary from those rooms accommodating 20–40 people, to those larger rooms taking from 70 to about 100. Facilities offered vary, for example, TV/VCR, overhead and slide projectors, screens, flip charts, microphones. Most offer catering for light refreshments and lunch.

For major functions, trade shows and conventions, the modern multi-purpose Cultural Centre takes up to 600 people with a smaller room for 200. Offering a sound system only, there are no catering facilities. The Royal Antiguan Hotel is the only one with a full size convention room, which accommodates 450 to 700 people. This can be divided in two, giving further capacities of 240 to 300, and 200 to 275. With all the necessary equipment available, they also offer catering to suit all requirements.

An entire itinerary for companies and corporations can be overseen by on-island destination management companies, including transfers and sightseeing tours (refer to Appendix, page 315).

For those seeking financial opportunities, Antigua has seen a tremendous growth in its investment and off-shore banking sectors and offers many advantages in both aspects (see Investment, page 289).

Antigua and Barbuda are represented by all the usual worldwide clubs, such as Rotary, and listings can be found in the Appendix, page 313.

DISABLED TRAVELLERS

If arriving by air, on leaving the aircraft, there is ease of access all the way through the airport and outside.

There is also designated disability parking for those who may be being picked up by private vehicle. For financial services, the large modern Bank of Antigua branch just outside the entrance to the airport is particularly accessible.

Most hotels have wheelchair accessibility to ground floor rooms and the Royal Antiguan Hotel has a lift to all other floors, although Club Antigua has units specifically designed for disabled visitors. Due to its flat surroundings and accessibility the Beachcomber Hotel also caters well to such visitors. Sandals has ground floor, 'user-friendly' rooms, with refurbished pathways around the property affording easy, short access to most areas. Rex Halcyon Cove provides two rooms specially built for the disabled, with or without wheelchairs. They can also provide a company cart and pathways are usable for wheelchairs.

Many restaurants have wheelchair access, notably Miller's By The Sea, Spinnakers, the Hub, Shirley Heights, to name a few. The Antigua Recreation Ground has a specific area for wheelchair spectators, and the multi-purpose Cultural Centre has ample access. The two main shopping areas in St John's, Historic Redcliffe Quay and Heritage Quay, both have wheelchair-width walkways, boardwalks and paths, with ramps where necessary, as does Jolly Harbour Marina and Shopping Centre and the Woods Shopping Mall. The Woods Shopping Mall also offers specifically designated disabled parking and has an easy access post office.

Many disabled people have enjoyed fun-filled holidays in Antigua, whether visiting from a cruise ship just for the day, or having flown or sailed in for longer stays.

Once here, you are welcome to meet people from the Association of Persons with Disabilities which holds general meetings at 5.30pm, on the fourth Thursday of each month at the Potters Community Clinic, Potters Village. Should you wish to contact them beforehand, Leslie Emanuel, the President, would be delighted to help with any queries regarding a trip. The Association is a member of Disabled Peoples International (DPI),

which has a membership of 120 national cross-disability organisations and many affiliates.

Leslie A. Emanuel Sr, President, Antigua and Barbuda Association of Persons with Disabilities, PO Box W123, Woods Centre, St John's, Antigua
tel/fax: (268) 461 7260
web site: www.abapd.org

DPI North America:
Toll Free 1-800-749-7773
web site: www.dpi.org

Antigua and Barbuda Society of and for the Blind, All Saints Road, St John's, Antigua tel: (268) 462 0663 tel/fax: (268) 462 3882.

TRAVEL, MEDICAL AND PERSONAL INSURANCE

Many tour companies include obligatory insurance in their package holidays (although this is being reviewed), however, you can purchase all manner of travel insurance from any travel agent, bank, your personal insurance company and the like. This is assuming you do not already hold an existing policy which will cover you against overseas medical costs (check the procedure on this; some insurances require you to call them, whilst abroad, to have any hospital stay or treatment authorised before they will guarantee covering you for such expenses) lost luggage, cancellation of flights and so on. Be sure to retain the necessary receipts relating to any insurance claim.

It would certainly be recommended to organise a travel insurance policy to cover against the possibility of all kinds of disasters, including theft, loss, medical problems, air ambulance or emergency flights home.

WHAT TO PACK AND WEAR

As described under Climate, the temperatures vary only slightly from winter to summer. During the winter months, the evenings are cooler and you may want a wrap, cardigan or light jacket. Simple, loose, preferably cotton, clothing is recommended all year round, and casual is the norm. Don't worry if your wardrobe at home is lacking such items; there are plenty of wonderful shops and boutiques on the island providing every style, type, budget of tropical day, evening and beach wear for men, women and children.

Standard business attire is the norm for formal meetings and presentations, but dependent upon your type of business, men are not expected to don jackets, or necessarily, ties. Local businessmen wear smart trousers, shirts (long or short-sleeved), sometimes a tie; women are very smartly dressed for business here and female business people should dress appropriately.

Dress is casual at all times; even for a good restaurant, the code is 'elegantly casual'. Beach clothes are essential, and possibly a beach towel, although even the smallest of hotels normally provide these, sandals or beach shoes for the hot sand and paving, and a sun hat.

Print and slide film (and processing) can be purchased on-island (see also Film and Photography, page 39), but it's probably wise to pack a good supply of your own favourite type of photographic film (and a polarising filter for the enthusiast, to increase contrast and bring out the vibrant colours and blue sea and sky).

Reading matter should be packed for general relaxation and for any unforeseeable delays.

If you wish to pursue any of the many sports on land or sea here, you may want to bring your own equipment and sports clothing. There are a number of walking opportunities (see Hiking and Walking, page 141) and if this gentle exercise interests you, bring suitable footwear, plus binoculars for bird watching, star gazing and general use.

A travel umbrella could be handy in the event of a tropical shower (the locals also use them as an essential item for offering good shade from the sun whilst walking). Packing an extra, light folding bag is always prudent – you never know what and how much you may see and wish to bring back!

Inevitably, visitors bring far too much clothing and on arrival find that the lined jacket, cocktail dresses and evening wear are just left hanging; don't forget that good laundry services and dry cleaning facilities are available in most hotels.

Starting a checklist a few weeks before departure is worthwhile; it's impossible to remember every little aspect at the last minute.

ELECTRICITY

Antigua has electrical supplies of 110 or 120 volts at 60 cycles per second, as well as 220 or 240 volts at 50 cycles. So, dual voltage electrical appliances are an advantage! Many hotels operate on the American system, so plugs would generally be of the two flat prong variety; either make enquiries beforehand, buy a plug adaptor at home or at the airport, or travel with the possibility of the hotel being able to supply the necessary electrical appliance or adaptor required. Do check the voltage before plugging anything in, to avoid a shortage and possibly ruining your appliance.

MEDICAL CARE AND HEALTH

Maintaining or achieving good health prior to travelling is the optimum goal, although sadly, the stresses of modern life often result in minor illnesses presenting themselves as soon as your defences are down once relaxing, and dormant illnesses can appear. So pack any necessary medical provisions you think you may require.

It makes sense to travel with one of the brand-name small healthcare kits, which include the most common medical needs. Ensure you are adequately prepared to travel with an ample supply of any drugs or health preparations you normally take; where imperative medication is concerned, travelling with a spare prescription would be advised in the event of loss or damage to your normal supply. Many good pharmacies exist on the island, mainly in and around St John's (see Appendix, page 319).

All hotels either have in-house doctors or doctors on call. Should you be unfortunate enough to incur an injury, there are first-rate specialists in back, joint, bone and sports related problems. Antigua has excellent doctors and practitioners encompassing all health aspects, both western and eastern, plus first-rate dentists and eye specialists (refer to Health and Beauty, page 148 and Appendix, page 319). Nevertheless, it may be worth the peace of mind to get a check up for your teeth and eyes prior to leaving home.

For those who wear glasses, take a spare pair, in case of loss or breakage – it would be dreadful to make the journey and not be able to fully appreciate the wonderful sights of this paradise! Having the prescription would also help one of Antigua's competent opticians quickly prepare a new set of glasses or contact lenses.

These twin islands have a confidential information line concerning HIV/AIDS, which aims to give help and information to people affected by and living with such illnesses (Monday–Thursday 8.30am–4.30pm, Friday 8.00am–3.00pm: (268) 462 5039 or for local calls, 462 5975/ 460 6209).

Alcoholics Anonymous meet in the Foundation Mixed School, on the corner of Independence Avenue and South Street, St John's on Monday (step meeting), Wednesday, Friday and Saturday (closed meetings), at 7.00pm; on Thursday at 7.00pm an open AA meeting takes place either in Falmouth or English Harbour. Al Anon/Alateen, help for families and friends of alcoholics, meet every Tuesday at 7.30pm at Cobbs Cross Primary School (if you need to speak to someone, call Gilly at 460 1726 or Louise at 562 1206). There is a possible Narcotics Anonymous meeting on Tuesday and Thursday at Ms Davis School. For both contact 463 3155.

HEALTH HAZARDS
DEHYDRATION/
HEAT EXHAUSTION/WATER
Antigua enjoys one of the world's healthiest climates but, nevertheless, as it is likely to be much hotter here than at home, dehydration is a potential hazard. Don't assume that

because you're not thirsty you do not need to drink water or (non-alcoholic!) fluids. The warm climate can be very deceptive, even if you don't perspire much, and you will feel noticeably better if you increase your normal intake of water. Bottled, purified or mineral water is readily available; however, the tap water (unless otherwise stated) island-wide is considered safe and generally used for ice cubes.

It may be necessary to increase your salt intake with salt tablets. Such deficiency can be evident by muscle cramps, tiredness, headaches and dizzyness.

STOMACH UPSETS/DIARRHOEA

Stomach upsets are unusual, but for the more susceptible avoid iced drinks in the sun, unusual foods and too much fruit until your stomach becomes more accustomed to local produce and cuisine. Knowledge of any past experiences will remind you to add to your personal first aid pack, any medical preparations which suit you best, otherwise, Antigua stocks most brands required to settle your stomach (for pharmacy listings, see Appendix, page 319).

Sea-sickness pills could be a useful addition too, as you're sure to be tempted by the many attractive catamaran, yacht and boat day trips.

Most incidences of diarrhoea can be relieved with readily available over-the-counter preparations, although they do not constitute medical treatment or cure. Should you experience vomiting or diarrhoea, your liquid and salt levels will be depleted and appropriate action should be taken immediately with a rehydrating solution to replace both vital minerals and salt lost. Almost all 'stoppers' for diarrhoea are not suitable for young children. If travelling with children, make sure to bring with you appropriate remedies recommended by your pharmacist or doctor – and read the label! If symptoms persist, contact your hotel reception and ask for a doctor (see Appendix, page 319).

INSECTS

Mosquitoes and sand flies ('no-see-um's') can certainly find the unsuspecting new visitor very tempting, particularly after dusk, so be armed with plenty of insect repellents (the most effective contain at least 80 per cent diethyl-toluamide, or DEET). Antigua doesn't have a problem in this respect generally, but it's always a possibility when being in the tropics, and all accommodation is regularly treated. Where your room has air-conditioning, you should not suffer at all, and if you have a fan, use it at night if you feel mosquitoes are around. Such rooms are normally supplied with mosquito coils (or electrical plug-in repellent devices), which when lit act as a deterrent.

If and when you are bitten, it may seem impossible but please do try to refrain from scratching the offending area. It just makes it red, angry and worse, and it can become infected and possibly scar. There are creams, lotions and sprays available both at home and here (locals use the economical Bay Rum liquid preparation) to soothe and allay that impossible itch.

'Fire' ants (red or black) are known here, so be careful when walking barefoot or sitting down for that idyllic grassy picnic; once bitten by them they can sting far more than any mosquito, but again, the remedies for mosquito bites apply (for pharmacy listings, see Appendix, page 319).

THE TROPICAL SUN

Whilst a suntan is still regarded as attractive and a sign of good health, we are all now well aware (or should be) of the mass publicity given to the dangers of too much sun and of taking insufficient protection against the sun's harmful rays.

Firstly, don't underestimate the power of the sun here, otherwise you could simply ruin your trip. You can get nasty sunburn from very early in the morning in a short space of time and the lighter your skin, the more damage you will suffer. Even shade or a cloudy sky offer only minimum protection. Many holidaymakers are seen to rush out underprotected in the mad quest for the deepest possible tan and it is a fallacy to believe that starting with a very high sun protection factor will reduce the danger of such a goal or should encourage a longer time in the sun. Sunscreens do not protect against skin cancer. The more sensible you are from the outset, the deeper and longer lasting your tan will be.

Please also strongly bear in mind that you should apply sun lotion at least 20 minutes before venturing out into the sun. It is a little known, yet vital, fact that it takes that long for the sun cream's protective properties to take effect, otherwise you can easily burn in that first foray and wonder why, or blame the ineffectiveness of the sun cream! Make sure your sun cream is both UVA and UVB effective, and at least with a SPF (sun protection factor) of 15. Young children should *never* be allowed to sunbathe or be out in the sun unprotected. Although sometimes more expensive here, the island's hotel boutiques, pharmacies, stores and shops all stock a wide range of internationally known brands, covering all protection factors, creams, oils, and preparations for watersports.

Whilst moving about, sightseeing and for sport, wear a wide-brimmed hat (particularly for those who get their hair braided, strips of burnt scalp look and feel awful) or a baseball cap and possibly something covering your shoulders. Good quality sunglasses are also highly recommended to protect your eyes from the glare, particularly when reflected off the beach and water. There is a plentiful array of styles and lenses available for purchase, and some duty free, from shops and boutiques island-wide.

You may be approached on the beach by vendors selling the raw juice or flesh of the aloe, a local cactus-like plant. Cosmetic and skin-care manufacturers have long known of its soothing qualities and there are many proprietary brands being sold containing extracts of this traditional healing plant, particularly useful in combating the drying effects of the sun. Certainly, do take advantage of the real thing – after your time in the sun, not during, as clearly it offers no sun protection at all.

HEATSTROKE

Beware of falling asleep in the sun and becoming unpleasantly, and sometimes seriously, ill through sun or heatstroke. Take time to acclima-

Manchineel tree

tise, avoiding excessive alcohol intake or very active sport in the heat of the day, when the body's heat regulating mechanism could be stretched to its limit.

Get medical advice if you feel you have a high temperature, become dizzy, flushed, feverish and have a headache; meanwhile, lie in the cool and try to drink water or fruit juice. Should symptoms increase whereby lack of co-ordination, delerium and even convulsions occur, contact immediately the hotel reception, a doctor or the hospital (see also Medical Emergencies, below).

DRUGS
Everyone is being made acutely aware of the tragic consequences of all forms of drug abuse from major publicity back home, and naturally Antigua cannot be the exception to the rule. Please do not encourage people to make a living selling drugs; there are severe penalties for the use of, or possession of, narcotic drugs.

HEALTH WARNINGS!
LAND
Fortunately, there are very few to deter the islands' image of paradise. The indigenous manchineel tree (*Hippomane mancinella*) seems to be most prevalent along beach fronts and, although perfectly harmless to sit under for shade, it must not be used as shelter from the rain as the sap from the apple-like fruits is poisonous and could cause

painful blistering. (Don't even leave your car under this tree because if it rains its water soluble toxic sap can remove paint.) The warrior-like Caribs in Antigua would dip their arrow heads in the toxic sap of the manchineel tree before hunting trips, and battles with the Arawaks and European settlers. Varying from a bush to 30-feet tall, it resembles the common crab-apple tree, and a suitable warning is often marked accordingly, but warn children not to try to pick up the fruit to nibble! If sap does get on the skin, wash it off immediately in the sea or at the nearest source of water. Do not even use the wood to make a fire as the smoke from burning it can cause irritation and even headaches.

There are no poisonous snakes or other nasties on the islands (the tiny lizards are far more afraid of you than you could ever be of them). There is the rare Antigua racer snake on Great Bird Island, but this is a completely harmless, gentle specimen (see Fauna, page 98).

SEA
Whilst an uncommon occurrence, do be very careful when walking amongst rocks and corals, as they can be home to the spiky sea urchin. They are rarely found at any hotel beach, unless you stray outside such designated safe areas or onto a reef. This hazardous underwater sea creature is the size of a golf ball and covered in long spines, normally black or dark in colour and

easily spotted (although the small baby ones can be quite hidden). If you step on a sea urchin, at least one of their brittle, hollow spines will become embedded in your foot (sometimes even through flippers and sandals) and once in, they extend an arrow-like head, making it impossible to simply pull out. Their toxic nature will sting for a good few hours and make it awkward to walk. Various local remedies include bathing the area in lime juice (light acid) or lighting a match to the end of the offending spike to 'kill' it. Alternatively, contact your hotel reception or a doctor (see Appendix for listings, page 319). If all else fails, they are naturally absorbed within a few days.

MEDICAL EMERGENCIES
Antigua has one main hospital for general and emergency care, the Holberton, located on the outskirts of St John's and equipped with the latest X-ray equipment and fully able to handle emergency cases. There is also a fully equipped and recently extended private hospital, the Adelin Medical Centre, situated on Fort Road, above St John's on the northwestern side of the island.

Mount St John's Medical Centre, overlooking St John's, high atop St Michael's Mount, is under construction for completion mid-2001. This massive, imposing structure will house one of the most advanced emergency departments in the Caribbean, with laboratories, pharmacies, teaching section and other support facilities. The state-of-the-art medical centre will include 177 acute care beds, ten observation beds and four medical/surgical units, pediatrics, obstetrics, neo-natal and intensive care, three operating theatres, comprehensive diagnostic facilities, amongst others.

Barbuda has a small casualty hospital, the Spring View Hospital in Codrington.

For all contact details, see Appendix, page 319).

If you are covered by suitable insurance, be sure to keep receipts for any medical care received, essential when making an insurance claim.

TAKING THE CHILDREN

West Indians adore children and Antigua is no exception. Naturally, travelling with babies and children of all ages requires forethought and planning but the airlines are all well versed in such care and many hotels here actively encourage family travel and welcome children. As mentioned earlier, the skin of babies and very young children should never be exposed to the sun. Hats and t-shirts should be worn even when they are in the water.

The numerous beaches and safe bathing present the perfect playground and there are many attractions and activities suitable for young ones. Most hotels have swimming pools and the larger establishments and resorts offer a children's programme of entertainment, and of course, children will always find other children to play with, wherever they are. These bigger places will also often provide a baby-sitter service.

For those self-catering, the supermarkets sell a variety of baby foods and fresh produce suitable for babies and young children's food preparation. They also sell copious quantities of disposable nappies; although they will inevitably be pricier than back home, the convenience of not having to haul packs over will probably outweigh the small extra expense. Quite a few hotels and restaurants cater accordingly, with children's dishes incorporated into their daily menus.

As with adults, but more so, the tropical sun can present a real danger to babies and children if normal and sensible precautions are not taken – be sure their sunhats, t-shirts and total sun block sun cream are with them at all times, along with plenty of liquids.

There are no harmful tropical reptiles or insects, although you would want to amply protect babies and children from any possible mosquito bites. Beware if your children are crawling or playing in and around tropical gardens as unfortunately, the splendour of a few highly coloured plants and flowers sometimes belies their poisonous attributes, notably the oleander, poinsettia and *Diffenbachia* (dumb cane). As mentioned in Health Warnings, the

manchineel tree, found all over the Caribbean and especially along shorelines, is not only to be avoided when it is raining. If a young child bites into one of the appealing tiny apple-like fruit, it could cause dire throat contractions. Thankfully, these are few and far between in Antigua and mostly marked accordingly with a warning sign.

PETS

Any pets arriving onboard by sea in private boats and yachts must not be taken off and onto the island. There are certain restrictions for those wishing to bring cats and dogs into Antigua from overseas. Pets from the UK, Australia, and New Zealand, may be admitted when accompanied by the necessary veterinary documents and animal health certificates, likewise for horses and ponies arriving by cargo ship from the USA or UK. Prior approval is required for pets entering from other islands and countries, although in principle, prior approval must be sought in all instances. Any enquiries can be made to the Government Veterinary Officer on (268) 460 1759.

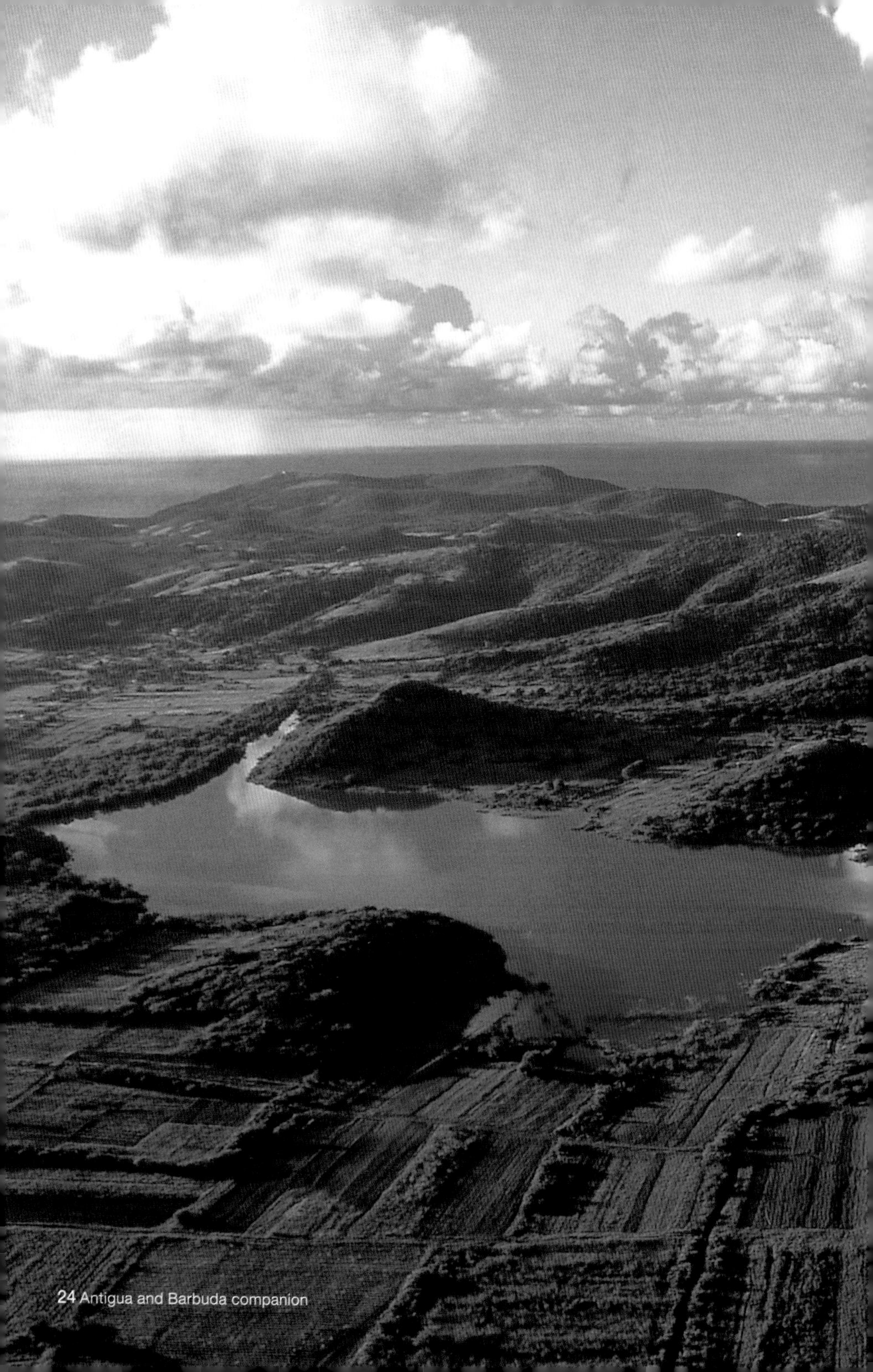

Easy reference practical tips

and useful information for visitors

LOCATION AND GEOGRAPHY

Antigua (pronounced An-tee'ga) and Barbuda are part of the Leeward Islands chain in the Eastern Caribbean, about 450 miles northeast of South America, and lie on the latitude 17°09′ north and the longitude 61°49′ west. Their combined 170 square miles are roughly situated at the centre of the Lesser Antilles archipelago, with neighbouring islands Montserrat to the southwest, St Kitts and Nevis to the northwest, St Martin and St Barthelemy to the north, and Guadeloupe to the south. Centrally located between the Greater and Lesser Antilles, giving it the description as the 'heart of the Caribbean', such a geographic position has made it important historically, and as the hub for regional airline connections.

Washed almost exclusively by the Caribbean Sea, Antigua's 108 square miles are encircled by 95 miles of indented coastline and comprise six parishes: St Mary, St John, St Paul, St Philip, St Peter and St George. Lying 27 miles off the northeastern coast of Antigua, is the smaller sister isle of Barbuda (see page 297), with an area of 62 square miles.

The state of Antigua and Barbuda's territory also includes the relatively little known half square mile of rock, Redonda, about 35 miles to the west and uninhabited, save for thousands of sea birds (see page 108).

Antigua developed from a volcano which rose out of the sea during the Oligocene period, about 34 million years ago. Coral began to grow on the volcanic rock, as the remainder gradually subsided; in time limestone was established towards the northeast of the island. The terrain is therefore varied, consisting of partly coral and its derivative limestone, and partly volcanic formation, separated by a central clay plain.

Such origins give the island the advantage of its many renowned beaches and at the same time unusually gracing everyone with a prettily undulating landscape, open plains, rolling hills rising to 1319 feet above sea level, verdant valleys and a lush evergreen deciduous rainforest area, all interspersed by meandering roads and lanes.

These unique physical characteristics have afforded Antigua many more archaeological features than any other island in the Eastern Caribbean. Over 60 aceramic sites of the first group of stone-tool making people have so far been discovered, as well as about 65 sites of a second group of agricultural and pottery-making people. Initially occupying Antigua in at least 3000 years BC, they lived well on the rich marine resources from the many reefs and mangroves.

The low-lying island of Barbuda is totally coral based and famed for its startling, long, empty pink sand beaches, lagoon and frigate bird sanctuary. Notwithstanding its flatness, with the highest point just 145 feet above sea level, and whilst scrubby in parts, this is not an uninteresting prospect. It is of great interest to explorers and walkers, comprising fascinating geological and archaeological facets, home to many caves, sinkholes and Amerindian sites. (See also page 298.)

Unusual in the Leewards, Antigua has a wealth of outer islands of varying size and uninhabited cays which fringe parts of the coastline, notably the northeastern area, all much loved and frequented.

CAPITAL

The city of St John's, with a population of 21,514, along with its outlying suburbs forming St John's rural with 14,121 (last census 1991), is situated on the northwest side of the island, about five miles from the airport. It

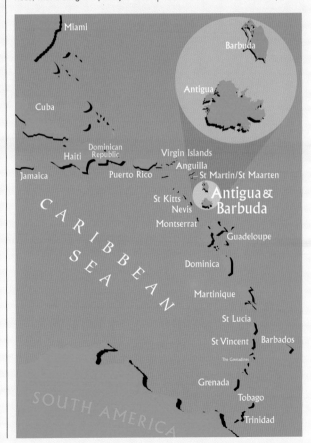

Produced by West Indies Publishing Ltd, PO Box 1245 St. John's, Antigua, W.I. Tel: (268) 461 0565/463 5550 Fax: (268) 461 9750. Email: wip@candw.ag   All rights reserved.

Antigua & Barbuda
© West Indies Publishing Ltd. 2001

is also where the principal port is positioned at Deepwater Harbour.

Barbuda's capital is the town of Codrington, where most of the island's inhabitants reside.

THE PEOPLE

Antigua and Barbuda has a population of 63,878 (last census 1991), with an estimated population as at 1996 of 68,612. The great majority are of African origin, their ancestors having been brought here in the seventeenth and eighteenth centuries to work on the sugar estates; a minority are the descendents of English and Scottish settlers, and fewer are of mixed descent (Syrian, Lebanese, Portuguese). More recently, there has been the influx of immigrants from North America, Europe and Asia. With a hardy, historical background, the people have a strong character and pride and are very friendly and courteous. From the last official figures available, the population annual growth rate is 0.18 per cent (1995), life expectancy at birth, male 71.9, female 75.2 (1994).

EDUCATION

Based on the English education system, there are 30 public and 27 private primary schools, nine public and five private secondary schools (comprehensive/grammar), where all children at the public schools receive free education (compulsory between the ages of 5 and 16). Once orientated towards achieving English certification and educational qualifications, their curricula now encompass aspects related more specifically to the Caribbean region. Hence Antiguans now sit the Caribbean Examinations Council examination, which is the equivalent of the former English O Level. The island's literacy rate is one of the highest in the Eastern Caribbean at 89 per cent (1994).

Further education is provided locally by the Antigua State College (pre-university and a first-year university programme), the Technical and Vocational Training Centre, the recently upgraded Hotel Training School, and the University of Health Sciences Antigua (founded in 1982), for those wishing to work in health related fields. Antigua is also a partner in the regional University of the West Indies. This provides higher education at the campus here for business studies, and for all other subjects at the various regional campuses in several CARICOM member countries. Overseas scholarships are provided each year by the government. A Youth Skills Training Programme offers a range of activities outside the formal education system.

RELIGION

The dominant religion is Christianity, mainly Anglican, with Methodist, Moravian, Roman Catholic, Seventh Day Adventist, Latter Day Saints, Wesleyan, Pentecostal, Lutheran, Evangelical and Baptist denominations represented and witnessed by the many churches in evidence. Sundays in particular prove a feast for the eyes as visitors notice immaculately dressed families making their way to the local church – and you are welcome to join them. Antigua has great religious tolerance, indicated by the free spirit,

diversification and melting pot of faiths practised, largely created by the influx of a relatively new cosmopolitan society.

Rastafarianism has been present here since the late 1960s, having been recognised in the Eastern Caribbean from around the late 1920s, when this essentially African-Christian movement was formed in Jamaica. Efforts to consolidate and centralise the Rastafari communities in the region culminated in early 2000, with Antigua co-hosting (with the Eastern Caribbean Rastafari Organisation ECRO) the Rastafari Millennium Summit. They derive their name from the late emperor of Ethiopia's pre-coronation name, Ras Tafari. Regarded as their god, he was later named Haile Selassie. True followers keep to themselves and are peaceful and friendly. Call the numbers below to find out the venue for their meetings, held on the last Saturday of every month.

Another faith which has a keen following, is that of Buddhism. Regular meetings take place at various homes on the island, where chanting and discussions on this globally popular faith take place.

Stated as 'the second most widespread religion on earth after Christianity', the worldwide network of the Baha'i Faith has a large base in St John's. The National Spiritual Assembly of the Eastern Leewards, established here since 1981, welcomes visitors to its headquarters. You are also able to join in the informal meetings there on Wednesdays at 7pm.

The Baha'i Faith, PO Box 352, Nevis Street, St John's
tel: (268) 461 2366/461 3331
fax: (268) 460 3667

SGI-USA Buddhist tel: (268) 461 4038

The Wadadli National Council for the Advancement of Rastafari (WNCAR), 49 St Mary's Street. St John's. Contacts: Ras Franki Tafari (Franklin Francis)

tel: (268) 461 0429
e-mail: franki@candw.ag or
Ras Shaka Tafari tel: (268) 460 3949
e-mail: francisrh@candw.ag

THE ECONOMY

The mainstay of the island's economy is dominated by tourism, accounting for about 70 per cent of the gross national product, 50 per cent employment, and 90 per cent of foreign exchange. Off-shore banking and insurance companies continue to establish at a fast rate and are much sought after by worldwide investors (see Investment, page 289). Light industry follows next and, although some way behind, it is developing at quite a pace. The existing mix of industries serving both domestic and foreign markets include electronic assembly, furniture, alcoholic and non-alcoholic beverages, foodstuffs, household appliances, paints, packaging materials and garment making. Agriculture is of increasing economic importance, although still a very

improvements, departing dramatically from the previously inherent and oft-joked state of Antigua's potholed roads. Apart from the increased general comfort and safety, such sleek new road surfaces encourage and ease the journeys of visitors wishing to reach the many beaches and attractions for their further enjoyment. Before tourism brought financial stability, economic pressure resulted in Antiguans going overseas; however, the increased employment since the 1970s (when tourism started to develop), has tempted many to return to their homeland, at the same time, bringing new ideas, experiences, talent and training with them. Antigua and Barbuda has also attracted people from neighbouring islands, to seek work and contribute further by bringing their skills here, with many eventually settling. Antigua and Barbuda is a member of the United Nations and also therefore, the World Bank, the International Monetary Fund, the Inter-American Development Bank and the Organisation of American States. Regionally, they have joined the Caribbean Community and Common Market, the 15-country regional body (CARICOM), and are a founder member of the Organisation of East Caribbean States (OECS).

THE GOVERNMENT AND JUDICIARY

The state of Antigua and Barbuda is a democratic republic, having initially gained independence in association with Great Britain on 31 October 1968 (when the United Kingdom was still responsible for its foreign affairs). Subsequently, Antigua achieved full sovereign independence on 1 November 1981, thereby having total control over its internal and external affairs, and defence. However, this twin-island state is still a member of the British Commonwealth, observing the traditions of a constitutional monarchy and the practices of a parliamentary democracy.

Barbuda was annexed to Antigua in 1860 when Christopher Codrington, an English planter, leased the island from the British crown. Barbuda has

young industry pursued mainly by small-scale and part-time farmers. Cash crops such as cotton and small quantities of fruits and vegetables are exported to neighbouring islands, plus the prized lobster. The principal trading partners for exports are the OECS countries. The main imports are fuel, food, machinery, transport and manufactured goods.

Antigua and Barbuda is a beneficiary under the Caribbean Basin Initiative (CBI), CARIBCAN, and Lomé trade preference schemes, qualifying for preferential market access to the US, Canada and the European Union for a wide range of products.

Despite a lack of exports and having to borrow from overseas, the inflation rate remains constantly under the 5 per cent level and unemployment rates are only just above this percentage. Foreign investment has played no mean part in contributing to this relatively stable economic performance, especially in the areas of tourism-related industries and services; well known brands of beer and soft drinks are also brewed and produced here under licence.

Over the last three to five years, in recognising the need to improve the infrastructure and create more for the visitor to do, see and spend money on, the government has spent an enormous amount investing in these areas. One such example is the EC$ 80–100 million visibly used in serious, long-term road

a strong local council and is represented in Parliament.

The British sovereign is head of state and is represented on the island by the Governor-General, HE Sir James Beethoven Carlisle, GCMG. As such, the queen's head is depicted on all monetary notes and there is still tremendous island-wide respect for HM the Queen and the royal family. (Princess Margaret honeymooned here and still visits and Diana, Princess of Wales, was a frequent visitor to these shores.)

The Prime Minister, the Hon. Lester Bryant Bird, leads the government as leader of the majority party, the Antigua Labour Party (ALP). The official opposition party is the United Progressive Party (UPP), whose leader is the Hon. Baldwin Spencer, MP. Additionally, there is the National Reform Movement.

Barbuda was formally annexed to Antigua in 1860 and up to 1903, influential land owners governed the island by lease; thereafter, the Antiguan authorities were ordered to govern it as a crown estate. From 1904 to 1976, a warden administered the island, after which time the Barbuda Council was established to allow a greater degree of internal self-government. The council

is empowered to make by-laws and administer all internal affairs, with the exceptions of land and security matters. The council, consisting of nine elected members, two Barbuda representatives to the national parliament, and a government-appointed member, is represented in Parliament by the Barbuda People's Movement.

Parliament has supreme legislative power and consists of two legislative chambers, the House of Representatives (the lower house), comprising a cabinet of 17 elected members representing the constituencies (including Barbuda), plus the Attorney General and the Speaker, and a Senate (or upper house), appointed by the governor-general on the advice of the Prime Minister and opposition leader. General elections are constitutionally every five years, through the democratic process of free elections. The election in 1994 reflected true political equality when four women were unprecedently appointed to Parliament, both in the upper and lower houses and were reappointed in 1999. Additionally the Governor-General's deputy is a prominent female, Her Excellency Ms Yvonne Maginley.

The government and the judiciary follow British guidelines and Antigua and Barbuda are members of the East Caribbean Supreme Court, with a High Court and an Appeals Court, with recourse to the Privy Council in the United Kingdom as the final court of appeal. Local magistrates' courts handle the majority of offences. The state's constitution, adopted in 1981 at the time of full independence, is also based on the British system of government, with ten articles and 127 clauses.

DIPLOMATIC AND CONSULAR REPRESENTATION

Antigua's diplomatic representation has increased over the years, whether it be with fully serviced embassies or honorary consuls. When travelling, it is always wise to photocopy the relevant pages of your documents: passport, driving licence, birth certificate and any other essential papers, keeping them separate from the originals, in the case of any loss or theft.

FOREIGN EMBASSIES AND CONSULATES

There are five resident diplomatic representatives, five non-resident,

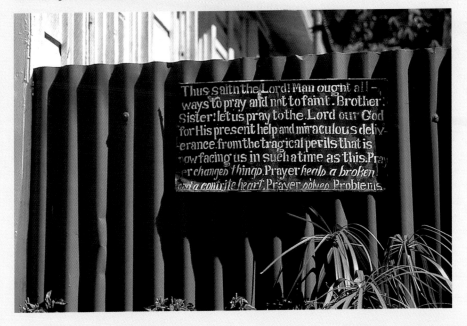

and 14 consular representatives. (These postings can change periodically.) See Appendix (page 314) for full listings and contact details.

SECURITY AND EMERGENCIES

GENERAL

The twin-islands enjoy a thankfully low crime rate, witnessed by headlines in the local papers for even minor misdemeanours. The Royal Police Force of Antigua and Barbuda is well able to deal with the islands' odd criminal but, clearly, as anywhere in the world, crimes do take place and you are well advised to take normal precautions. Lock your doors and windows when leaving your room; keep your valuables, passport and traveller's cheques in the hotel safety deposit box and don't make an issue of showing bankrolls of dollars in public. Similarly, lock your car when leaving it and do not leave valuables lying around in it for all to see. On the main resort beaches, you may be approached by people selling tours, souvenirs, beach clothes, aloe, coral necklaces, hair braiding services and the like. These are invariably services appreciated by visitors and have not become a problem. However, should you not be interested in what they have to offer, a polite but firm 'no' will send them elsewhere. Begging is virtually unheard of.

WOMEN TRAVELLERS

Antigua and Barbuda are perfectly safe for women travellers but some may be the target of attention from local males. This largely depends on the demeanour and dress of such female visitors, as despite their apparent flamboyance, Antiguans are largely conservative and so women in provocative attire would understandably attract a response. It has to be said many local men receive considerable encouragement in this direction. Just behave as you would anywhere else, taking normal care and precautions.

POLICE

Headed by a six-member Police Service Commission appointed by the governor-general, Antigua has five police sub-divisions with ten police stations (plus one on Barbuda) and a divisional headquarters on the eastern outskirts of St John's (see Appendix, page 320).

BUSINESS HOURS

COMMERCIAL

Most general retailers are open from 8am to 4pm, Monday to Saturday and closed on Sundays. However, stores and shops in resort areas and at Heritage Quay and Historic Redcliffe Quay may vary these times – in fact if there is a cruise ship in on a Sunday, many of the major stores in St John's will open. A few of the more traditional, old established shops and businesses may close in the middle of the day for lunch and only open for half a day on Thursday.

Supermarkets vary from opening at 8am to closing at 7pm and the larger, the later, up to 10pm, seven days a week.

GOVERNMENT

Offices and departments are open Monday to Friday, 8am to 4.30pm (3pm on Fridays).

BANKING HOURS AND SERVICES

As banking hours and services differ, refer to Appendix (page 312) for comprehensive information and complete listings of all banks in Antigua and Barbuda.

ANTIGUA

All the main banks are in St John's, some with branches at Woods Centre, the airport, English Harbour and Jolly Harbour, but not found elsewhere on the island, so be sure you have enough cash and small change before you set off. All banks will change cash and traveller's cheques to EC dollars, but for those which accept credit cards, a passport, or means of identification and identification with a photograph, must be shown at the bank at the time of the transaction. Instant money is available through Automated Teller Machines (ATMs), which are a recent blessing to the island and an absolute boon to visitors who are well versed with obtaining cash at home in this convenient and time-saving manner. Another source of receiving money in minutes (on a pre-arranged basis) is via Western Union Money Transfer, who have offices in Antigua and more than 100 countries worldwide.

BARBUDA

There are branches of the Antigua Barbuda Investment Bank and Antigua Commercial Bank on Barbuda, which can handle currency transactions.

TELECOMMUNICATIONS

TELEPHONE

The Antigua Public Utilities Authority (APUA) operates a reliable island-wide local telephone service (as well as the water and electricity supplies).

The worldwide company Cable & Wireless is responsible for all external telecommunications including digital direct-dialing facilities, fax, Internet, data access services, telex, paging and mobile phone services. With continual commitment to upgrading, a massive investment was made on their part with a state-of-the-art submarine fibre optic cable system linking 17 Caribbean islands and allowing provision for high operating transmission of services such as international direct dialling (IDD), credit card calls, operator-connected calls, cardphones and even more sophisticated switching services for ISDN, video conferencing and data network service (DNS 2000).

The many easy-to-use, public call boxes are quite widespread and provided by both APUA and Cable & Wireless. The APUA public telephones accept either 25-cent and one-dollar coins and can only be used for local calls. Call boxes with the blue Cable & Wireless logo accept the widely used and popular Cable & Wireless Antiguan phone cards. Overseas calls can be made from these public phones. Prepaid calling cards are available from Cable & Wireless and can be used to make international calls from any touch-tone phone; such calls can also be charged to Mastercard, Visa and Discover credit cards.

Phone cards can be purchased,

in varying EC dollar denominations, at the Cable & Wireless office on the corner of Long and Thames Streets, St John's, and Antigua Yacht Club Marina, at two Cable & Wireless vending machines located at the airport, plus at selected shops, major supermarkets, pharmacies and some banks island-wide.

They are a particularly economical option as international calls made from the Cable & Wireless office in St John's, private or hotel phones are charged by the full minute (plus an additional 20 per cent government tax, and hotel charges where applicable). Using the card bypasses this, deducting only those minutes and seconds used, from the time allocated on the type of phone card purchased.

Phone books, with tourist and yellow pages sections, are easy to come by at hotels, villas, apartments and private homes, and the local directory enquiry operators (411) are usually very helpful.

Dialling 0 for the overseas operators will put you directly in touch with the efficient Cable & Wireless operators who will assist you in placing overseas calls, or connect you to the operator in the required country for any international directory assistance. Cable & Wireless can also arrange connections to their Quick Reach Beeper Service pager.

Cable & Wireless Customer Front Office, Cnr Long and Thames Streets, St John's
tel: (268) 480 4000
fax: (268) 480 4240

Antigua Yacht Club Marina
tel: (268) 480 2626
fax: (268) 480 4323

OPERATOR ASSISTED INTERNATIONAL CALLS
When placing your overseas call through the operator (all carrying a minimum three-minute charge), you will need to state which type of call you require:
a Person-to-person: when you wish to speak to a particular person. Give the operator the name, and once connected to that person and conversation begins, the charging commences.

b Station-to-station: when you wish to speak with anyone who answers the number given. Charging begins as soon as a response is heard, whether from a person or an answering device.
c Collect: give the operator the name of the party to authorise the acceptance of the charges.
d Credit card: a very convenient means of payment. Give the operator the information requested from your calling card or credit card.
e Ship: calls are possible to ships at sea. Give the operator the necessary details.

CELLULAR PHONES
That ubiquitous and increasingly necessary appendage is available here, should you suffer withdrawal symptoms or need to be accessible. Visitors can hire a cellular phone from either Cable & Wireless Caribbean Cellular or APUA PCS, enabling you to relax yet still stay in touch with business, family and friends both on island and overseas.

Should you be island hopping, they have a 'one number roaming to the Caribbean' service which makes it possible to make and receive calls on your cellular phone when you are outside the home service area. Previously, visitors had to obtain a separate cellular number for almost every island they visited in the Caribbean. There is a surcharge for this service but it is far less expensive than call-forwarding calls from one island to the next.

If visitors have an AMPS-compatible cellular system at home, pre-registering is possible (USA 1-800-262-8366; Canada 1-800-567-8366; elsewhere 1-268-480-2628). Once arrived, simply dial '0 SND' for instant over-the-phone access. A division of the island's own national telecommunications company, APUA Telephones Division, has a full range of cellular phones and services available from APUA PCS. This offers full facilities using GSM technology, whereby anyone with a Triband GSM phone can obtain a SIM card and make and receive local and international calls, by purchasing a prepaid calling card from APUA. For a visitor from the USA or Canada with a GSM 1900 (unlocked), the same

applies as for the GSM Triband. For those visitors wishing to rent an APUA prepaid cellular phone, for making and receiving local and international calls, these can be obtained from APUA PCS in St John's and Nelson's Dockyard with outlets planned island wide. Check their web site for full information.

Airtel has a cellular phone service for visitors who have a TDMA or Dual Mode phone. They can programme the phone on a prepaid service for local and overseas access.

Airtell Cellular
Friar's Hill Road,
Gambles Medical Centre, St John's
tel: (268) 480 2050

APUA Personal Communications Service (PCS)
Long Street, St John's
tel: (268) 727 2782
fax: (268) 480 7476
e-mail: vwhyte@candw.ag
web site: www.apuatel.com

Cable & Wireless Caribbean Cellular
Bencorp Building,
Independence Avenue, St John's
tel: (268) 480 2600
fax: (268) 480 2629
e-mail: info@caribcell.com

Cable & Wireless Caribbean Cellular
Woods Centre
tel: (268) 480 2628
Antigua Yacht Club Marina
tel: (268) 480 2626

AREA CODES
The international dialling code is 268. When calling from the UK, dial 001 268 and then the seven-digit local number; calling from the USA or Canada, dial 1 268, followed by the seven-digit local number.

When calling the UK from Antigua or Barbuda, dial 011 44 before the UK number and calling the USA from here, dial 1 before the US number. The local phone book gives comprehensive coverage of dialling codes and charge bands for worldwide destinations.

FAX
Faxes may be sent from most hotels and a very useful public service is

offered by Cable & Wireless for the sending and receiving of faxes. At the St John's main office you can take advantage of their Bureaufax facilities by sending a fax directly from there or enquire about the receipt of one. Various yacht service companies and cyber cafés will also offer fax facilities. Naturally, the information already covered relating to both local and international telephone calls, applies to faxes sent from private or hotel fax machines.

Cable & Wireless Customer Front Office
Cnr Long & Thames Strs, St John's
tel: (268) 480 4000
Bureaufax Service: (268) 480 4236

Cable & Wireless
Antigua Yacht Club Marina
tel: (268) 480 2626
Bureaufax Service: (268) 480 4323

INTERNET AND E-MAIL

Again, Cable & Wireless provides a one-stop global telecommunications network, not exactly a cyber café but offering all the latest technology just the same. At their office on Long and Thames Streets, St John's (details above), you can browse the Net, access your e-mail, print out information or work on a project. Use your own laptop or one of their desktop PCs.

There are also a few other places offering Internet and e-mail services, amongst others.

Cyber Stop
Antigua Yacht Club Marina
Falmouth Harbour
tel: (268) 463 2662
fax: (268) 463 0825 VHF: 68
e-mail: anna@antiguarent.com

Internet Connections
Upper High Street, St John's
tel: (268) 480 3000
fax: (268) 480 3003
e-mail: demo@candw.ag

Mad Max Video Cyber Café
Putters, Dickenson Bay
tel: (268) 562 3456
fax: (268) 560 4653
e-mail: dickensonpark@hotmail.com

Parcel Plus
14 Historic Redcliffe Quay, St John's

tel: (268) 562 7587
fax: (268) 562 7588
e-mail: plusfive@candw.ag

Skullduggery Expresso Bar and Internet
Antigua Yacht Club Marina
(and at Nelson's Dockyard),
English Harbour
tel: (268) 463 0625
e-mail: skulldug@candw.ag

SOS Asis
50 Church Street, St John's
tel: (268) 562 1585
fax: (1) 530 618 7165
e-mail: sosasis@hotmail.com

POST OFFICES, MAIL AND RELATED SERVICES

OPENING HOURS

The main post office in Long Street, St John's is open Monday to Friday 8am to 4pm (5pm Friday). There are sub-post offices at the airport, Woods Shopping Mall, Nelson's Dockyard, in All Saints, and a branch in Codrington, Barbuda – all are open from 8am to 4pm weekdays.

Postal rates are incredibly low compared with rates in the USA, Canada and the UK – so you can happily while away a few hours writing to friends and family back home. Stamps are also on sale at most hotels. You can purchase very economical Antiguan aerogrammes from post offices.

PHILATELIC BUREAU

This is located at the main post office in St John's for first day covers and special issue stamps. To join the mailing list, obtain the necessary form from the bureau, whereupon you will receive the current stock list of stamps available and their prices, along with a standing order form. Stamps remain on sale for six months or until supply is exhausted; only the cost of the stamps and postage (where applicable) is payable. Enquiries can be addressed to the Postmistress-General, General Post Office, High and Long Streets, St John's, Antigua tel: (268) 462 0023/4 fax: (268) 462 1622

POSTE RESTANTE

For those wishing to receive mail, rather than just send, there are poste restante services at the post offices island-wide and on Barbuda. Mail should be marked with your date of arrival in Antigua or Barbuda, addressed to you (emphasising your surname), c/o General Delivery, name of post office, Antigua, West Indies. You will need identification when you pick up such mail.

American Express cardholders, or those with Amex traveller's cheques, can have mail held for them at their office at Antours, PO Box 508, St John's, Antigua, addressed similarly as the general delivery mail to the Post Office (above).

PACKAGES

Be warned that if anyone sends you a package or parcel, it will be held at the main post office in St John's and will have to clear customs. They will ask you to open it in front of them and very likely charge duty, which could be as much, if not more, than the value of the goods. So, wait until you get home for that birthday present!

COURIER SERVICES

There are a number of internationally known courier services offering the usual facilities of speedy door-to-door

INTERNATIONAL PEN FRIENDS

There is a very active, local representative of this worldwide organisation, based at Christian Hill. With headquarters in Dublin, Ireland, the aim of International Pen Friends is to bring the world closer together by pen and paper. There is a membership book of 300,000 people in 210 countries, covering eight languages; the subscription fee varies according to age. Send your name and address, together with any requests of type of person and country you wish to communicate with – members include people of all ages and from all walks of life: schoolchildren, university professors, business owners, politicians, clergy, and so on. To join or gain further information, contact Alva Carlos or Keitha James, IPF Chairperson tel: (268) 463 3269

delivery of mail and small packages, both regionally and worldwide.

DHL Worldwide Express
tel: (268) 462 2034
fax: (268) 462 2035

Federal Express tel: (268) 562 7587
fax: (268) 562 7588
Barbuda tel: (268) 460 0465

UPS (LIAT) tel: (268) 480 5735
fax: (268) 480 5860

NEWS AND MEDIA

NEWSPAPERS AND MAGAZINES
There are various newspapers: The *Antigua Sun* is a comprehensive paper covering local news, events, sport, regional and international news items; *The Daily Observer* carries local and international news and both are published Monday to Saturday; *The Outlet* publishes political and local issues each Tuesday and Thursday; *The Workers' Voice*, the government mouthpiece, comes out every Friday.

The official publication of the Antigua Hotels and Tourist Association and the Department of Tourism is a large, square-shaped 'coffee table' type magazine called *Life in Antigua*. This is available, on a complimentary basis, through all hotel rooms, suites, apartments and villas on Antigua, plus through the main ground handling tour companies. This striking and colourful publication encompasses all you need to know whilst on the island, as well as carrying unusual and interesting articles and 'snippets' of island life. So, if staying in a hotel or apartment-hotel, be sure to obtain this (not all hotel issues carry the main title of the magazine on the front cover, having fully personalised it for their guests). You may well be able to pick up other smaller free magazines and maps about Antigua, whilst on your travels around the island.

Quality magazines are also produced for the famed Antigua Sailing Week Regatta and the Classic Yacht Regatta (see pages 119 and 123), available from the major travel shows around the world, and distributed on the island from the beginning of each year. Major titles of international colour magazines,

news periodicals and books are available from the following:
First Editions
Woods Centre
tel: (268) 462 9246
fax: (268) 462 9363
e-mail: firstedition@candw.ag

Island Newstand
Bob Camacho's Arcade,
High Street, St John's
tel: (268) 462 2457
fax: (268) 462 2458

Lord Jim's Locker
Antigua Yacht Club Marina,
Falmouth Harbour
tel: (268) 460 1147
fax: (268) 560 4093
e-mail: lordjim@candw.ag

P.C.'s Book Review
St Mary's Street, St John's
tel: (268) 462 1545
fax: (268) 480 4240

RADIO
The government radio station ABS (Antigua and Barbuda Broadcasting Service), broadcasts on AM 620 with news, information and entertainment. The BBC World Service is widely listened to, and is found on 89.1mhz FM, and 6.195mhz, 5.975mhz, 17.840mhz AM (depending on time of day). Nationally broadcast US channels are available and there are various other commercial local and regional stations offering music, chat shows and news. Probably the most popular of these local stations are GEM, broadcasting on FM 93.9, Sun FM on FM 100.1, ZDK on FM 99.0, all carrying an hourly news service and Caribbean and international music; Voice of America is on 15.575mhz AM, and Radio France Internationale can be found on either 9.800, 11.615, 13.625, 15.530, 17.630. 17.860 or 21.645mhz AM; the local Caribbean Radio Lighthouse station broadcasts mainly programmes with a religious slant on 1160mhz AM. As cricket is the national game, radio coverage can always be found on ABS at 620 AM whenever there is a cricket series anywhere in the Caribbean.

HAM RADIO
Enthusiasts can tune in to 3.815 mhz on the 80 metre band where twice

daily at 6.30am local (or 10.30am GMT) and again at 6.30pm local (or 22.30 GMT), there is a general roll call beginning with Guyana in the south up to the Virgin Islands in the north. As with other countries worldwide, Antigua has a reciprocal licence arrangement. Operators are granted a temporary licence which allows them to use their home call in combination with the Antigua country code (V2). A normal procedure is followed to obtain such a licence, involving a formal application to the Ministry of Telecommunications. The application form requires specific details of the operator's country of birth, call sign, class of licence, expiry date and must be accompanied with identification and a copy of the person's valid licence.

For those visitors interested, there is a local ham operator who facilitates amateur radio operators who would like to participate in the very popular worldwide operator contests. Providing an antennae farm, he is able to accommodate most requirements.

Campbell Mickey Matthew
Telecommunications Officer
tel: (268) 460 5552/462 1113
fax: (268) 481 1672
e-mail matthewm@candw.ag

Roy Carty tel: (268) 462 0982

MARINE VHF
Where would 'yachties' (and those without phones) be without this vital and much used form of communication? For local news and weather, switch to channel 06 at 9am for English Harbour Radio, entertainingly broadcast by the locally famed English sailor and raconteur, Jol Byerley. For general communication, use channel 68.

With respect to safety related communications, yachting communities try and avoid using channel 16 for calling shore based stations or other yachts. When in Antigua channel 68 is used and once contact is made, callers switch to another working channel.

TELEVISION
There is one island television station, the government owned Antigua

and Barbuda TV Station (ABS), which broadcasts in colour. Most of the larger hotels have cable or satellite television, whether in-room or in the lounge area.

VIDEO TAPES, TELEVISION AND VIDEO RENTALS
Video-tape rental outlets are quite common around the island, and the Hitachi Centre has colour televisions and video machines for rental on a weekly basis.

Television Hire
The Hitachi Centre,
Market Street, St John's
tel: (268) 462 1371
fax: (268) 462 4849

Video Hire
DJ's Video Club, Games and Electronics Centre
tel: (268) 460 5685

First Run Video Club
tel: (268) 460 5888/463 0825

Mad Max/Putters
tel: (268) 562 3456

Neighbourhood Video Spot
tel: (268) 462 9506

Super Video Club
tel: (268) 462 2267

CINEMA
There is a good, recently refurbished air-conditioned cinema situated in High Street, St John's.

The Deluxe Cinema Movieline
tel: (268) 462 3664

BOOKS
The largest and most comprehensively stocked book shop on the island is First Editions at Woods Mall, just north of St John's, with a branch at Galley Boutique, Jolly Harbour; they also stock most of the hotel shops and boutiques. Worthy of comparison with any international bookstore, you will find the latest bestseller, a vast selection of all types of subjects, including a good range of books on Antigua and other parts of the Caribbean.

In St John's, Island Newstand is centrally located for a wide range of newspapers, magazines and books; the Map Shop caters to those seek-ing educational, religious, travel and other subject matter books, and carries a good selection of maps. The Gift Shop at the Museum of Antigua and Barbuda, St John's, stocks a wonderful range of locally published stories, folklore and poetry, along with many excellent publications by local historian, Desmond Nicholson.

The Best of Books
Benjies Mall,
Redcliffe Street, St John's
tel: (268) 461 2369
fax: (268) 462 2199

First Editions, Woods Centre
tel: (268) 462 9246
fax: (268) 462 9363
e-mail: firstedition@candw.ag

Galley Boutique, Jolly Harbour
tel: (268) 462 7693
fax: (268) 460 1333

Island Newstand
Bob Camacho's Arcade,
High Street, St John's
tel: (268) 462 2457
fax: (268) 462 2458

MAPS
Lord Jim's Locker
Antigua Yacht Club Marina,
Falmouth Harbour
tel: (268) 460 1147
fax: (268) 560 4093
e-mail: lordjim@candw.ag

The Map Shop
St Mary's Street, St John's
tel: (268) 462 3993
fax: (268) 462 3995

PUBLIC LIBRARIES AND ARCHIVES
There is only one main public library, located in Market Street, St John's; it is sadly lacking in good, up-to-date stocks, funding and facilities and only available to residents, or those able to borrow on behalf of a resident.

There is also the admirable effort of a small library, created by a local student, situated in the Greenbay/Donovans area. He started the Village Library in August 1997, having learnt how to run the facility from his school's library-skills programme. From the basic premises he initially created, the Optimist Club of Wadadli erected a larger, solid, purpose-built structure. Found there most days and some evenings, Marlon Carr is often visited by tourists who, having heard of him, seek him out to donate their holiday reading and offer support.

Visitors interested in the life and history of Antigua will find a visit to the National Archives well worthwhile. An air-conditioned modern building houses information relating to education, the government, the Antiguan people through family records, including the famed Codrington Papers. Regular exhibitions are held throughout the year of two weeks' or a month's duration. Conveniently situated on Factory Road, near the Cenotaph in St John's, it is open Monday to Friday.

The comprehensive reference library at the Museum of Antigua and Barbuda welcomes visitors. Overlooking the main museum exhibition area, you will find a wealth of information amongst the hundreds of documented books and computer records. Adjacent to the National Archives will be the location for the new state-of-the-art Public Library, complete with computers, research and study rooms.

Antigua and Barbuda Library Association
(Mr Noval Lindsay, President)
tel: (268) 462 3946

Law Library
St Mary's Street, St John's
tel: (268) 462 0626

Museum of Antigua and Barbuda
Long Street, St John's
tel: (268) 462 4930
fax: (268) 462 1469

National Archives
Factory Road, St John's
tel: (268) 462 3946
fax: (268) 462 4959

Public Library
Market Street,
St John's tel: (268) 462 0229

FILM AND PHOTOGRAPHY
A veritable photographer's paradise abounds on these islands. Intense sunlight can cause over-exposure and so safer times for taking pictures would be early morning or later in the afternoon; otherwise

filters could be used. Avoid leaving your camera in direct sunlight, by a window or in the car and have film developed immediately upon your return home. If using specialised or professional film, it's a good idea to keep this in the fridge, should one be available where you are staying (see also important note under Travelling To and From Antigua, page 6).

There are excellent photo-processing centres in Antigua, many with a one-hour, or at least a one-day, service. This is also where you will find print film (plus at hotel boutiques, local shops, supermarkets) and, in a couple of the larger establishments, slide film. Internationally known brands of cameras, equipment, lenses and filters can be purchased both inside and outside duty-free Heritage Quay.

Benjies
Heritage Quay, St John's
tel: (268) 462 3619
fax: (268) 462 3803

Carib Foto
Woods Centre
tel/fax: (268) 562 0142

Island Photo
Redcliffe Street, St John's
tel: (268) 462 1567
fax: (268) 462 7726

Photogenesis
Michael's Avenue, St John's
tel/fax: (268) 462 1066

GETTING AROUND AND PUBLIC TRANSPORT

> The use of travelling is to regulate imagination by reality, and instead of thinking how things may be, to see them as they are.
>
> Dr Samuel Johnson

First-time visitors are invariably surprised by the many things to explore, see and do whilst in Antigua and how you travel depends on how adventurous you feel: you can either freely go round on your own, let someone else take you or book an organised tour.

HELICOPTER

Helicopters are relatively new to the travel and sightseeing scene, and

very successful too. Enquiries for private charters to nearby islands can be made directly with the helicopter company or through a travel agent. For short to longer shared tours, viewing by helicopter gives a unique slant on the island and offers a breathtaking trip, accompanied by a personal running commentary. Since the unfortunate volcanic eruption in Montserrat, helicopter tours to this neighbouring island have also become popular.

Caribbean Helicopters
Jolly Harbour
tel: (268) 460 5900
fax: (268) 460 5901
e-mail: helicopters@candw.ag

CAR HIRE

The most popular way for visitors to see the island is by car or four-wheel jeep rental ('R' or 'RA' on the number plate denotes an official rental vehicle that can be legally rented) and you are well advised to book these in advance during the peak periods. This form of transport allows you to come and go as you please, at whatever pace you choose and is highly recommended if you are staying for more than a day or two. Getting around Antigua's uncongested roads is not at all difficult and no point on the island will be far from your base. Do not put off the opportunity to drive yourself around the island for fear of getting lost – as it is only a small island, you can always ask someone for advice en route and even if you do find yourself temporarily misrouted, this may just add to a memorable adventure.

Book through your home travel agent or at the airport upon arrival, through your hotel or direct with the car-hire office – they should all deliver your choice of vehicle to your hotel free of charge. Ask the car rental company to provide a copy of the full colour, easy to follow *Antigua and Barbuda Tourist Map*. This comprehensive, colourful island map (see also page 174), includes all hotels, petrol stations, points of interest and three coded sightseeing routes plus a good street guide of St John's, complete with the one-way traffic system.

A local temporary 90-day driving licence is required by law, easily obtained upon presentation of your own valid driving licence and a fee of EC$ 50.00 (US$ 20.00). This can be arranged through the car-hire company, at the Transport Board in Factory Road, St John's (tel: 460 8300) or at the police stations at Coolidge (near the Airport tel: 462 3185), American Road (St John's tel: 462 3913), English Harbour (tel: 460 1002) and Bolans (near Jolly Harbour tel: 462 1080).

Refer to Appendix (page 315) for the many international and reliable local car-hire companies, which offer a variety of vehicles, including manual and automatic transmissions, air-conditioned cars, sporty four-wheel drive vehicles; some rental companies have vehicles for seating larger numbers. Naturally, rates differ with size and type of vehicle and with the time of year. At the time of taking over the vehicle, check for any scratches and bumps already made (then there's no risk of you being charged for them), and that there is a fully inflated spare tyre and a jack provided. You should check the insurance cover as well.

Filling stations are relatively numerous, although understandably less so in the rural areas, and often closed on a Sunday. Check your petrol level before leaving on a trip (petrol is sold by the gallon).

SCOOTERS AND MOTORBIKES

These are a more liberating and adventurous mode of transport, but being completely out in the open, don't forget to apply copious sun cream on bare arms or legs!

As with any self-driven transport, care must be taken to avoid careering into an unexpected wandering roadside herd of cows or goats, children playing around a corner, dogs darting out in front of, or beside, you, and more. The apparently quiet roads can lull one into a dangerous false sense of security. Nevertheless, scooters and motorcycles do offer great flexibility. Again, a temporary local driving licence is required and you have to be over 25 years of age. Crash helmets are provided (see Appendix for listings, page 315).

BICYCLES

These are an excellent way for the fit to explore the island and its less accessible regions, when you have the advantage of savouring the scenery and the opportunity of local contact. Extra caution should be taken though, when cycling on the road, as it can be somewhat hazardous to the vulnerable cyclist, with vehicles swerving to avoid animals and potholes! Remember to wear a wide-brimmed hat or baseball cap to avoid the risk of sunstroke, and be well protected with sunscreen lotion on exposed skin. Also bear in mind, that the bikes you hire may not have lights, in which case be especially careful at night.

Extensive ranges of bikes, including mountain bikes are available for hire by arrangement, plus guided tours, from companies in St John's and Jolly Harbour (refer to Appendix, page 315).

ROAD RULES AND ADVICE

Driving on the left is the first rule of the road here. There are parking restrictions in the capital, St John's, but these do not pose a problem, especially if you are prepared to park a short walk from the centre. Failure to comply with the painted parking areas would result in a parking fine, even if the offence is eventually forwarded through to the car rental company at a later date, in which case, it would be added to your charges. With some 650 miles of open paved roads and light traffic, there are no restrictions elsewhere on the island.

In the more rural areas, there are many unpaved roads and tracks to tempt those with four-wheel drive vehicles, scooters and bikes. Whilst these can lead to quaint little villages and secluded groves, do be aware that you may end up trespassing on someone's back garden! Also take care when ascending and descending some of these steeper tracks as rainfall can cause considerable erosion, loose stones and boulders.

You're likely to emulate the unhurried pace of the locals and following their example is the best way to make the most of your drive – besides, what's the hurry? Speeding

is ill advised anywhere, but particularly here in Antigua when you never know when you may come across goats or cows crossing the road, an impromptu cricket or basketball match on the tarmac, or even a vehicle on the wrong side of the road avoiding a pothole!

It is not unusual here for the driver of the car in front to stop suddenly, without warning, for a chat with a friend, turn without signalling or park awkwardly; this is simply characteristic of the people and the island, so please also be prepared for these eventualities. Many roads are unlit at night, so a steady speed is sensible, as is the use of your main beam to spot the odd pedestrian or animal along the roadside ahead. However, a word of warning: invariably local drivers have a habit of keeping their main beam on even when a car approaches in the opposite direction. Whilst this is happening slightly less often, when it does, it can be very dangerous, totally blinding you; if it is obvious this may happen, a common preventative is simply to flash your main beam at the offending driver,

who often as not, will oblige by switching it off until he or she passes you – as is the normal, courteous practice elsewhere in the world.

There is a law here regarding the wearing of seat belts, with a EC$ 500 fine if prosecuted by the police for not doing so; it is advisable to use seat belts at all times, just as you would back home.

Should you be unfortunate enough to encounter a breakdown, call your car-hire company, which will assist you. In the unlikely event of an accident, you must leave your vehicle in its position at the time of the accident, and phone the police, as well as your car-rental company immediately, which will help you in dealing with the situation. Do not be tempted to move your vehicle, even if it is blocking the road, as the insurance company needs the police report, and you could otherwise invalidate your insurance.

Although not particularly obvious, there are drink/driving laws and heavy penalities that could be levied if convicted, especially if there was an accident.

DRIVING AROUND THE ISLAND AND DIRECTIONS

Antigua has a good network of uncongested roads and whilst some of the minor roads are still in a state of disrepair, the major roads have benefited from major long-term road resurfacing improvements. But, the odd pothole along the country lanes merely adds to the charm and character of the island, rather than having spaghetti junctions of sleek surfaced roads.

Once totally devoid of directional signs, Antigua now has large green and white signs at the main intersections around the island. The island's relatively small size makes it virtually impossible to get completely lost and, remember, if all else fails, the sea is also there to guide you.

There are often hotel, restaurant and tourist attraction directions posted on many telegraph poles. Don't hesitate to ask a passing local for help, and should you take a wrong turn in getting from place to place, it can only enhance your touring adventure.

St John's street signs have also increased in numbers, thus aiding getting around town.

Barbuda has no surfaced road system, rather dirt roads and tracks and no signed directions but plenty of people to help you find your way.

TAXIS

These are much used by those preferring to be chauffeured, to freely enjoy the journey (as it is difficult for the driver when sightseeing to fully appreciate the drive's sights and sounds) and at the same time not have to concern yourself with where to go and how to get there. These are recognised by 'H', 'HA' or 'HB', on the registration plate. Taxis can be ordered from your hotel or with a call directly to the taxi firm (refer to Appendix, page 315). Their fares are unmetered but the government fixes standard rates island-wide and it is wise to establish both the amount and the currency before setting off. These mostly privately owned vehicles tend to congregate around St John's, Woods Centre and the airport in the north, at Nelson's Dockyard in the south, at Jolly Harbour in the west and are available at all times. If you are being dropped off at a bar or restaurant, it is just as well to arrange in advance for return transport.

Any one of these knowledgeable drivers is only too delighted to escort you on short or long sightseeing tours, often accompanied with entertaining local tales and folklore. Hired by the trip, the hour, half or full day, prices are negotiable for such sightseeing trips. You may prefer a mixture of driving around at leisure during the day and travelling by taxi in the evening.

MINIBUSES

These 14- to up to 28-seater buses mainly ply the north–south, St John's to English Harbour main route, and will pick up and drop off on request. Sometimes very noisy with loud music, nevertheless, they are an economical (and usually extremely quick) privately owned form of travel. Operating prescribed routes as assigned by the Transport Board's unofficial system of routes, they connect outlying parts of the island with St John's. Originating from two main bus stations in St John's, they operate from early morning to dusk, Monday to Saturday and less frequently on Sundays and holidays. Passengers pay their fares on entering, with children under twelve paying half the adult fare and no fare for infants in arms.

East Bus Station is situated near the Cenotaph, Independence Avenue, St John's.

West Bus Station is in Market Street, St John's.

BUS

This form of public transport has a somewhat erratic service, with no timetable and rarely any marked stopping places but it is an extremely cheap and fun way to travel. Many visitors get tremendous enjoyment from this local form of travel and it presents a great way to meet and chat with the villagers.

They will gladly help with where you should, or should not, get off. Once you do, it's a question of merely waiting for another bus to come along to continue this interesting, casual trip, or attracting the attention of both car and taxi drivers by pointing to the ground or in the direction you wish to continue.

Using the same two main bus stations in St John's as the minibuses: East Bus Station, Independence Avenue, near the Memorial, serves both the north and the east of the island, West Bus Station, by St John's market, the villages in the southern and western parts of the island and English Harbour.

The local people will be well versed in the main routes served, which tend to start from very early in the morning to around 6pm, although the central All Saints to St John's route normally continues until quite late. The bus services are reduced at the weekends, being quite scarce on Sundays.

CONDUCTED SIGHTSEEING TOURS

One of the easiest ways to see especially the lesser known, more rugged and historic parts of Antigua is with the growing number of four-wheel drive escorted tours available (see page 212).

ETIQUETTE

Local customs and values may differ from home and misunderstandings are best avoided for a happy and pleasant holiday or business trip. A high moral standard abounds on an island where the church is still very much a focal and social point. Therefore, to the average conservative Antiguan, topless bathing is generally frowned upon and could attract unnecessary and unwanted attention; resort hotels are the occasional exceptions. So too, understandably, inappropriate attire, such as swimsuits, bikini tops and the like, are not appreciated in town.

Antiguans, particularly the older generation, have an innate sense of traditional manners and politeness. It is not unusual for someone to enter a shop, waiting room or any other public place, and greet those assembled (even if all strangers), with a 'Good morning', or 'Good afternoon'. This is an absolutely delightful tradition, which humbles one into realising just how impersonal and impolite the pace of the later twentieth century has made some of us. Certainly, if you wish to ask directions or a question, you will have far more respect and cooperation if you greet the person appropriately first, instead of just abruptly firing off your request despite your eagerness for the answer. The maxim anywhere in the world should be to treat all others with the same respect as you would wish to receive.

On an island of such great beauty, both in sights and people, visitors naturally wish to take many photos and record video footage. However, taking into account the hundreds of thousands who follow similar routes, it can be quite offensive to villagers when tourists are intrusive in their desire to capture a local at work or play (imagine trails of folks peering into your window or garden, let alone with camcorder or camera!). So, if you wish specifically to take a picture of anyone, please respect local sensibilities and ask permission; it is often given and such courtesy is sometimes further rewarded, if desired, with conversation.

WHAT TO BUY

There is a wealth of locally made goods and luxury duty-free bargains to be recommended, whether for personal use or as gifts. Selections of these can be found in St John's, Jolly Harbour, English Harbour, resort and hotel boutiques and at other spots around the island (see also page 229).

There's a burgeoning arts and pottery scene with an extensive variety of styles and items, which can either be bought direct from the artist, sculptor and potter, or from one of the many retail outlets stocking their wares.

Not surprisingly, one of the most durable and inexpensive souvenirs is a t-shirt and Antigua offers an inexhaustible range of screen and hand printed or painted, in all manner of styles and sizes. The island also boasts an increasing number of gifted clothing designers, and wonderful tropical outfits for the whole family have become very popular buys.

Vendors line some of the streets in St John's, likewise along some of the more popular beaches, offering amongst other handicrafts and items, locally created jewellery made from soaked, baked, and/or painted seeds, shells, beads and the like, all frequently purchased by the eager visitor. Another sought-after item with multiple uses is the ubiquitous sarong dress, to fit all sizes and often seen colourfully strung out along washing lines.

Local shops and the market are a good source of locally made tropical jams, jellies, chutneys, sauces and spices, to help maintain that Antiguan flavour once back home. With a history of sugar cane and rum making, it is no surprise to find various brands of popular (and extremely low priced) Antiguan rum – perfect for rum punches back home, or for spicing up desserts.

Selecting your purchases from local goods and handicrafts is of especial value to Antigua and Barbuda, boosting the local economy and benefiting all. Last minute buys can be made from the small range of excellent and diversified shops at the airport.

TIPPING AND TAXES

This is an accepted practice the world over, including Antigua. Most hotels and restaurants add a standard service charge of 10 per cent, and it is purely up to the individual as to whether they leave more; just check whether it has already been included or not. There is also an 8.5 per cent government tax which will be included. The price quoted on any goods is the price to be paid; there is no VAT or service tax to be added.

Taxi drivers, again as the norm elsewhere, usually receive 10 per cent of the fare. Hotel guests often leave something for the maid, and villa guests tend to tip more.

SUNRISE AND SUNSET/ 'THE GREEN FLASH'

Antiguan sunsets are legendary, but like the sunrise, happen very quickly and so are not very long lasting. Maybe that's why 'sundowner' drinks are so popular, affording great photo opportunities and enable one to totally savour every second. Many also practise this ritual for the possibility of a glimpse of the illusive 'green flash'. This is best spotted on or near the sea, when the last sighting of the sun disappearing behind a cloudless horizon can result in a luminous green strip, slightly more than the width of the sun, zapping across the surface of the sea for no more than a split second. The Travel Channel (USA) recently named Antigua as having one of the top five best beach sunsets in the world.

Being so close to the equator, days and nights are of about the same length. So the glowing sun disappears under the horizon, around 6–6.30pm, as quickly as it appears, 6–6.30am at dawn.

History and
heritage

History and heritage

On his second voyage to the New World in search for a route to India, Christopher Columbus sighted a previously uncharted island, from nearby Redonda, on 11 November 1493. While historians generally accept that he did not land on the island, he is credited with naming this island, Antigua, in homage to a famous miracle-working saint in Seville Cathedral, Santa Maria de la Antigua.

It was during this latter part of the fifteenth century that Columbus unfurled royal banners and planted Christian crosses, taking possession of other neighbouring islands. Henceforth, the Lesser West Indies became part of European history.

However, what he 'discovered', whilst a world new to Europeans, was a world with people and with a history thousands of years old. It is thought to be around 4000 years ago when the first hunters and gatherers arrived on Antigua, probably from South America. The islands then were much larger so the distances between them were shorter and more navigable than today. Archaeologists have uncovered evidence suggesting that this tiny island had been inhabited, although not continuously, since this time.

Archaic Amerindians arrived by primitive canoe having threaded their way between Antigua and Barbuda's barrier reef to land on sandy beaches (see also Barbuda History, page 298). These seafaring people existed on the abundant fauna and flora of shore and ocean, fishing and living with skilfully made stone and shell tools. They had paddled from their native South America in 100-foot long canoes, first arriving in Trinidad and Tobago, from whence they slowly made their way north to arrive at these islands. Sea levels were then at least 275 feet lower than they are today so Antigua and Barbuda were joined.

The carbon dating of ancient camp-fire charcoal found in the Jolly Beach area, later led to the belief that the earliest known tribe lived here about 1775 BC. These were an archaic pre-ceramic people. Nomadic wanderers, these archaic Amerindians collected marine resources mainly around North Sound, an ideal area for collecting the necessities of life.

For the next 1000 years, Antigua appears to have been completely uninhabited, until the seafaring, semi-nomadic Arawak began migrating from their original home in South America to the islands of the Caribbean. They settled here around Indian Creek, Mamora Bay, Mill Reef, Coconut Hall, Blackman's Point and at Spanish Point in Barbuda. Another 40 settlement sites are known in other parts of Antigua, where they found conditions reasonable for raising their newly introduced plants and crops of cassava, corn, sweet potato, and fruits such as soursop, guavas and pineapple. They tended to live next to shallow waters and lagoons, subsisting on the waters rich in shellfish and fish.

These pottery making, rural people lived a peaceable and industrious pastoral life, organising a surprisingly advanced agricultural society until around 1200 AD. Archaeological digs and various finds have revealed examples of shell adze, shell middens and their distinctive pottery, decorated with a white paint, dated about 300 AD. From such archaeological explorations, the site at Indian Creek with its abundant supply of natural resources, would seem to have supported around 50 people.

Then, firstly, the Indian Creek mangrove swamp and site eventually silted up, killing off the marine life and, with fresh water in short supply, their agricultural way of life was threatened. Second, around the same time, the Ignimis branch of the warlike Carib Indians, or Calibi as the Indians called themselves, were advancing through the Windward Islands.

Initially responsible for the Arawak's exodus from South America, they were long the Arawak's enemies. These ferocious warriors periodically raided and plundered the islands, stealing the Arawak's food, carrying off women and children as slaves and murdering the men. Forced to flee north to such islands of the Greater Antilles as Puerto Rico and Jamaica, the docile Arawak tribe evolved to become the more advanced society of Tainos.

In a French–Carib dictionary published in 1660, written by a missionary who lived in Guadeloupe and Dominica for many years from 1628, it stated that these nomadic Caribs called Antigua by the name of Waladli. Barbuda was called Wa'omoni, and Redonda, Ocanamanru. It is presumed that it is from their own name, whence the term Caribbean (Sea) came from.

The wild Caribs made no attempt at permanent settlement in Antigua or Barbuda. They did, however, use the islands for the collection of food and other necessities unobtainable in the neighbouring islands where they lived, and as bases for attacks on other nearby islands. Thus, in the sixteenth century, when the major colonial powers in the region, the French, Spanish and Dutch, fought for control of the Caribbean and landed in Antigua, they found nothing of value – no gold or silver here, nor fresh water. Harassed by the Calibi, none made any attempts at colonisation.

Antigua, St Kitts, Nevis and Barbuda were taken under the protection of England in 1625 and two years later, the Earl of Carlisle claimed Antigua, but decided to settle in Barbados instead. He had obtained a grant for both islands from Charles I in 1627. The English, Dutch and French continued to possess these newly discovered lands and for a very short period in 1629, a French privateer, Captain d'Esnambuc settled in one part of the island, and a friend of the Earl of Carlisle, a Mr William, settled on Claremont in the Carlisle Bay Valley.

It was not until 1632 that a serious attempt was made to colonise Antigua. In that year, the English sent over a party from St Kitts, led by a Captain Edward Warner, the 22-year-old son of General Sir Thomas Warner, who had established the first colony on St Kitts several years earlier. He had been granted 'rights of warrant' by the Earl of Carlisle. So upon landing on the island, where he found Mr Williams in the area also now referred to as Old Road, he established a settlement at Falmouth and the colonists duly claimed Antigua for the English crown.

The fierce Caribs soon attacked but despite repeated and often bloody raids over the next 50 years, these redoubtable English colonists persevered and finally fought them off. The English settlers lived much as the Arawak had before them, cultivating cassava, sweet potato, ginger and maize and reaping a bountiful harvest from the sea.

By now, Sir Walter Raleigh had introduced tobacco to England and succeeded in convincing Queen Elizabeth I that the weed he had found the Indians smoking was potentially very viable. The early English colonists began to grow it for export to England and so created Antigua's first cash crop. Indentured bondsmen, faced with either prison or deportation, and poor Englishmen, formed the hard labour in the tobacco fields, having signed on to work in the colonies for a minimum of three years.

However, overproduction of tobacco throughout the Americas soon made it unprofitable to grow, and the crops were beginning to suffer from soil exhaustion. The fledgling colony needed a crop replacement in order to survive. The answer came in the form of a relatively unimportant secondary crop which was imported from Brazil, via Barbados – sugar cane. Already grown in small quantities since 1640, it began to grow in importance as sugar became popular throughout Europe as an inexpensive substitute for honey.

Nevertheless, whilst the English tobacco planters recognised the opportunity for enormous profits, they realised that the growing and harvesting of sugar cane was very labour intensive. Those previously given 'transport to the colonies' instead of the gallows would not be sufficient for the quantity of hard labour required in the cane fields, particularly as sugar cane flourished on the Antiguan soil.

Cotton planters in the southern parts of the North American colonies, along with colonists elsewhere in the Caribbean had already turned to the West African slave trade to fulfil labour requirements – and the Antiguan colonists followed suit. The population living on Antigua in 1646 was about 750, rising to 1200 ten years later and increasing to 39,600 in 1787, of which

Cutting Sugar Cane, Bendals.   Antigua, B. W. I.

Antigua, B. W. I. „Last Sugar Wind Mill", „Renfrews" (from South).

there were only 2600 whites.

Lord Willoughby obtained a grant to settle in Antigua in 1663 and founded Parham, named after his town in England. In April 1668, an Act was passed proposing that a town be built at St John's Harbour. However, nearly ten years later, Falmouth was still the main settlement, having the only church on the island, which had the dual purpose of a court house.

But colonial rivalry was not yet at an end. During this period, with sugar increasingly important to European countries, the Dutch fought for Antigua in 1665 and only the following year, the French attacked, both destroying sugar plantations and taking slaves.

The island was nearly devastated, with English military leaders captured by the French, and Caribs from Dominica kidnapping the settlers' wives. By the end of 1666, the Treaty of Breda ended the war, finally giving the now impoverished island to England. Whilst a poor winnings at the time, the treaty gave international recognition to English sovereignty over Antigua, which helped foster an era of prosperity.

From 1667 to 1680, Antigua was ruled by one of the best colonial governors, Colonel William Stapleton (to this day, there is a lane named after him in St John's). Refugees arrived from Surinam, then a Dutch possession, and with this new populace increasing the work force, he was able to pursue an ideal. He ensured that Antiguans did not devote themselves entirely to one crop and with the success of not being dependent on one staple trade, Antigua quickly rose as the wealthiest and most prosperous of the Leeward Islands.

A decade earlier, whilst it was Governor Christopher Keynell in the early 1650s, who established the first sugar plantation here, it was Sir Christopher Codrington, when he took over this plantation in 1674, who made it so successful. An established planter in Barbados, he came to Antigua and named the plantation Betty's Hope, for his daughter (now a popular visitor attraction, see page 198).

His modernised sugar plantation, benefiting from the latest methods of refining sugar learnt in Barbados, began to encourage other planters. This soon resulted in sugar becoming the island's most important crop and half of Antigua's population consequently consisted of black imported slaves.

There began the infamous 'triangle of trade', between Europe, Africa and the New World; manufactured goods went from England to Africa and were exchanged for slaves secured by African coastal tribes. The slave ships then crossed the Atlantic, with the trade winds speeding their passage, and sold the slaves to the West Indian sugar cane estates. Vast profits from this transaction were made and added to the lucrative spoils of the final part of this exchange – the sale of sugar, molasses and rum to England.

To accommodate the maximum number of plantations, it was the Europeans who, by 1705, had sadly deforested the once verdant hills and lush valleys of Antigua to make way for vast cane fields. That year there were 27 mills, increasing to 74 by 1710 and reaching their zenith in 1748, with 175 windmills and 64 cattle mills, all worked by the veritable army of slaves. Many of these mills erected for cane crushing, at first oxen-driven, and later powered by sails, still stand testimony to such massive cultivation and established wealth, but also as reminders of the strength and dignity of the enslaved workers.

Such valuable arable resources made the English aware of the need for fortification of Antigua, as the West Indian sugar islands continued to be attacked and change hands. They began to construct a number of outposts and harbours, also useful to keep the still marauding Caribs at bay. Over 40 military installations were created (see Antigua and Barbuda National Parks, page 199) along the deeply indented and beach-rimmed coasts of Antigua, which were easy prey as ideal landing places; as a cannon ball could only travel about a mile, it was also a practical consideration.

Many defences still abound, but the most famous is English Harbour, where Nelson's Dockyard remains as a fine example of the only Georgian working naval dockyard in the world. Named after the renowned admiral Horatio Nelson, commander of the Northern Division of the Leeward Island Station in Antigua,

Betty's Hope

1784–1787, it is a must for all visitors to the island (see also page 205). It was the early English settlers who originally built the long, straight road from English Harbour, branching out to Five Islands in the west and Nonsuch Bay in the east, as a direct line of communication to any point of defence, in the event of attack.

Sir Christopher Codrington had become the largest landowner and the richest planter and, a devoutly religious person, was said to have been one of the most sympathetic of slave masters. On 6 January 1685, he leased the sister island of Barbuda from the English crown for an annual fee of 'one fat sheep if asked'.

For over 200 years, this annex to his estates was mainly for the purpose of cultivating imported fruit, vegetables, herbs and spices, producing livestock and draught animals and for fish and timber supplies, thereby negating the importation of the immense quantities of foodstuffs required to feed the slave population and his own extended family of planters.

Furthermore, Barbuda represented an even more lucrative opportunity in the way of shipwrecks. The Codringtons had carte blanche to salvage the many ships which ran aground on the perilous reefs off Barbuda and kept a full inventory of men, boats and all equipment required for such profitable operations.

Barbudan slaves became proficient workers in the areas of agriculture, hunting, fishing, animal husbandry, wood and leather handicraft occupations. Operating pretty much on an independent basis, they were freely able to enjoy the fruits of their labours in the form of fresh provisions and meat. Conversely, the lot of the slaves in Antigua constantly created revolts, conspiracies, rebellions and escape, resulting in brutal and inhumane punishments. It is certainly noted by historians that despite the repugnant system of slavery, their lives in Barbuda weren't tainted by the same

tyranny as those on the Antiguan sugar plantations and so they understandably vociferously resisted any deportation to the main island.

Codrington had initiated the link between Antigua and Barbuda and it was about 200 years later that the relationship was cemented when, by order of the British monarchy, Barbuda was officially annexed to Antigua on 1 August 1860. It was also Codrington, as governor, who guided an Act through the Antiguan Assembly in 1681, to divide the island into five (now six) parishes. Within each was the provision for the erection of a church, the first built being St John's, within the compound of the present cathedral and churchyard. These churches became the focal point of life in Antigua and they all ministered to the slave population.

During the seventeenth and eighteenth centuries, sugar in the West Indies became the gold and silver of the Europeans and Americans. At the time of US independence, Adam Smith wrote that 'the profits of the sugar plantations in any of our West Indian colonies are generally much greater than those of any other cultivation that is known either in Europe or America.'

However, by the beginning of the nineteenth century, the reign of 'king' sugar was about to be toppled. Too dependent on its monopoly held in selling sugar to the mother country and the colonies, the free import of sugar from Cuba and other West Indian territories not under British rule proved a real threat. Tradespeople and consumers resented its high price, artificially due to protective laws and tariffs, but the final blow was due to the just revulsion in Britain over the slave trade.

In early 1807 Parliament passed a law pioneered by William Wilberforce making it a crime for any Briton anywhere in the world to trade in slaves. On 1 August 1834 slavery itself was abolished in Antigua with the release of 23,350 slaves (at that time there were just under 2000 whites and around 4000 free coloureds).

Mindful of previous incidents of slave uprisings, many of the vastly outnumbered planters

feared for their lives. However, they were relieved when the newly freed slaves went to church on such a victorious day to 'Tank God for make we a free!'

The churches up and down the island saw the planters, too, visiting to offer best wishes to 'their people'. Slaves in Antigua were the first to be emancipated in the British West Indies, for Antigua had by-passed the four-year apprenticeship period suggested by Britain and was the only island in the Leeward Islands to do so. It was a time of great gratitude and celebration: one such church, Grace Hill, was filled to capacity with 1000 more standing outside.

It was the revolutionary demise of the slave trade and the demand for free trade in sugar which combined to cause a collapse of the sugar estates, and therefore the economies, not only of Antigua but throughout the West Indies.

Unjustly, the plight of the black slaves continued despite total emancipation. Legally they were free but the mixed blessing was that there were no opportunities of work for them except on the plantations. Consequently, most continued to work for the remaining plantation owners, except that now they were responsible for their own subsistence and lodgings. This forced them to create shantytowns amidst an appalling setting of civil strife, periodic rioting and the bankruptcies of most of the large sugar mills. Others bent on supporting their families in the best way possible, migrated to the huge sugar cane estates in Cuba and Santo Domingo, which were being eagerly wooed by American investment.

Ironically, freedom of the slaves was an advantage to the planters who were no longer responsible for those unable to work through sickness or age, plus these estate owners received compensation from the British government. Many former slaves found themselves either thoroughly exploited or landless and moneyless. Serving as rector of St John's Parish (1827–1850), the Reverend Robert Holberton of the Anglican church founded an infirmary to care for the destitute in times of sickness and death and set up the crucially needed Daily Meal Society (the island's main hospital is named after him).

Antigua Slipway and Dow's Hill

Notwithstanding such dire economic and turbulent surroundings, the determination of the freed slaves started to manifest itself in the creation of villages such as Liberta, Freetown and Freemans Village. Ownership of land was vital to their development, but available land for them to live on and cultivate was sparse, as the estates still commandeered most of Antigua. But as the sugar industry continued to decline, so more land became available. Some people settled around the churches and schools, which had played such an important part in their lives, establishing villages such as Bethesda, All Saints, Bendals, Jennings and Newfield.

Former slaves were slowly surfacing from the pressures of extreme exploitation and degradation, to acquire land and become householders; sterling efforts against all odds resulted in over a thousand houses being bought on hire purchase, in 27 villages, less than five years after emancipation. Even the disastrous earthquake of 1843 did not deter the people from continuing to build their independent settlements.

The majority of these houses were built on the 'lift system', a local form of an unofficial cooperative, where all worked together for the common good. These villages formed the basis upon which the map of Antigua stands today and this unchanged rural scene is evident in their cultivated plots and flower gardens which can still be enjoyed in such early 'free' villages.

Adversity and struggle were the watchwords of the second half of the 1800s for all, as the Antiguan sugar industry was virtually priced and legislated out of existence and the workers were reluctant to return to the back-breaking toil they had known. The remaining planters welcomed labour from as far afield as Madeira, Portugal and even China.

Modern knowledge and equipment elsewhere aggravated the Antiguan sugar industry depression further. However, after a Royal Commission appointed in 1896, a modern central sugar factory (Gunthorpe's) was established, in 1904, on the outskirts of St John's.

St John's Cathedral

The earlier production of muscovado sugar was rapidly replaced by grey crystals, which by 1915 formed 86 per cent of Antigua's total sugar export (a revival of the cotton industry, molasses, limes, onions and logwood made up the balance). The new central sugar factory brought about a timely change in the fortunes of the local workers as they were brought together once more and learnt new skills.

Nevertheless, reports of the truly miserable conditions under which the majority of the freed slaves were living prompted a Royal Commission investigation, led by Lord Moyne. Upon arriving on the island, the commissioners were staggered at the extent of the atrocious living and working conditions.

It was such findings which ultimately led to the formation of the first trade union for Antigua, when one of the members of the commission, Sir Walter Citrine, held a public meeting in the Anglican cathedral school room in St John's on 3 January 1939. He earnestly entreated the people to form such a union in order to secure the rights of an organised labour force.

Subsequently, just a couple of weeks later, the Antigua Trades and Labour Union (ATLU) was formed on 16 January 1939. Reginald St Clair Stevens, a local jeweller became the first president, and Vere Cornwall Bird, an executive member (42 years later he became the first prime minister of Antigua). A Trade Union Act was subsequently passed on 3 March 1940, affording workers the right to negotiate for higher wages and better working standards.

Of further, and immediate, impact on Antigua, World War II brought the Americans (about 40,000) to the island. Via the Lend-Lease Act of 1941, as agreed with Great Britain, they established military bases offering local labour better wages than those of field hands. Construction workers were required to build the roads, deep water piers and an airfield, and unique opportunities became available on these bases for skilled and unskilled workers. Conditions improved slowly but steadily with the newly acquired material wealth, and a feeling of true liberation was in the air.

"Homeward Bound", Antigua, B. W. I.

Fashionable Wedding, Antigua, B. W. I.

An era of change began in Antiguan history. There began to emerge a new, free society of black people creating a dynamic infrastructure of labour, demanding honest wages for honest work, the opportunity for education and a place in the political life of the island.

Following the war, the crucial point was reached regarding the political, social and economic future of Antigua. The Antigua Trades and Labour Union set about addressing the problems of such new opportunities and training, following the almost total divorce from the sugar era. The governor of the Leeward Islands, from 1950 to 1957, Sir Kenneth Blackburne, remarked to the Antigua Legislature, that through the trade union's success, the previously experienced squalid living, working and educational conditions had been reversed in merely a few years. A new generation of university educated Antiguans began to return from abroad and involved themselves in the island's politics.

A ministerial system of government, based on Westminster, was introduced in 1956, with increased membership of the Legislative Council and the appointment of a Chief Minister in 1961. In the same year Barbuda was made a separate constituency having been previously attached to St John's.

By 1966, this crown colony was ready for independence and a constitutional conference held in London, when Vere Cornwall Bird represented Antigua as Chief Minister, resulted in Antigua and Barbuda (and Redonda) becoming the first associated state in the Caribbean, on 27 February 1967. Antigua was finally free of colonial rule for the first time in three centuries and autonomous in the conduct of its domestic policies, although foreign affairs and the defence of the islands remained the responsibility of Great Britain.

The sugar industry ultimately failed completely and the central sugar factory was closed in 1971; employment improved with the advent of tourism, bringing an increase of hotels, diversification of related services and factories for light industry. The state's economy began to make steady progress.

Thus, with established strength to fully handle its own affairs, Antigua and Barbuda achieved full sovereign independence on 1 November 1981, thereby gaining total control over internal and external affairs, and defence. For the first time in 328 years, the Union Jack was lowered and the Antiguan flag raised. This great ceremony took place at the Antigua Recreation Grounds amid an extensive display by the Royal Navy, and finishing with a spectacular firework display.

The day after, Prime Minister V. C. Bird formally received constitutional freedom in Antigua from HRH Princess Margaret, as the representative of Her Majesty the Queen. Her Royal Highness duly delivered the 'throne speech' at the state opening of the first parliament of this newly independent nation.

Today Antigua and Barbuda is a free nation within the British Commonwealth, growing and prospering in many directions. Sugar is no longer king, but a thriving tourist trade and its associated service industries affords the islands one of the highest standards of living in the Caribbean.

Historical and Archaeological Society, Museum of Antigua and Barbuda, St John's, tel: (268) 462 4930 tel/fax: (268) 462 1469 e-mail: museum@candw.ag web site: www.antiguanice.com

Christopher Codrington has created a web site entitled, 'Historic Antigua and Barbuda'. This is a meeting place for all those interested in the history, archaeology and genealogy of Antigua and Barbuda. e-mail: coopcod@village.ios.com web site: idt.net/~coopcod

The Historical and Archaeological Society of Antigua and Barbuda (HAS)

– discovering yesterday today, preserving the past to enrich the future

The Historical and Archaeological Society of Antigua and Barbuda (HAS) was born in 1956, after Dr Fred Olsen and Mr Happy Ward discovered an Amerindian site at Mill Reef Club. The society subsequently began publishing the 'Mill Reef Diggers Digest' in 1965. By 1966, the society was registered in the name of the Antigua Archaeological Society (AAS). The main function at the time was to raise funds for the excavation of the Brook Site at Mill Reef, coupled with a general archaeological focus to discover and excavate pre-Columbian habitation in Antigua and Barbuda. The old Mill Tower at Mill Reef's Gate was converted into a museum, where Dr Olsen lectured to raise money for excavating another newly found, important site at Indian Creek.

In 1971 the society elected Desmond Nicholson, President and the Hon. Basil Peters, Minister of Education, Vice-president (and the first Antiguan-born member). By 1985, the society expanded its activities, becoming ensconced in its present home, the old 1750 court house on Long Street (along with the Museum of Antigua and Barbuda), in the heart of St John's. Its chairman in 1985 was Mr Reg Murphy, an Antiguan national (with a doctorate in Archaeology from Calgary, Canada), but still, at that time, the membership consisted of very few other nationals. It was also during this year that lecture tours of historical sites developed. In 1986, the name of the society was changed to include the word 'historical', in the hope of attracting more local membership.

In this same year, Dr and Mrs Earl Mitchell

of the USA spearheaded the Betty's Hope tourist attraction project with HAS coordinating it with the Antigua Department of Tourism. This was formed into a separate trust in 1990, aiming to restore parts of the old Codrington plantation, Betty's Hope (see page 198).

Having created awareness and interest to look after the nation's magnificent environment responsibly, through the museum and HAS, a meeting was hosted in 1989 on environmental matters, coinciding with a pollution exhibit. It was at this point that the nucleus of an environmental body emerged, soon developing into an established environmental group called the Environmental Awareness Group (EAG), which now has a small office in the museum.

HAS has also helped to create a small museum at Jumby Bay on Long Island, to demonstrate the importance of this small offshore northeastern island in Caribbean pre-history. Another small project on this haven, operating as an exclusive resort, is an ongoing 'save the turtle' programme (see page 103) concerned with the conservation of an endangered species of Caribbean turtles which only nest and lay eggs on this part of Antiguan land.

Happily, the society has now become very well subscribed and, indeed, the museum itself has become 'national', in the sense of providing vital information and facts related to the history of this island state and serving to establish a national identity through cultural research.

Admission is free to the main museum and the complete library and research centre, provided by HAS is on the second floor of the museum building in Long Street. Here you may learn more about the unusual and little known facts of the island, such as the delicious (and still available) 'bush tea', interesting shipwrecks, what High Street looked like in the last century or learn to identify artefacts.

The library contains over 2500 publications on Antigua and the greater Caribbean, along with masses of photographs. There are 24 databases, totalling over 25,600 entries, including such subjects as Antiguan and Barbudan history, people, culture, newspaper articles, flora and fauna. This is a most fantastic source of remarkable variety, with knowledgeable staff to assist you.

One of the aims of HAS is to design and develop public outreach programmes, including brochures, guides and other collateral materials. The society has an ongoing programme relationship with all the government schools, whereby weekly visits are made to the museum by school children. An associated body restores the old steam engines and locomotives at the former sugar factory.

HAS sponsors special lectures and exhibitions, slide presentations, video showings, lectures by university lecturers and exhibitions of works of renowned artisans, fundraising auctions and luncheons. These special events take place in the open gallery space on the second floor of the museum throughout the year. There are so many diverse monthly activities and exhibitions that it is best that you telephone or call by to see what is happening during your stay.

Extraordinarily illuminating are the monthly field trips, which the society supports and conducts for the general public, where participants explore many intriguing sites each month. Some of these trips are hikes, exploring caves and trails into the Shekerly Mountains, for instance, in the southwest of the island. Others allow an opportunity to view at first hand and understand the impressive restoration work of, for example, the Betty's Hope mills, or to be unearthing and analysing minute grains of earth for specimens, hundreds, maybe thousands of years old, with a

pair of tweezers. But all of them offer a chance to explore a part of Antigua that most have not seen, whilst collecting more information about the lore and artifacts of the Amerindians in Antigua. All field trips are conducted at the weekends with a guide, and members take their own picnics, swimming gear where necessary, and have a fabulous day out.

The Historical and Archaeological Society, a private non-profitmaking organisation, also operates the Museum of Antigua and Barbuda. The government of Antigua and Barbuda provide the building, utilities and some of the staff, but the annual overheads and remaining staff salaries are solely the responsibility of the society.

In order to continue expanding the vibrant and educational programming that serves the community and, indeed, provides much stimulating enjoyment and recreation for many visitors, the society depends on the revenue generated from membership, donations and the museum's gift-shop sales.

You don't have to live here to become a member and apart from contributing to the continuance of such worthy voluntary work for the good of all, you will find much to amuse you and learn from the quarterly newsletter, which will be sent to you upon joining. To become a 'friend of the Museum, the annual fee is a mere EC$ 40.00 to enable you to support the necessary and ever increasing programme.

See end of History and Heritage article for further contact details.

National flag

In 1966, a national flag competition was held and Reginald Samuel, artist, sculptor, painter and art teacher, won with his design, submitted amongst 600 entries. This was for the occasion when the country became a state in association with Great Britain in early 1967.

The golden sun symbolises the dawn of a new era. Its seven points represent Antigua's six parishes plus Barbuda.

The mainly red background of the ensign symbolises the life blood of slave forefathers and dynamism of the people.

The blue band symbolises hope and the black, that of the soil and African heritage.

The colours gold, blue and white collectively represent Antigua and Barbuda's tourist attractions, sun, sea and sand.

The 'V' in the design is the symbol of victory at last.

The national coat of arms and motto

The colourful and intricate design of the coat of arms was originally created in 1966 by Gordon Christopher, a prominent Antiguan painter, printmaker, graphic designer and art teacher whose works have been exhibited both nationally and internationally.

His design, significant of the year 1967, when Antigua and Barbuda were proclaimed a state in association with Great Britain, was subsequently modified by the then financial secretary, Don Cribbs, in order to meet certain stipulations required for the crest.

The top image of the pineapple represents the famed Antigua black pineapple. The surrounding red hibiscuses are symbolic of the many luxuriant varieties which bloom here.

The centre of this heraldic image with the golden sun and the wavy blue and white bands depicts the sun, sea and beaches for which Antigua and Barbuda are renowned.

The old sugar mill and the stem of sugar cane echoes the historic production of sugar, once Antigua's main industry.

The right hand century plant or dagger log, with its shower of clustered yellow flowers, was part of the historic emblem of Antigua and the Leeward Islands. The fallow deer was brought to Antigua in the 1700s by the Codringtons and is unique to Antigua and Barbuda.

The scroll underneath bears the motto of the nation, 'Each endeavouring, all achieving'.

The motto was composed in 1976 by James H. Carrott MBE, then Permanent Secretary in the Ministry of Trade, Production and Labour. His concept was 'to provide inspiration to each Antiguan and Barbudan to recognise that the development of the whole country would be a benefit to all, but that development required the effort of each individual'.

National anthem

To celebrate becoming a state in association with Great Britain in 1967, a competition was held in which Walter P. Chambers, a church pipe organist and piano tuner, won the music section, and Novelle H. Richards, a well-known trade unionist, poet, journalist and author won the words section. In 1981, at the time of full independence, the original six lines were modified to include Barbuda.

Words by NOVELLE H. RICHARDS

Music by WALTER P. CHAMBERS
Arr. by H. A. Kenney

Not too fast

1. Fair An-ti-gua and Bar-bu-da We thy sons and daugh-ters stand
2. Raise the stan-dard! Raise it bold-ly! Ans-wer now to du-ty's call
3. God of na-tions, let Thy bless-ing Fall up-on this land of ours;

Strong, and firm in __ peace or dan-ger To safe-guard our Na-tive Land
To the ser-vice __ of your coun-try, Spar-ing noth-ing, giv-ing all;
Rain and sun-shine __ ev-er send-ing, Fill her fields with crops and flowers;

We com-mit our-selves to build-ing A true na-tion brave and free
Gird your loins and join the bat-tle 'Gainst fear, hate and pov-er-ty,
we her chil-dren do im-plore thee, Give us strength, faith, loy-al-ty,

Ev-er striv-ing, ev-er seek-ing, Dwell in love and un-i-ty.
Each en-deav-our-ing, All a-chiev-ing Live in peace where man is free:
Nev-er fail-ing, all en-dur-ing, To de-fend her lib-er-ty.

National symbols of Antigua and Barbuda

For some years it was thought that Antigua and Barbuda should name and publicise their national symbols in order that their rich heritage and environment was fully recognised and valued. To coincide with the Independence celebrations in 1981, the dream became a reality when 13 national symbols were sanctioned by the Cabinet.

The following descriptions explain the importance and significance of the symbols, whilst at the same time identifying the social settings out of which many of these symbols emerged. It was once said, 'a clear sense of national identity gives a nation collective strength and is the surest defence of its liberty. The weaker the national identity becomes, the more easily can undemocratic forces pick a nation off.'

Not all the symbols are merely a historical document and you are bound to see some interesting examples, which are not difficult to spot, whilst travelling around this twin-island state.

National animal

The European fallow deer (*Dama dama*) is believed to have been introduced from Norway into England during the reign of James I. The Codringtons imported them onto Barbuda in the early eighteenth century, and later to Guiana Island (off the northeast coast of Antigua) In 1740, there were about 1000, increasing to 3000 in 1784 but, considered a nuisance for stripping the vegetation, only about 300 remained a century later. After thriving for centuries and despite gracing the national coat of arms, today only a few exist.

National bird

The frigate bird (*Fregata magnificens*) is also referred to as man-o'-war, as it snatches food from other birds, or weather bird as it flies inland at the approach of bad weather (see also page 108).

This quite spectacular bird is one of the most valued assets to Barbuda's tourism, coupled with the island's stunning miles of pinky-white sand beaches (see page 302). The vast mangrove area situated by the Codrington Lagoon, on the east side of Barbuda houses some 2500 pairs. Visitors are taken in boats to view these incredibly photogenic birds, the oldest known being 34 years old. Relatives of pelicans and cormorants, during the mating season the males blow up an enormous and distinctive scarlet throat sac to attract a female mate.

National dish

Pepperpot and fungee were made in deep clay fire pots by the first people of Antigua, the Amerindians, as a means of preserving food. This highly seasoned stew was made with a rich sauce and various vegetables, into which cassava bread and meats were dipped. Called tomali (toma – sauce, ali – clay pot) by the Amerindians, they would keep this cooking, adding to it the next day. Another school of thought indicates that the island's forefathers combined an assortment of wild bushes and other easily obtained ingredients to feed their families and stave off hunger. Today, it is a delicious stew typically containing marrows, spinach, aubergine, peas, pumpkin, okra, salted meat and dumplings. Fungee is a paste-like ball delicacy of cornmeal and okra.

Every good fungee no meet good pepperpot.
(Not every person meets a suitable companion.)

National dress

This was originally worn for special occasions such as weddings and market day, particularly by cakemakers and market vendors, around the post-emancipation era (1834–1940). The female ensemble features a starched white apron over a

Madras dress. These were traditionally sewn by hand, utilising frills, tucks and lace and with various headwear such as headwraps or a cotta, worn when carrying items on the head. The male attire consists of a Madras waistcoat over a starched white shirt, black trousers and a straw hat sporting a Madras band. Madras was brought to the Caribbean from India and the red, yellow, green and black colours in this outfit represent the island people's dynamism and African heritage. Many Antiguans proudly display their national pride by wearing their traditional dress to fairs and special events. On National Day, when stalls are set up with local food and drink, and national prayer services are attended, most people wear their national outfits to work.

National flower

The dagger log (*Agave karatto*), a member of the lily family, found scattered across the gentle, rolling Antigua hills and coasts, is a hummingbird's delight.

One of the most extraordinary of Antigua's flora, this initially stemless rosette known for its long erect dagger-like leaves, grows for years in pursuit of its true crowning glory. Normally after ten to 20 years and growing only a few leaves each year, an

enormous terminal bud emerges, growing rapidly to a height of 20 feet or more. The flowering stalk of this Agave (derived from the Greek word meaning noble) produces a very large compound inflorescence bearing a cloud of brilliant yellow flowers. Not just attracting numerous pollinating hummingbirds by day, its flowers act like bright beacons, attracting pollinating bats by night. Thriving in dry conditions, these tall plants can frequently be seen standing sentinel on coastlines around the island. After the plant blooms around April and fades, vegetative bulbils (instead of seeds) are produced. The whole plant eventually dies, having given everything for the next generation. Thereafter, from the individual bulbils, suckers eventually flower in the same lengthy 10–20 year time frame.

In Amerindian times, the fibre of the leaves was used extensively for hammock strings, cords, ropes and handicrafts. Later, the white interior pulp of the leaves made a fishing tow bait, and the dead dried-out logs on which the flowers bloomed, were spiked together with a length of hard wood, to make 'dagger rafts'. In Barbuda, these rafts are called 'batta logs'.

A fine tinder was made from the powder at the base of the leaves, which was used during World War II, when matches were scarce. Medicinally, the plant was used for treating tuberculosis. Today, these plants are used pharmacologically in the synthesis of cortisone and oestrogen, and the sap from their leaves has been used by herbalists for years. Further uses are in food, soap and shampoo.

National fruit

Antigua black pineapple (*Ananas comosus*) was originally introduced to Antigua by the South American Arawak Indians and was believed to be food for the gods. The thorny leaves were used for making twine and cloth and a tasty wine was made from the fruits. The juice is used locally for fever, stomach pains, urinary complaints and wasp stings, and the leaves as a poultice for sprains. As early as 1640, settlers in Antigua cultivated the black pineapple near English Harbour, and they have been cultivated ever since on the south side of the island, particularly near Cades Bay and Claremont. The pineapple was often seen adorning many fine pieces of furniture in colonial times as a heraldic symbol denoting hospitality. Known as 'black', the Antigua pineapple has a dark green/blackish colour when young, then glows golden when ripe. Whilst smaller than most commercial types, it is renowned for its particularly sweet and luscious fruit and is not to be missed.

National historic symbol

The sugar mill tower was used to house the sugar cane grinding rollers. Worked by armies of African slaves during the seventeenth to nineteenth centuries (see History and Heritage, page 50), these grinders squeezed juice for the manufacture of sugar at the boiling houses. Huge sails, powered by the trade winds, turned these strong mills (see Betty's Hope, page 198), of which about 114 sugar mills can easily still be seen dotting the landscape. These sentinels now stand as mute witness to the days of wealth and enslavement, when the island was a sea of waving green cane. The first mill is said to have been built at Claremont, probably by the Piggot family from Ireland, who were the first sugar mill tower builders, while the mill at the Savannah near Cobb's Cross is another very old one.

National music

The fife band was originally conceived as a form of entertainment in the eighteenth century. It was always played under the wide shadow of a tamarind tree, whilst spectators would dance, performing the traditional 'heel and toe' jig. In such economically harsh times, materials for all these homemade instruments were easy to obtain: they included a piece of old pipe blown one end for the 'boom pipe' (playing bass), a 'grater' or 'grudge' made out of metal or tin, and a piece of bamboo, which they called the 'fife'. This is a small flute with six to eight holes on top which plays the the diatonic scale. A larger flute, a homemade Yuca-

lili (ukulele) and a traditional guitar are the other instruments used in the fife band. This typical Antiguan music is unchanged today, performed for the enjoyment of all, particularly by the Rio Band. Playing since the 1930s, this famed seven-member team of players, often seen performing at various hotels, is especially experienced and has now increased its repertoire to include traditional tunes, as well as local and regional folk songs.

National sea creature

The hawksbill turtle (*Eretmochelys imbricata*) was much prized by the Amerindians, perceived as a gift from their gods. Of the 250 worldwide species of turtles, only eight are sea turtles and all, commonly found in the Caribbean, are endangered species (see page 103). Between 400 to 500 eggs are laid annually around Antigua and Barbuda by 80 to 100 Hawksbill females. Distinguished from other turtles by its narrow pointed beak, they are solitary in their behaviour and consequently are generally difficult to observe. This species grows to about three feet in length, with the largest, at a weight of 175 lbs, found on the 100 fathom line over the insular shelf in the ocean. Healthy coral reefs are imperative to their survival, where they sleep and feed on sponges and other encrusting organisms, living anything up to 50 years.

National song

The benna is thought to have been derived from a typical song-dance brought to the plantations by the African slaves. Steeped in African rhythm, the benna (or ditti) followed a one-verse repetitive song, from which the later folk-style calypso probably originated. Peculiar only to Antigua and Jamaica, it provided relief and solace from the endless work in the sugar-cane fields, giving the slaves an essential means of expression. Accompanied purely by the banjo, it was often sung in a 'call and response' mode with an audience. The benna remained around until the 1930s and 1950s, when a colourful, sometimes controversial local character, John Quarko, made his mark. The legendary town crier of St John's became the master of the benna, ringing his bell to command attention. He would announce sales or events, advertise services for a small fee, generally entertain with folk songs and benna, and fearlessly relate local gossip, which once landed him in jail for slander!

Typical benna of 1924 by Thomas Joseph
Man Mongoose dog know your ways,
Mongoose go in a Forrest kitchen,
Thief out one of he big fat chicken,
Put um in he waistcoat pocket,
Man Mongoose.

Note: 'Mongoose' was a local scamp, William Forrest, a merchant in Scots Row (now Thames Street), St John's, and an amateur geologist and archaeologist.

National stone

Petrified wood found here is around 25 million years old, belonging to the geological Oligocene period. Trees and wood buried in mud, often containing volcanic ash, for millions of years, produce such fossils. Silica, iron and manganese from the ash, preserve the wood's original form by filling in the spaces within, thus hardening it like stone. Part of the earth's crust, petrified wood fragments may still be found in scattered places over Antigua's central plain, particularly around All Saints and Freemansville. This confirms that the island was once much forested. Indeed, a whole petrified forest lies buried beneath a twelve-inch layer of volcanic ash at Corbison Point, near the island's northwest channel. The most delicate microscopic details of organisms, shell forms and forest structures, silicified during a fatal explosion in Antigua's volcanic district, remain visible – although this rare phenomenon is slowly slipping into eternity through erosion by the sea. It is a preciously guarded non-renewable source and a fine example of this endangered item, a large petrified tree trunk, may be seen on display at the Antigua and Barbuda Museum in St John's (see also page 176).

National tree

The whitewood tree (*Bucida buceras*) belongs to the combretum family, related to the mangrove and almond tree. It is a large, horizontally widespreading, ornamental shade tree, growing from 30 to 70 feet in height, with a three-foot diameter trunk. Being very hard and strong, with a specific gravity of 0.93, the olive-brown wood was formerly used in making gun carriages for the forts. Then called black Gregory, whilst difficult to work, this decay resistant wood was excellent for lathe turning and much utilised for durable construction. Making a good grade of charcoal and with the bark used for tanning, its many properties caused its demise and now only a few are left, although thriving in damp areas such as dry river beds and in coastal areas. This is another symbol with great history and heritage requiring the utmost respect and care.

National weed

Not what one would expect to be lauded by being chosen as a national symbol, but the widdy widdy (*Corchorus siliquosus*) was an essential high protein addition to slave food over the centuries. This was confirmed when a Mr Luffman sent a letter from Antigua to England in 1787, describing the 'weedy weedy' bush as part of the slave's diet. Its value was later appreciated by the sugar workers who favoured this wild bush plant boiled with cockles when they went on strike for better wages and conditions in 1951. Also known as 'popololo', the older leaves were especially good and nutritious, and often added to the pepperpot. Requiring little cooking, this rather sticky potherb, a type of broomweed belonging to the *Tiliaceae* family, was once used as a tea for asthma and colds, and reputed to be an excellent laxative.

Calendar of events and public holidays

There is always something happening on the island year-round from local festivals and activities to major sporting events. Look out for posters, flyers and in the local papers for important diary dates (please note that some holidays and festivals may affect the working hours of government offices, banks, shops and stores). Local and overseas tourist boards (see page 5) will be able to give you up-to-date details of events, festivals and activities – the regular ones are listed below, alphabetically for each month:

JANUARY

Anjo Insurance Golf Open Championship – Cedar Valley Golf and Country Club (see Active Traveller, page 140) tel: (268) 462 0161.

Annual International Hot Air Balloon Festival – (see page 82) for further information contact the Antigua and Barbuda Department of Tourism tel: (268) 463 0125/6/7 or Todd Challenger Balloons, UK tel: (44) 1 473 448048.

Art exhibition – at Harmony Hall (see page 191) tel: (268) 460 4120.

Art exhibition – at Island Arts Gallery, Aiton Place, Hodges Bay on the third Saturday in the month, 5–8.30pm (see Arts and Crafts, page 187) tel: (268) 461 6324 for details.

Official start of the cricket season

Official start of the netball season

Official start of volleyball season – at the YMCA Sports Complex, corner of Cross and Bishopsgate Streets, St John's. Visitors' participation welcome every Saturday morning. For further information contact Wilbur Harrigan tel: (268) 462 0827.

1 January – New Year's Day – public holiday

FEBRUARY

Art exhibition – at Harmony Hall (see page 191) tel: (268) 460 4120.

Art exhibition – at Island Arts Gallery, Aiton Place, Hodges Bay on the last Saturday of the month, 5–8.30pm (see Arts and Crafts, page 187) tel (268) 461 6324 for details.

Valentine's Day Grand Prix Regatta – a 2-day event consisting of four classes and seven short races at Jolly Harbour tel: Commodore Nick Maley (268) 461 6324.

MARCH

Art exhibition – at Harmony Hall (see page 191) tel: (268) 460 4120.

Art exhibition – at Island Arts Gallery, Aiton Place, Hodges Bay on the last Saturday in the month, 5–8.30pm (see page 187) tel (268) 461 6324 for details.

APRIL

Annual Model Boat Race Competition – the Catamaran Club, Falmouth, an unusual opportunity to see these perfectly scaled down marine works of art compete, and be proudly shown by their owners, boatbuilders and skippers (see page 133). For further information contact Elizabeth Mason, Department of Tourism tel: (268) 463 0125.

Antigua Classic Yacht Regatta – one of the foremost classic yacht regattas in the world, including events such as the Parade of Classics, Tall Ships race, Heritage Festival and gig-racing (see page 123). For further information contact the Antigua Yacht Club tel: (268) 460 1799.

Annual Sailing Week – the world's finest sailing craft meet for this famed week of competitive racing and beach parties (see page 119) tel: (268) 462 8872.

Art exhibition – at Harmony Hall (see page 191) tel: (268) 460 4120.

Earth Day – guided walk for nature with talks, 8am start, to celebrate Earth Day (started in the United States in 1970) and to highlight the fragility of the last undeveloped areas of Antigua. All welcome to join in and see parts of Antigua that you may never otherwise experience. For meeting place and route, contact the Environmental Awareness Group (see page 114) tel: (268) 462 6236.

Good Friday – public holiday (can also fall in late March)

Easter Monday – public holiday (can also fall in late March)

Keithly Sheppard Youth Soccer Tournament – YASCO, Old Parham Road, St John's. For date and further information tel: (268) 562 1102.

MAY

Anglican Food Fair – the Deanery grounds, a variety of stalls and stands with a feast of Antiguan and Caribbean fare. For further information tel: (268) 462 0820.

Annual Antigua Tennis Week – Curtain Bluff Hotel. Join international tennis professionals for a stimulating combination of world-class tennis and instructional clinics. For further information tel: (268) 462 8400.

Blindness Awareness month – the main fundraising period for Antigua and Barbuda Society of and for the Blind (see page 176), with various activities helping to raise local and visitor awareness of the blind or visually impaired tel: (268) 462 0663.

Liberation Day Rally – the Rastafarian community of Antigua and Barbuda, under the umbrella of the Wadadli National Council for the Advancement of Rastafari (see page 31), join African peoples the world over in celebrating African Liberation Day with a rally/march through St John's.

Labour Day – public holiday (first Monday in the month).

JUNE

Antigua and Barbuda Sports Fishing Tournament – the Catamaran Club (taking place every Whitsuntide weekend and so can fall in May). Boats and anglers from across the Caribbean compete to land the record catch for a great number of trophies and prizes to a value of around EC$ 100,000 (see page 151). For dates and further information contact the President, Francis Nunes, Jr tel: (268) 462 0649/1961.

Calypso Spektakula – an increasingly successful annual calypso show with international West Indian artists. For date and further information contact Mr Gordon tel: (268) 462 0471.

Barbuda Caribana Festival – five days of festivities in Codrington, Barbuda, including the

> Get a feel of the island and meet some residents. The Historical and Archaeological Society at the Museum of Antigua and Barbuda holds an evening lecture series throughout the year, on the second Saturday of each month from 7.00pm. These cover myriad topics with different speakers, some from overseas. Wine and nibbles are included in the EC$ 10.00 requested donation. Check the local papers; call in to the museum, or telephone (268) 462 1469/4930.

Caribana queen show, calypso competition, dancing in the streets and lots of action. Falls on Whitsuntide weekend and so can fall in May.

Final Jump-up – in Barbuda to end Caribana Festival.

Jolly Harbour to Barbuda Cruise and Race – race to Barbuda, overnighting Saturday and Sunday at Spanish Point on Barbuda. Games, barbecue on the beach, racing back to Jolly Harbour on Monday. Party and presentation at Dog Watch Tavern, Jolly Harbour. For further information tel: Commodore Nick Maley (268) 461 6324.

Mr and Miss Antigua Bodybuilding Championship – for date and further information contact Wesley Barrow, President tel: (268) 462 3681.

Olympic Day Run – starts at the Antigua Recreation Grounds, St Johns. For further information contact the Antigua and Barbuda Olympic Association tel: (268) 462 3476/2988.

Red Cross Week – is usually held during the first week, when fêtes, bingo sessions and dinners take place and volunteers with their familiar Red Cross tins collect donations (see page 294) tel: (268) 462 9599.

Wadadli Day – an annual celebration of all that is Antiguan including local cuisine, arts and crafts, dance groups, drama, fashion, poetry and games, trade and agricultural fair.

World Environment Day – tree planting activities.

For further information contact the Environmental Awareness Group (see page 114) tel: (268) 462 6236.

Whit Monday – public holiday (eighth Monday after Easter and can also fall in late May).

JULY

Antigua Carnival Celebrations – a time of non-stop music and dance culminating in a spectacular costume parade (see page 79) tel: (268) 462 4707.

Holy Family Catholic Parish Bazaar and Food Fair – St Michael's Mount, St John's; international food, culture, games and competitions for a good family day out tel: (268) 461 1127.

International Show Jumping and Dressage – teams from Barbados, Jamaica and Trinidad, joining Antigua as members of the Caribbean Equestrian Association to compete for the sponsor's Carib Cup prize (see page 143). For further information call Spring Hill Riding Centre, Falmouth Harbour tel: (268) 460 1333.

Caricom Day – public holiday (first Monday in the month).

AUGUST

Antigua Carnival continues.

Official start of football season – Antigua Recreation Grounds. For further information contact Chet Green tel: (268) 480 3232.

The Royal Antigua and Barbuda Police Force Week of Activities – beginning with a church service highlighting the different aspects of police work including a talent show tel: (268) 462 0360.

Carnival – public holiday (first Monday and Tuesday in the month).

SEPTEMBER

OECS Bridge Championships – open to locals and visitors, including the Open Pairs Championship, Open Teams Championship and the National Teams Championship (locals only). Awards and trophies will be given and Master Points compatible with ACBL Master Points (from the USA) will be awarded (see page 145). For further information contact the Chairman, Mr Al James tel: (268) 462 1459.

Turtle Watch – for further information contact the Environmental Awareness Group (see page 114) tel: (268) 462 6236.

OCTOBER

Annual Kite Flying Competition – all kites must be homemade. Free to enter, children and adults. Contact the Independence Committee tel: (268) 773 3190.

Jolly Harbour Annual Regatta – four races, different categories, primarily for local yachts and a great spectator event. Contact Jolly Harbour Yacht Club tel: Commodore Nick Maley (268) 461 6324.

National Warri Festival – held in the first week, up to Independence Day (1 November) (see page 283). For dates and further information contact Trevor Simon, Antigua and Barbuda National Warri Association tel: (268) 462 6317.

Heritage (National Dress) Day – from two weeks preceding this day, schools, companies and government buildings commence decorations for judging; there is the official launching of celebrations, a service of thanksgiving, various programmes and events up to 31 October, which is National Dress Day, with food fair and exhibition, ceremonial parade on 1 November.

NOVEMBER

Antigua Open Golf Tournament – open to all members and visitors. For dates and further information contact The Cedar Valley Golf and Country Club (see page 140) tel: (268) 462 0161.

Independence Day (1 November, public holiday) – the Prime Minister's Soccerama. For further information contact Chet Green tel: (268) 480 3232.

DECEMBER

Champagne Party in Nelson's Dockyard – for something completely different and fun! An annual tradition – many visitors and locals gather here from noon onwards for partying to live bands, quaffing reasonably priced bottles of champagne (kept in a ice-filled bath), with all proceeds going to the Hourglass Foundation charity. Join in for a historical, colourful, festive day!

Nicholson's Annual Boat Show and Marine Fair – the world's oldest charter yacht show where boats from all over the world converge on English Harbour, Falmouth and the St James's Club. From sloops and cutters to schooners and catamarans plus big power craft (see page 130). For further information contact Nicholson's Yacht Charters tel: (268) 460 1530.

25 December – Christmas Day – public holiday
26 December – Boxing Day – public holiday

SPORTS CALENDAR

January–July	netball, cricket
January–December	volleyball
February–July	basketball
September–February	football

Cricket fever!

I tole him over an' over
Agen; watch de ball, man, watch
De ball like it hook to you eye
This ain't no time for playin'
The fool nor makin' no sport;
this is cricket!
Islands, Kamau Brathwaite

Taking on an almost religious zeal, cricket is everywhere, evidenced by the number of formal international or regional matches, a rudimentary knockabout with bat and ball on some obscure street corner or on the beach, or just in the local talk. Antigua boasts many globally respected superstars and whilst commanding awe from the Caribbean to Bombay and from London to Melbourne, they can often be found watching youngsters at play on a makeshift pitch. Cricket is much more than just a game to Antiguans and Barbudans. It binds the exceptional sportsperson and the society to which he or she belongs; it inspires, motivates, creates self-confidence, dreams and instigates a national pride.

Gravy

The game of cricket was introduced to the Caribbean by the English two centuries ago and has since been ably mastered by West Indians, becoming a national religion. Both then and now, it is seen as character building, encompassing discipline, noble qualities, spirit and good sportsmanship, hence the term, 'It's not cricket', meaning 'It's not the done thing'.

Antigua is immensely proud of its cricket heroes, none bigger than 'Master Blaster' Viv Richards. Former captain (and first Antiguan captain) of the all-conquering West Indies team, Sir Isaac Vivian Alexander Richards commands a rare majesty and for over a decade was the world's best batsman. As a wonderful ambassador for Antigua, his smiling personality is always open to the attention of his legion of fans. There is a street named after him in St John's, as there is for another Antiguan test great, the legendary Andy Roberts.

Now retired from the game, Roberts was the pioneer of the present generation of fast bowlers which made the West Indies feared wherever they played. The successive star-studded list of Antiguan cricketers includes the recently retired strikingly tall fast bowler and national hero, Curtly Ambrose, and the great batsman Richie Richardson, with many fresh, young Antiguan faces, such as Ridley Jacobs ready to join these illustrious ranks.

Visitors can gain a unique insight into the culture of Antigua, by witnessing the spirit and fervour of official local matches held across the island on Thursdays, Saturdays and Sundays, which are interspersed with regional and international matches.

To be in Antigua during a test match is to witness the exciting spectacle of world-class players amid an extraordinary atmosphere. The irrepressible enthusiasm of the Antiguans becomes so wildly infectious. It hits all who attend as soon as they get near the ground – you simply cannot leave.

It was former West Indies captain Richie Richardson who opened the ultra-modern Antigua Commercial Bank double-decker stand, in his name, at the Antigua Recreation Ground, where all test matches have been staged since 1981. One of the leading international test venues in the world, it has benefited from rebuilding and refurbishment to the tune of over EC$ 7 million. Upon completion of the next phase, this outstanding facility will be regarded as one of the most modern cricket pitches in the world, with an electronic scoreboard and lighting for night cricket.

Thrilled at the refurbished bleacher stands, where dancing crowds roar and cheer, waving flags and merry-making, overseas fans are always impressed with the fun-loving, cricket crazy Antiguans and Barbudans, who are obviously out for a good time.

Even England's failure to win on these grounds in 1998 – where 13 years prior, Viv Richards plundered the English bowling for the fastest century (off 56 balls) in test history – could not dampen spirits of the 6000 English supporters. How could this happen with the famed Chickie's Hi-Fi, renowned cross-dresser cheerleader 'Gravy', comedian 'Mayfield', and 'Papie' on the bugle? There is all this and more during a test match in Antigua. There are food stalls of every description, souvenir stands, iron bands, horns, drums, costumes, music and entertainment to feed the soul.

West Indian cricket feeds the voracious appetites of the wildly appreciative, fanatical Caribbean spectators, creating a true carnival-like scene. The participation response is the best ever seen, especially in the West Indies Oil Company double-decker stand, which hosts Chickie's Hi-Fi, the Red Stripe/Guinness Posse and Gravy, often joined by local calypsonians, and top musicians like David Rudder. Here, for the price of a ticket, everyone gets a souvenir t-shirt and unlimited free beer! It's 'party, party' for everyone on into the late hours, long after the day's cricket.

The stand rocks and rolls with spectators gyrating and partying as DJ Chickie's resounding music blasts across the ground. This cricket carnival could also not be complete without local comedian Gravy on his podium, who struts and prances in time, acknowledging every boundary or wicket.

The popularity of these cricket characters has earned them much attention from the media, including television stations, all adding to the spontaneous and electrical atmosphere surrounding the unique spirit of test cricket in Antigua!

CATCH THIS ... THE CARIBBEAN CRICKET CENTRE

March 1998, saw the opening of this ultra-modern cricket facility, built on the Jolly Beach hotel complex. The Caribbean Cricket Centre boasts six practice pitches with nets and a playing strip, much used since its opening by visiting teams.

Hoping to encourage more young West Indians to become top-class cricketers, the West Indies Cricket Board sees the facility, the first ever cricket centre of its kind in the Caribbean, as the hub of its development programmes. Directors of Club International believe it will woo visitors to its comprehensive all-inclusive hotel, and are offering scholarships to young cricketers throughout the region to stay and benefit from the excellent training and tuition.

Housing the best qualified coaches both locally and regionally, the Caribbean Cricket Centre plans an expansion programme to include a pavilion, press area, physiotherapy and fitness room, bar and sports shop, plus a library featuring the history, records and rules of the game, as well as a video room.

The Caribbean Cricket Centre
tel: (268) 460 5893
Jolly Beach Hotel
tel: (268) 462 0061 fax: (268) 462 1827

A carnival of celebration

Antigua's Carnival is one of the high-spots of the year, as well as one of the Caribbean's greatest summer events, a veritable kaleidoscope of colours, costumes and parades of smiling faces. A cast of thousands joins this traditional festival, celebrating Antigua's heritage.

On 1 August, 1834, when slavery was officially abolished in Antigua (the earliest in the British Caribbean), the people took to the streets to dance and sing and give expression to their joy at attaining freedom. For some years, sporadically, informal gatherings and celebrations were held to commemorate the event but not until 1957 was the first official Antigua Carnival organised. Since then, this evocation of folklore which recalls African roots and the anniversary of emancipation, has traditionally been held annually, commencing during the last week of July and culminating on the first Monday and Tuesday in August. An official programme covers ten full days of pageantry through music and dance, giving an opportunity to all those participating to expose their inherent cultural attributes and illustrate their skills, beauty and innovative talent.

Carnival combines many facets of Antiguan culture, an intermingling of the traditional with the modern. But what it's really all about is a week-long celebration of uninhibited dancing and singing, of grand spectacle, flamboyant costumes, a 'jump-up' in the streets, calypso and reggae and steel bands.

Taking place in the heart of St John's at 'Carnival City' (Antigua Recreation Ground), the capital's streets crackle and pop with the energy of all the festivities. The huge floodlit stage begins construction in early June for Carnival City and, as the crowds need plenty of refuelling, not far from Carnival City a festival village is set up. Loud music adds to the electric atmosphere of various bars and foodstalls and it is here that many retreat during Carnival from the frenetic watching of the shows and to make new friends with whom to debate the latest winners' fortunes and those to come.

Planning the masqueraders' outfits starts early,

almost as soon as one carnival finishes. Participants spend the next 51 weeks preparing, designing, creating and building these fantastic costumes for the bands (the street parades) in their 'mas camp'. The themes, characters, music and dance all have to be decided up to a year in advance. There is much prestige to be gained when a band or singer gets the crowd behind them and wins, and so all competition participants are totally committed in their quest for these coveted titles.

Steel band members and arrangers have also worked hard most of year, both on their steel pans and on their music. You're surely in for a treat with the repertoire they always have to offer, all vying for a place in the finals.

The calypsonians release their songs on the radio and, during June and July, play at weekends in the calypso tents. Calypso lovers from far and wide congregate at these venues to hear the amusing, graphical and provocative lyrics, some to be heard for many a month to come.

The best of these singers take part in the semi-finals of the nationwide calypso competition the day before the official opening of Carnival.

Prior to the Carnival, the widely known musical group, Burning Flames return to their annual spot, Jampond, on open pasture just outside St John's. Here, on the Saturdays preceding the main event, devoted fans catch their latest carnival sounds, for free. The atmosphere further intensifies as the headquarters of the Lions Club, on Cross Street, near Carnival City, becomes the next major haunt of this exciting band. Hundreds of people from all over the island come to the 'Lion's Den', to feast on the many hits of soca, zouk and reggae, as they dance throughout the crazy nights of Carnival. And thus the build-up of activities creates an all encompassing, infectious spirit as Carnival opens with a street parade on the Saturday. Ten days follow of non-stop partying, when few sleep.

Events during the following week, such as the Village Pageant, Female Calypso, Teenage Pageant, Carnival Queens' competition, Children's Carnival, Junior Calypso, Steelbands Panorama competition, Jaycees Caribbean Queen show,

Calypso Finals and the King and Queen of the Band competition lead up to the explosion of 'J'ouvert' (meaning 'daybreak' and pronounced 'Jouvay') on the following first Monday in August (Antigua's emancipation day in 1834).

One of the more traditional, well known mas bands is the Vitus Mas Group who always make a particular point of highlighting Barbuda. One of their main goals is to keep Carnival 'moral and merry', avoiding lewdness so often prevalent at other carnivals worldwide. Thereby they encourage all ages, types and nations to rebond, welcoming strangers and celebrating life in its fullness. Carnival is for people of all nationalities and walks of life, gathered together to have spontaneous, harmonious fun.

Don't worry should you not feel like jumping, dancing or don't like crowds; there are plenty of spots to sit and gaze in wonderment at the spectacle before you and plenty of tempting aromas from the terrific food and drink available to keep you satisfied and revived.

The Carnival Office, Long Street, St John's tel: (268) 462 4707

Challenger Hot Air Balloon Festival

This spectacular, gloriously colourful annual event heartily supported by the Ministry of Tourism, draws increasing numbers of international balloonists who eagerly participate with their unique balloons. Since its inception, visitors and locals have feasted their eyes upon the grandeur, serenity and exotic colours of a galaxy of balloons in all flamboyant shapes and sizes.

The oldest form of manned flight, hot air ballooning was brought to Antigua in 1995, when Todd Challenger, an Antiguan based in Suffolk, England, created the first festival of its type in the Caribbean.

Having recently started to organise balloon festivals in Barbados and Jamaica, Todd Challenger and his marketing director, Nova Alexander, have succeeded admirably in their quest of 'bringing ballooning to the people of the Caribbean' by also arranging a professionally run passenger flight operation.

Commencing at the beginning of 2001, for the first time in the Caribbean, you can experience this extraordinary form of flight for yourself. Challenger Balloons have obtained an air operator's certificate enabling them to operate fare-paying passenger rides year-round in Antigua.

With a very early get-up call, typical of all balloon gatherings, the ascents start around 6am (depending on weather conditions), when the winds are at their lightest. The day starts even earlier for the ground crews who have to wrestle with the acres of balloon cloth, first filling them with powerful gusts of air from huge fans, used whilst the 'envelopes' are lying on the ground, then as they inflate, to 'anchor' the basket and balloon to its standing position. To

see and feel the blasts of heat shooting from the propane burners situated in the baskets is tremendous – it is well worth arriving early to take in this unforgettably bustling, exhilarating scene!

Once fully inflated the cluster of balloons rise in unison. There is nothing to compare with the almost ethereal sight of this kaleidoscope of colours drifting up and floating over the tropical islands.

With the headquarters at Glanvilles, typical launch sites are in line with the trade winds from the northeast and would include such bases as Newfield, Willikies, Betty's Hope, Emerald Cove, Freetown and Bethesda. Decisions are made on a daily basis to ascertain the most suitable launch site; in the event that the wind direction changes to the southwest, all balloons will be launched from Old Road or Jolly Harbour Marina.

Traditional at all major balloon events, night-time displays during the festival complete the end of the day, when the breathtaking Night Glow exhibitions take place. It is a major

spectator event, lighting up the dark night sky, when each tethered balloon is inflated, whilst remaining on the ground. The 'envelopes' take on an appearance of huge electric light bulbs as long flames from the burners inside light up the huge multicoloured balloons the size of two-storey houses. This fantastic festive scene is taken around the island each evening to various hotels, on to the beach and with all the balloonists even going over to Antigua's sister-isle, Barbuda, for a truly unique Night Glow show!

At such venues as Jolly Beach Hotel, St John's East Bus Station, Miller's by the Sea, Lashings and more, you will have the chance to admire at close range and inspect the workings and operations of a hot air balloon. Meet the balloonists who will be taking part from all over the world and feel free to ask questions and even climb into the wicker baskets. Challenger Balloons will be actively working with local charities such as Crossroads and the Fiennes Institute to help raise funds while the festival events take place.

Gasps and numerous exclamations can be heard upon first sight of these majestic multi-hued, nylon creations – and you can share this exciting spectacle at the celebrations of the annual Challenger Hot Air Balloon Festival held in Antigua.

Already bringing balloonists and visitors from around the world to the twin islands, this has added another dimension to Antigua's attractions as the festival continues to grow from strength to strength year after year.

For further details contact Todd Challenger, Antigua: Challenger Balloons, Glanvilles Village, PO Box 2468, St John's tel: (268) 724 2752 fax: 01 978 926 5964 or in the UK: Challenger Balloons tel: (44) 1473 743118 fax: (44) 1473 241710 e-mail: todd.challenger@hotmail.com website: www.challengerballoons.co.uk

The story of Christmas in Antigua

The absence of snow does not detract from the infectious festive scene generated in Antigua during the Christmas period. Shops and stores are draped with tinsel and brightly coloured lights. Christmas trees are glitteringly decorated. Homes are richly festooned and, of course, the hotels enter fully into the exciting spirit of Christmas and New Year fever. The island is liberally sprinkled with gestures of goodwill and feelings of hospitality and fun, making it an especially memorable event.

It is a fabulous time to experience the islands, and whilst many global traditions are dying out, Antigua continues to maintain the joy and character of the most popular customs from its yesteryear.

The cultural forms of 'old time Christmas' were often community based, involving crowds of celebrating people watching or participating in the performances of the masqueraders, play-actors, clowns and bands. New Year's Day was one of the main highlights, when the crowd would throw down money to the parade of steel bands, iron bands and performers which moved throughout the city into the Point area. Stretching back to the mid-1800s, following emancipation, the most well-known included:

JOHN BULL
Many felt the delight and terror of being chased by this frightening character. An impersonation of an African witch doctor, he was dressed in dry banana leaves, masked and horned. Often accompanied by a whip man, who would keep everyone in order, John Bull would run after him too, as well as 'charge' the crowds.

CAROL TREES
Resembling a Christmas tree, this consisted of a stick with several crossbars on which were hung lighted lanterns. These were paraded by carol singers as they serenaded homes and residents, sometimes joined by an accordion.

HIGHLANDERS
Part of the Scottish legacy in Antiguan culture, these colourful masqueraders always attracted the largest audience. Whilst their ancestral kilts were proudly worn as if for a Highland fling, they were flamboyantly bedecked with headdresses of beautiful peacock feathers mounted on their caps, red, long-sleeved shirts with colourful ribbons sewn to the backs of their shoulders, pink, fine mesh wire face masks and sported cow-hide whips.

MOKO-JUMBIES
One of the most sought after forms of Christmas entertainment, this tall, brightly costumed figure perched on stilts, pranced and jigged to the rhythm of a tambourine band. The old art form of

stilt-walking was reintroduced in 1994 by the Vitus Mas group in an effort to keep the talent alive. Fortunately their efforts to revitalise what would otherwise possibly have become a lost art form have resulted in an ever-increasing group of enthusiasts.

LONG GHOST

These were yet another frightening yet irresistible Antiguan figure of fun, again on stilts. They became so tall they could entertain the merchant families in town, who lived on the second storey above their shops. As this white cloaked character loomed above street level through upstairs windows, children would gaze at its waving long arms, operated like a puppet, whilst below, others would run behind the 'ghost' at a discreet distance.

BANDS

These are as diverse in sound and composition as the nationalities present in Antigua who played them. The jazz band was a very common sight, with conventional instruments and the string bands with fife, guitar, banjo, ukelele, triangle, cymbals, iron, plumbing pipe, and drums, the Caribbean version of the British and French military bands of the seventeenth and eighteenth centuries. Others included the Portuguese band in traditional red and yellow costumes, minstrel bands, monkey bands, mas bands, Highlanders in plaid kilts, Belgians, oriental soldiers, Native Americans, cowboys, and the clowns, which dominated the Christmas scene.

Christmas Day was ushered in from as early as 4am, with the sounds of fiddles and drums played by groups of people as they went through town, and from the end of the nineteenth century, the holiday season was lengthened from three days to one week.

Festive fare was, and is, elaborate and covers a multitude of different meat and vegetable dishes, followed by traditional rich Christmas

MASQUERADE/MAS BANDS

'Mas' is short for 'masquerade', derived from the word 'masque', which is defined as a 'form of theatrical play often performed in the sixteenth and seventeenth centuries for kings, queens, or noblemen … with music, dancing and song'. This term covers several varieties of troupes which were the main events of the regular Yuletide celebrations.

cakes and puddings, often infused with plenty of local rum, accompanied with homemade guava cheese, sweets and fudge. You may come across a very traditional seasonal drink made from the berry of the Sorrel plant; every family seems to have its own special recipe.

An island Christmas is perfect for couples and families. Antigua has much to entertain and enthral. Look at noticeboards and check the newspapers for a comprehensive list of activities and events. Churches welcome visitors to their seasonal worship, late-night services and carol singing. Shops in St John's stay open very late up to Christmas Eve, creating that initial sense of party time. Island-wide, there are poetry and song recitals, theatre, concerts, raffles, bingo, dances, fairs, fêtes and, of course, Santa Claus.

There are many wonderful events during Christmas and New Year which may provide a glimpse of the past, and in any event, you cannot fail to be entranced by the different festive sights and ambience as you pass through town or drive around the island.

Peace, love and light to all, 'tis the season to soak up the rich, hospitable atmosphere of this exotic festive time in Antigua.

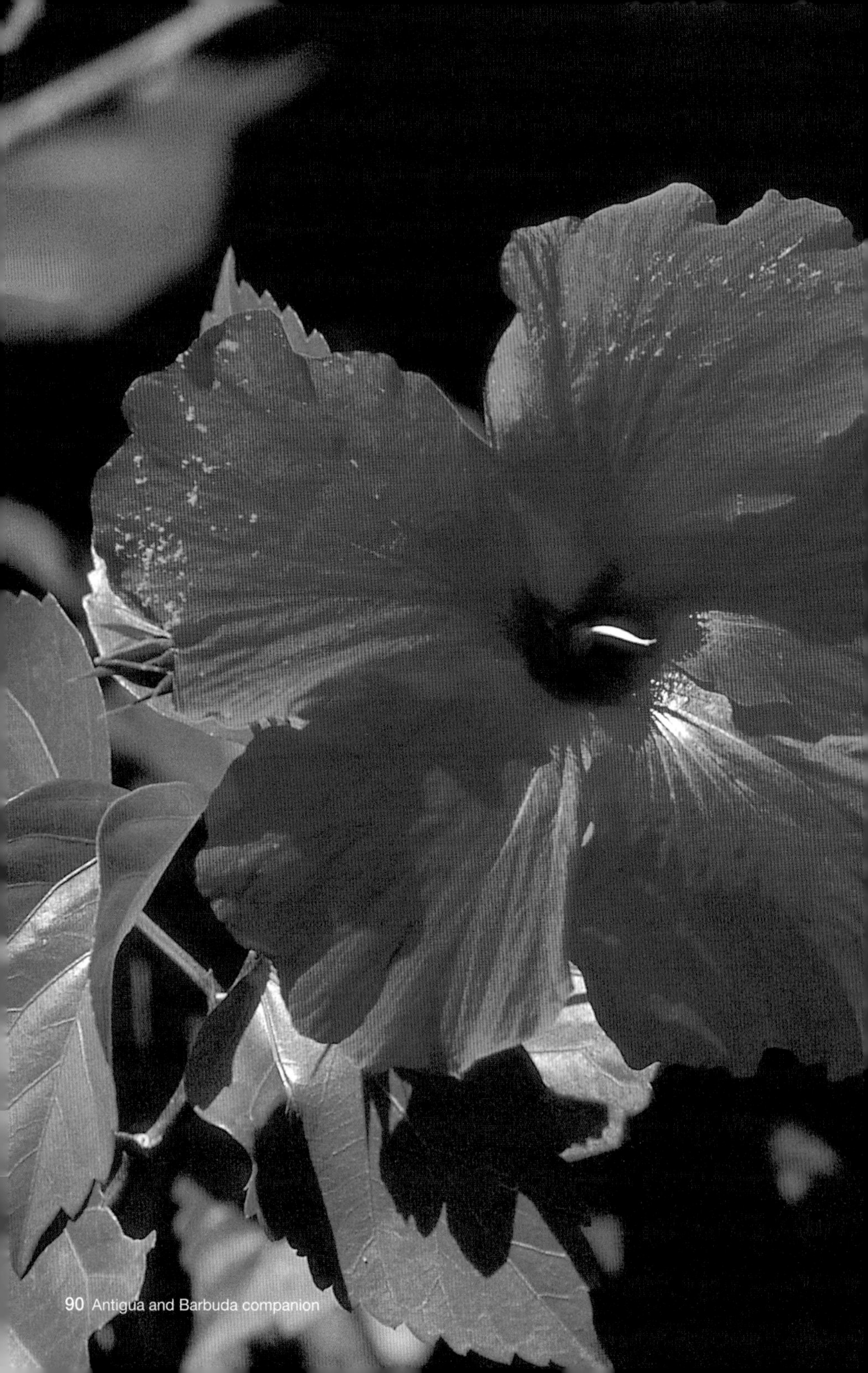

Flora and fauna

Flora and fauna

Through the ages, a selective process changes the balance of the ecosystem, whereby at each stage, there is both loss and introduction of various species of flora and fauna. Added to which, on these islands, is the introduction over the centuries of alien species. As one may expect, due to such aspects, plus change of habitat and degeneration of habitat from both natural and human activities, animals once found in these islands, such as the rice-rat, iguana and agouti, are sadly now extinct here. Naturally, the extinction of just one species can have far reaching consequences, leading to a 'domino' effect of further extinctions through the ecosystem. The Environmental Awareness Group (EAG; see page 114) has made sterling efforts to preserve and protect all manner of life on these islands.

As islands much inhabited and invaded in the past, Antigua and Barbuda have an interesting range of flora and fauna, some introduced by colonists and others indigenous to the area. Whether this is your first visit to Antigua and Barbuda, or one of many, you cannot fail to be absorbed by the prismatic colour of the tropical flowers and fascinated by the varied animal life. This section describes both common and rare examples you are likely to encounter.

FLORA

Given the history of these islands, it is not surprising that many of the flowering plants, shrubs and trees originating in other parts of the world have been transported here over the centuries. Whilst the majority of flora is native to Central and South America, others have come from tropical areas as far away as Southeast Asia, Africa and the Pacific islands.

Most of Antigua is now used for grazing livestock, cultivation or is developed for business and housing. Only in the southwestern part does there remain considerable evidence of Antigua's native flora. Almost every type of tropical flower, plant and tree can be found here. Some flower all year round, some are seasonal, others are fruitbearing.

However, don't expect year-round carpets of flourishing flora. There is a dry season here and not all the vegetation is lush, either. Parts of Antigua are open pasture, covered with the perennial, prickly acacia bush, locally called 'cassie'; others are rather scrubby due to lack of surface water. But then some of the rockier coastal areas can boast cacti and succulents such as the tall dagger log or century plant, (see National Symbols page 65) Antigua's national flower, and the curious looking Turk's head cactus. Nevertheless, often acting as natural decoration, the flowers, plants and trees noted below can still be found in abundance in the landscaping surrounding most hotels, in private gardens and whilst touring through the countryside.

Flowers, plants and gardens

Antiguans love gardening and take great pride in cultivating a profusion of colour, no matter how small their garden may be. Visitors may recognise many of the more familiar tropical flowers, shrubs and plants: allamanda, amaryllis, angel's trumpet, bird of paradise, bougainvillea, chenille plant, firecracker (or Antigua heath), frangipani, ginger lily, heliconia, hibiscus, ixora, morning glory, orchid, oleander, periwinkle, plumbago, poinsettia and spider lily.

The rainfall in Antigua tends to become greater going from north to south, so many of the splendidly colourful informal village gardens increase in richness of variety at the southern end of the island.

Trees

Sadly no primeval forest remains in Antigua, having been systematically destroyed over recent centuries to make way for the vast acreages of sugar cane. Following king sugar's demise, the majority of Antigua is now covered in grass and scrub. However, a few areas in the wetter

Traveler Palm, Botanic Station
Antigua, B. W. I.

Developed extensively today in the skincare and cosmetic world, a familiar name to you may be the multi-purpose plant, the aloe (*Aloe vera*), seen in abundance here. First recorded for its medicinal usefulness in 400 BC, its health-promoting properties were recognised by the ancient Greeks and Egyptians, and Mahatma Ghandi utilised the aloe's therapeutic advantages to survive his long fasts.

Rediscovered in the 1930s, when it was found to heal radiation burns from X-rays, a decade later it alleviated the discomfort suffered by atomic fallout victims, following the Nagasaki and Hiroshima bombings. Its long, smooth, spiky-edged, fleshy leaves produce a pungent, but exceptionally soothing, clear gelatine. Once the leaves are cut or broken, this sticky substance can be applied to every type of burn, sore, insect bite, sting or rash and is claimed to relieve such other ailments as ulcers, bowel disorders and painful joints. Vendors sell it on the beach as an instant remedy for sunburnt visitors (however, please also refer to page 20 on sun care) and many locals use the sap as a hair conditioner.

ant trees are in magnificent bloom. Look for vendors selling the flamboyant's two-foot long seed pods, which rattle when dried, as highly painted, wonderfully inexpensive souvenirs – locally called shak-shaks.

Common trees seen around the island include: bauhinia, calabash, cassia, dogwood, frangipani, Indian laburnum, Indian rubber tree, ironwood, jacaranda, lignum vitae (tree of life), locust, neem, Norfolk Island pine, pink cassia, pride of India, queen of flowers, sandbox, silk cotton, Spanish oak, tamarind, turpentine, 'wattle', West Indian almond, West Indian mahogany, white cedar, yellow elder.

The following are commonly planted trees along the coastal areas and shores, often acting as useful soil retainers, the habitat of many birds and insects and providing useful shade for visitors to the beach: the tall, graceful 'whispering' casuarina tree, the cordia tree, sea grape and the highly toxic manchineel tree (perfect for beachside shade when the weather is dry, but to be avoided when there is rain, see page 22).

As one would expect, Antigua is covered with various palms and palm-like trees: the slim-trunked cabbage palm, often reaching heights of over 100 feet, the tall stately royal palm, the popular coconut palm, the giant leaved, open fan-like traveller's palm and the primitive, cone-bearing, short cycad.

Fruit trees of several varieties are to be found in Antigua and many households have at least one or two in their garden. The market in town and roadside stalls will display the more common fruits, some seasonal and some producing year round. Whilst travelling around the island you will see some of the following: avocado, banana, breadfruit, cashew, grapefruit, guava, lime, mango, orange, pawpaw (papaya), soursop and sugar apple.

The Antigua and Barbuda Horticultural Society meets the third Thursday of every month either at the Museum of Antigua and Barbuda or on a field trip, president: Vincent Bell. **For further information contact Patricia Fraser, Treasurer, tel: (268) 463 2074 or Vice-president, Bruce Nodine tel: (268) 463 7586.**

regions, such as the hills around Fig Tree Drive, including the Wallings watershed (see page 197), have remained largely undisturbed for nearly 100 years, with some trees attaining a height of 50 feet or more. Cool, shady lanes wind through these scenic, lush hillsides.

If you are from a temperate country, you will be pleasantly surprised by the striking abundance of colourful flowering trees, particularly from June to August when the floral glory of the scarlet crowns belonging to the flamboy-

FAUNA

Amphibians

Two small tree frogs, also called piping frogs, (*Eleuthrodactylus johnstonei* and *Eleuthrodactylus martinicensis*) are the only extant native amphibians to the country. When you first arrive, you may think that you are only hearing crickets after the sun sets. However, what you are also hearing are the exceptionally loud two-note chirps coming from these adorable tiny frogs, given that they are only the size of a thumbnail! You will particularly be aware of this constant night-long chorus after a shower of rain. Put another way, should there ever be a total silence after dusk from such active, singing amphibians, you've either had too much rum or it is their warning of an imminent hurricane!

The marine or giant toad or crapaud (*Bufo marinus*) was introduced from Central and South America to Antigua as a biological defence against vermin in the agricultural fields. Often seen at night and after rain, they are highly toxic beings, known to have killed curious dogs with the poison which is secreted in glands around the eyes. Weighing up to two pounds, these huge toads are one of the largest in the world. However, the most notable feature is their extraordinary digestive system – capable of consuming almost anything from the most poisonous, offensive insects to any available pet food, which they doggedly favour. An extremely high reproductive rate during the wet season can result in great numbers of giant toads in certain areas, often creating a road hazard and much swerving.

Reptiles

Some 17 reptiles have been recorded from Antigua and twelve from Barbuda. A common species to Barbuda, a tortoise (*Geochelone carbonaria*), is presumed to have been introduced from South America by Arawak or Carib peoples.

Common to both islands, there are three geckos or woodslaves: *Hemidactylus mabouia*, *Thecadactylus rapicauda* and *Sphaerodactylus elegantulus*. Initially offputting, these plump, almost transparently pinky-white nocturnal lizards with squat legs and head, are nothing to fear. The timid gecko is indeed a friend; it scales vertical surfaces and glass with velcro-like pads to catch even large flying and crawling insects.

Small members of the *Iguanidae* family, which you can't fail to notice, are some of the varieties of defenceless lizard, the ground lizard (*Ameiva griswoldi*), and the more common tree lizard or green lizard, (*Anolis bimaculatus* or the brown *Anolis wattsi*). Mostly brown coloured with black specks, the foraging, sun-loving ground lizards will rustle in the undergrowth as you walk by. The conspicuous tree lizard is a harmless carnivore here which frequents gardens, verandahs and most inhabited areas. Environmentally adapting itself by chromatic variation, this nimble rustler could appear green, turquoise, buff, grey or brown. The female can grow to about six or seven inches and the stockier, sturdier male, to about nine or ten inches. Should you see a lizard raising itself high on the tips of its toe pads and swaying threateningly, sporting a bright yellow or orange dewlap (throat fan), this is the male either about to attack another male who is probably threatening his territory, or he is frantically courting! After copulation, which can last for hours, the female will produce soft eggs in holes in the ground. After several weeks, tiny, two-centimetre hatchlings appear.

Bird Island is the sanctuary of the harmless and precious Antiguan racer snake which was driven to extinction on mainland Antigua in the 1890s by the introduction of the mongoose. This very attractive, gentle, one-metre long *Alsophis antiguae* grass snake, has a population of just about 150 individuals, confined in exile on this island's 0.083 square kilometres. Despite their name, 'racer', they are a slow moving ground dwelling snake, feeding mainly on lizards and other small animals. As the world's rarest snake (indeed one of the world's rarest animals), in obvious need of protection, and with the impact of constant visitors to the idyllic Great Bird Island (see page 222), a conservation project began there in October 1995, developed by the EAG, the Forestry Division, and various regional international partners.

Mammals

In the late 1800s, the mongoose (*Herpestes auropunctatus*) was introduced to these islands from India to kill the rats which were seriously damaging so much of the sugar-cane fields. But the unforeseen happened and the nocturnal rats which used to live on the ground learnt to climb trees. So, the poor mongoose was left standing at the bottom gazing at the rats overhead! As a consequence, the daylight foraging mongoose started on the keeper's fowls, ground nesting birds and as mentioned earlier, on the racer snake.

Because of this, mongoose were later maligned as pests and an eradication programme was established in many British colonies. Nowadays, more happily, visitors can often see them running across the road. About 16 to 18 inches long, they are light brown furry creatures with long bodies, short legs and a bushy tail. These appealing, intelligent animals resembling ferrets are from the *Piperrieae* family. Such sprightly, cunning creatures live on fruit, eggs, reptiles, amphibia, rodents and, when they can, farmyard fowl.

The European Fallow Deer (*Dama dama*) is one of Antigua's national symbols (see page 64) and was introduced in the early eighteenth century to provide game for hunting. Sadly now only a very few exist on Guiana Island and on Barbuda.

Moving onto creatures of the night, bats are frequently seen flying about after dusk. Antigua and Barbuda each have colonies of the same seven species (a high number for a small land mass). These comprise three different insect eating bats, three fruit bats and one fish bat. The common house bat, a small insect eating bat, lives under the roofs of many houses: the other is the common fruit bat. The other five species are less common and often restricted to certain parts of the islands.

A lesser known aspect of all bats is their importance as pollinators, crucial to the continued survival of many plants and trees. They are strong flyers and able to carry pollen for long distances, particularly from one of their

favourites, and one of the national symbols, the daggerlog or century plant.

The bat, an ubiquitous insect eater, can be seen darting around at low level at sunset. Possibly unbeknown to you, this species is your best friend. An individual bat can consume about 3000 insects in one night – imagine life without these airborne pest controllers! All the insect bats are quite small, each having a wingspan of one foot or less. The smallest, the tiny funnel-eared bat, weighs less than a 25-cent coin.

Two of the larger fruit eating bats have up to an 18-inch wingspan. Mango is the food of choice, while the smaller long-nosed fruit bat, with its long tongue, specialises in feeding on nectar, like a hummingbird. Superficially, you can tell the difference between a mango eaten by a bird and one eaten by a bat. The bat eats at the bottom, because it hooks on up at the top; the bird stands up and punches from the top and at the side. All the fruit bats have a 'nose-leaf', a small fleshy pad on the tip of the nose which is used like a transmitter to direct their ultrasound.

The fish eating bat, also called the bulldog bat because of its likeness to that breed of dog, is the largest. With a wing span of up to two feet or more, it can be found along the coast or around secluded freshwater ponds and reservoirs, such as at Wallings. If you stop near the sea whilst passing down the coast, you can sometimes smell fish eating bats. They live in caves and come out late in the afternoon, flying along the coast. When the fish breaks the surface of the water, making ripples, the bat dives down and picks up the fish with its hind legs, like the osprey.

Domestic animals

Given the rural nature of Antigua and Barbuda,

it is not unusual to see a classic pastoral scene of fields of grazing cows and sheep. Confusingly, the sheep you will see here resemble goats and are referred to as 'hair' sheep, not being of the 'wool' variety. One easy way to tell them apart is that sheep tails are 'down', whilst goat tails are 'up'!

Goats seemingly roam indiscriminately – don't be surprised should you see a small herd traversing St John's! It's all part of the charming country character of these islands.

Donkeys are still a common form of village transport, particularly in the southern half of Antigua, where they are also seconded as pack animals. Horses are tethered here and there, either used for visitors to ride or for the occasional horse race at Cassada Gardens (see page 142). In and out of town, many people keep chickens and cockerels, referred to as 'yard fowl', mainly for food purposes. Dogs and cats are popular pets although the lack of education and financial means often prohibits the neutering of such animals and whilst not the problem of India or Indonesia, stray animals are prevalent (see also the Antigua and Barbuda Humane Society, page 110, and PAAWS, page 112).

Marine life

This could be summarised in one word – abundant! Well, Antigua is an island nation, after all, and the waters here are rich in coral, seaweed, fish and other marine life. The coral reef habitat is one of the most dense and diverse on the planet, even rivalling the Amazonian rainforest in complexity and number of species. The Antiguan marine world is amongst the most beautiful in the world, much appreciated by snorkellers, whilst the larger marine animals are only likely to be seen while diving (see page 157).

Whale and dolphin watching

Some 27 species, a third of all whales and dolphins, have been recorded in this relaxed warm-water setting. Whilst Antigua does not have specific whale and dolphin watching tours, if you participate in any of the diving and sailing charters here or are a yachtsman or woman, you may well be accompanied by dolphins following your boat, or riding the bow waves, and perhaps see them congregating on offshore fishing banks.

The best time to see whales and dolphins in Antiguan waters conveniently coincides with the high tourist season, January to early April. Following their 2000-mile journey from the cold north Atlantic, the humpback whales are frequently seen arriving here around January, en route to their mating grounds, and even more so in February and March on their way back. The other main species of whales which may be sighted are sperm whales, pilot whales, minke whales and even various beaked whales which all feed on squid. The striking orcas, pseudorcas and pigmy killer whales may also be seen.

Numerous tropical dolphins abound, feeding inshore around the many bays and coral

Nathalie Ward

end in April, are provided with forms to fill in with details of any whale sightings. These are subsequently relayed to the Whale Desk and on to a database at the Antigua and Barbuda Museum in St John's, where you are welcome to obtain any such information (the museum also supplies all such information to the Marine Education and Research Centre, Eastern Caribbean Cetacean Network, in St Vincent).

Main lookout points

These are on the south coast, off Shirley Heights, east of English Harbour and off Dieppe Bay, west of Falmouth. Humpback whales and bottlenose dolphins can sometimes be seen at the mouth of Indian Creek. Minke whales are seen in deeper waters during the winter.

There are reasonable opportunities to see short-finned pilot whales in the offshore waters to the east, and Atlantic spotted dolphins both here and off the west coast, occasionally close inshore.

On Barbuda's southeast coast, north of Spanish Point, Atlantic spotted and bottlenose dolphins can sometimes be found inshore in Pelican Bay.

Humpback whales, even mothers with calves, can be seen in the shallows inshore near the west coast of Barbuda, especially between February and April.

For further information contact John Fuller tel: (268) 461 3085 e-mail: fullerj@candw.ag or the Eastern Caribbean Cetacean Network (St Vincent) e-mail: eccn@caribsurf.com or Nathalie Ward (USA) tel: 508 548 3313 fax: 508 548 3317 e-mail: nward@mbl.edu

reefs and in the fragile mangrove forests. Here in Antigua, the name 'dolphin' generally means the dolphin fish, a common dish on Antiguan menus, and so be assured it is not the 'Flipper' dolphin which is being served! Remember to specify that it is the mammal and not the dolphin fish you wish to see when on a day cruise, although sightings can understandably never be guaranteed. Patience is also the watchword, but the spectacle of a breaching whale or leaping dolphins at play is a just reward.

Skippers participating in the famed Antigua Sailing Week Regatta, held from the last week-

SEA TURTLES

Sea turtles are native reptiles to Antigua and Barbuda and include green (*Chelonia mydas*), loggerhead (*Caretta caretta*), leatherback (*Dermochelys coriacea*), and the hawksbill (*Eretmochelys imbricata*) turtles. Of the 250 species of turtles, only eight are sea turtles, mainly found in the Caribbean and all are endangered.

In existence since dinosaurs roamed the

earth (200 million years ago) and the only ancient sea reptile to survive today, sea turtles can live, if allowed to, up to 100 years or more (sea turtles have a life span estimated to be close to a century). Undisturbed for centuries, flotillas of female sea turtles would crawl out of the surf to commence their traditional nesting ritual and carve their sandy nests on the very beach where they were born. Sadly, this is not so now.

Despite few natural enemies, the sea turtle population has declined dramatically as a result of over harvesting (for meat, shell, leather, oil and eggs) and other threats. On most Caribbean islands, there are now strict laws enforcing the protection and very survival of these majestic, lumbering giant marine chelonian reptiles and their precious nesting sites. Able to navigate their way through thousands of miles of open sea, they are driven back to their natal sites by a powerful hereditary homing instinct.

Here, the Antigua and Barbuda Fisheries Regulation provides for an annual closed season for sea turtles and declares certain activities

illegal including disturbing, taking, selling, purchasing or possessing turtle eggs, interfering with turtle nests and taking, selling, purchasing, possessing undersized turtles and/or undersized turtle shell.

The loggerhead is considered vulnerable; the other three turtle species are endangered. Whilst other species become sexually mature at approximately 15 years old, the slow-growing green turtle has a longer wait. Unlike the other turtles, which feed on sponges, jellyfish, molluscs, crustaceans, fish and squid, the green turtle is a herbivore, feeding on turtle grass and seaweeds.

Weighing as much as 1400 pounds and around six feet long, the leatherbacks are the world's largest ocean-going (pelagic) turtles and the only species with a soft, flexible shell, unlike the hard shells of the others. Insulated by a thick layer of fat, it is this unique outer skin which eliminates waste gases, affording such long periods under water, coupled with their ability to convert salt water to fresh water. This unusually adaptable turtle has been observed laying eggs on the southwestern coast. Please let the EAG know if you see one, particularly if on a hotel beach where the light will disturb the turtle and probably prevent laying of eggs.

Unlike the leatherbacks, the hawksbills, on average about three-feet long and weighing around 160 pounds, do not migrate long distances between feeding and nesting grounds. Turtle nesting sites are reported island-wide but Jumby Bay (Long Island), a privately-owned offshore resort island in Antigua's North Sound area, is host to an impressive hawksbill turtle conservation and monitoring project, set up in 1986.

Located on the island's Pasture Bay, it is noted as the best studied rookery of nesting hawksbill sea turtles (listed as the most endangered reptile worldwide since 1970 in the world), and the only one of the few that is feasibly able to tag every female.

Providing vital research information on these turtles with their distinctive beak-like mouth, the Hawksbill Sea Turtle Research Project (HSTRP) has been sponsored by Cable &

Wireless for the last three years. They have been responsible for funding the University of Georgia to train and give lecture series in Antigua, as well as contributing to the transport of equipment and presentations to schools. Additional funding comes from Jumby Bay and individual donations, under the direction of a professional marine biologist and the Long Island Residents Association (LIRA). This tiny island's environmental sensitivity to its endangered marine visitors even extends to great consideration being taken with respect to the construction of houses and lighting, ensuring the turtles remain undisturbed.

During a Cable & Wireless clean-up and beach improvement project at Jabberwock Beach, in the northeast of Antigua, Dr Jim Richardson of the University of Georgia discovered that this, too, was one of the beaches sea turtles favoured as a nesting place. Along with comprehensive beautification plans for this popular coastal stretch, a portion will be designated as a sea-turtle nesting sanctuary with educational and informative signage.

Turtle watching involves keeping a vigil from early evening through the night to dawn, to be able to witness the nocturnal nesting process. It is a fascinating study and a great privilege to watch the emergence of a new generation of such an endangered and ancient animal.

Further information can be obtained, and donations made, to any of the following people: Dr Jim Richardson, Jumby Bay Hawksbill Project, Institute of Ecology, University of Georgia, Athens, Georgia 30602, USA tel: (706) 542 6036.

Long Island Residents Association, Jumby Bay Island, PO Box 243, St John's, Antigua tel: Corina Edwards-Sealy (268) 462 7849 or 462 6000.

Birds

Wetlands and coastal habitats of these islands are both a permanent home and frequently the first landfall for over 100 species of migratory landbirds and waterfowl, particularly from North and South America. Valuable salt ponds and mangrove swamps attract such birds, and are the subject of many Environmental Awareness Group (EAG) projects and surveys aimed at conserving and restoring such unique ecosystems.

Among the 173 species of birds noted from Antigua and Barbuda, one of the most important seabird colonies of the West Indies is the magnificent frigatebird (*Fregata magnificens*) nesting colony on Barbuda (see page 108). The island has benefited from two professional studies: one on Adelaide's warbler (*Dendroica adelaidae*) and the other on the subject of the breeding behaviour of the frigatebird colony, which thrives in an area of rich food supplies, the Barbuda Bank. The latter is also home to the rare and beautiful West Indian whistling duck, found also on other offshore islands.

Barbuda's Codrington Lagoon and the satellite ponds of the island's interior offer the perfect refuge with a variety of feeding habitats and extensive pond edge. Apart from a great number of migratory species, which may be expected annually, Barbuda's native shorebirds include: Wilson's plover (*Charadrius wilsonia*), willet (*Catoptrophorus semipalmatus*), black-necked stilt (*Himantopus mexicanus*) and killdeer (*Charadrius vociferus*).

Included in the list of families or species of birds you may see on Antigua and Barbuda, or at sea, are: pelicans, herons and egrets, ducks, ospreys, hawks, rails, gallinules and coots, plovers and turnstones, oystercatchers, stilts, snipe and sandpipers, moorhens, pigeons and doves, jaegers, gulls and terns, kingfishers, woodpeckers, tyrant flycatchers, swallows, cuckoos and anis, caribs, warblers, nightjars, swifts, mockingbirds and thrashers, grebes, shearwaters and petrels, storm-petrels, tropicbirds, boobies and gannets.

Good spots for birdwatching in Antigua are the many coastal ponds, creeksides and salt ponds on the west coast, around Five Island harbour, Parham harbour and other wetland sites on the eastern coast. Pelicans, boobies, sandpipers and terns are frequently seen in and around the Jolly Harbour area, stretching up to

Ffryes Bay. It is the offshore islands which are host to numerous species of migratory seabirds, especially from February to June. The best spots in Barbuda would be Codrington Lagoon, Bull Hole and inland mangroves.

Particularly common, the cheeky, bold sparrow-like Lesser Antilles bullfinch (*Loxigilla noctis*), the cheerful, vocal bananaquit (*Coereba flaveola*) and the purple-black rather arrogant, strutting Carib grackle or blackbird (*Quiscalus lugubris*), are regular visitors to the breakfast table of visitors and the subject of many amusing pictures. You are likely to see the long-necked, graceful, large white common egret (*Casmerodius albus*) swooping across the rolling pastures to join the smaller cattle egret (*Bubulcus ibis*), which settles on and near grazing cattle. Also, with three species frequently seen but less able to be photographed, is the enchanting hum-mingbird, the only bird able to fly backwards!

The Caribbean has many resident birds occurring nowhere else and Antigua is no exception, being honoured, for instance, as the home of the subspecies of broad-winged hawk (*Buteo platypterus insulicola*), which is unique to the island. Should you wish to have further information of the islands' avifauna, do not hesitate to contact the EAG.

Of course, books can be written, and are written, covering the enormous variety of tropical flora and fauna. Those species included here may well inspire you to seek further sightings and information. As a visitor to these islands, the best way for you to help the fragile ecosystem and environment is simply to enjoy it and not participate in the taking, buying or eating of any rare species; this helps us to preserve the precious remaining unspoilt natural areas.

Barbuda's frigate bird sanctuary

Barbuda's high spot for nature lovers and ornithologists is the Codrington Lagoon Bird Sanctuary, not far from the airstrip, in the lime-green waters of Codrington Lagoon.

This sanctuary also forms the nature reserve of the magnificent frigate bird (*Fregata magnificens*), where literally thousands of these unmistakable large birds breed. These are quite spectacular, particularly during mating time in early winter or in the spring, when the pure white chicks are hatched. You may also hear the frigate birds referred to as 'man o' war' birds. The name has developed from their keen ability to allow other birds to do the fishing. They deftly swoop down in aerial combat and grab their catch, or trouble the other bird until it drops its bounty, to their benefit.

Codrington Lagoon is also home to approximately 400 bird species, where waterfowl flourish in the large lagoons, creeks, swamps and mud flats, and to which many migratory North American species are attracted. You may well see the endangered West Indian whistling duck, and countless common brown boobies and pelicans, but the frigate birds are the main attraction.

A local boat operator will take you on a guided tour of the lagoon. It is a short 20-minute ride from the wharf over to the frigate bird sanctuary, whereupon the boat glides through the mangrove narrows towards the north end. Numbering over 4000, this is one of the largest nesting colonies of the glossyblack magnificent frigate bird in the world (the other is in the Galapagos). The mangroves spread for seven miles by about two miles, still perfectly intact and completely unpolluted, supporting this fantastic rookery and marine life.

The history of such majestic birds can be traced back approximately 50 million years and, despite having a weight of just a few pounds, they are endowed with a tremendous wingspan of up to eight feet. This gives them the greatest wing area in proportion to their weight, of any bird in the world. It is said that they cannot take off from the sea or land, but once airborne from the mangrove trees, the streamlined frigate bird can soar at up to 22 miles an hour to an altitude of 2000 feet. Professional studies have confirmed that the birds live up to 33 years, however, scientists believe they can live up to 50 years.

With surprising quietness, the adult males swoop and whirl, trilling and making smacking noises, with softly flapping wings, creating a most serene atmosphere. It is truly a fantastic spectacle, watching thousands of these striking, aerial denizens overhead.

Visitors can watch the males with their flamboyant and distinctive scarlet throat pouches, blown up to the size of a balloon, try to attract a female mate; when she appears, the wings tremble, showing the undersurface flashing in the sunlight, whilst the male also emits a drumming sound. A raucous scene can be witnessed at mating, when birds argue over the twig nests, perch ownership or even landing rights! Such courtship rituals take place from September

to January, when egg laying also occurs. However, the colonies are active throughout the year because frigate birds have one of the longest chick-rearing periods of any bird species – being not fully independent until about eight to ten months old.

Tickets to visit the frigate bird colony can be purchased in Barbuda at the Tourist Booth at the Lagoon Wharf.

Unquestionably, it is well worth taking the short flight to visit this quiet and charming neighbouring sister island (see Barbuda, page 297) and to visit the marine haven of its special bird sanctuary.

The Antigua and Barbuda Humane Society

Formed at the end of 1991 by Canadian-Antiguan lawyer, Karen Corbin, and Antiguan veterinarian, Dr Radcliffe Robins, this registered charity has made tremendous inroads in the prevention of cruelty to animals. The Humane Society's goals encompass the bringing about of fundamental changes in local attitudes towards animals, their role in society, and the respect and care with which they should be treated.

Associated to the world renowned Royal Society for the Prevention of Cruelty to Animals (RSPCA), the Humane Society is also an associate member society of the World Society for the Protection of Animals (WSPA). It was thanks to the help of the RSPCA overseas fund and local contributions that a dog and cat shelter was constructed with labour provided by the Department of Public Works. It is hoped that this will further improve the re-homing programme, which has already been successful for hundreds of animals.

Donkeys are adorable creatures, but due to their longevity can become unwanted. The respected Donkey Sanctuary in England (through the International Donkey Protection Trust) assisted the Humane Society in fencing a five-acre area for such donkeys and also donated a much needed livestock trailer. The society even cares for a very unusual species, not normally found in the Caribbean – Chilean llamas. A herd of these lofty, gentle animals was abandoned in Antigua whilst en route to the USA.

As a visitor to Antigua and Barbuda, you are likely to see sheep, goats, donkeys, cattle and horses roaming on unfenced land and along the roadsides of this rural community. Viewed as countrified and charming, noticing an ill or stray animal can also be distressing. Animal welfare and humane animal control is in its infancy here. Taking action to stop indiscriminate breeding of dogs and cats, for instance, is costly to owners and does not take precedence above other pressing social needs. The islands are only just beginning to appreciate the joys of animals as pets and companions, capable of showing unconditional love and requiring care and respect.

In 1997, the Humane Society addressed this aspect by conducting its first neutering clinic, where locals paid a token amount to have their animals spayed or neutered. It had a good response and is expected to become an annual event.

However, such animal shelters and programmes in this small nation require considerable funding – impossible without the co-operation of worldwide animal societies and the kindness and generosity of visitor donations.

Some take it further by 'adopting' a dog or

cat found wherever they are staying, and having fallen in love with it, then decide to take it back home. This is actually both possible and easy as, thankfully, there is no rabies on these islands. Dogs and cats can enter many countries, including Canada and the USA, simply with a rabies vaccination and a health certificate from the Chief Veterinary Officer. For entry into the UK, however, the animal must adhere to the six-months quarantine regulations there. Whilst the society does not particularly encourage these options (there will be unwanted animals needing homes in the visitor's home country), it does help with any request for the necessary arrangements.

A 35-acre animal sanctuary, near Bethesda, in the south, is the Humane Society's base and home to the donkeys, llamas, and the dog and cat shelter. It is among these rural grounds where visitors may also enjoy the small livestock farm, containing an assortment of young animals, particularly lambs and goat kids being hand raised and bottle fed. You are most welcome to call in to observe the society's efforts and delight in the abundance of animals; large directional signs in this picturesque area will guide you to the entrance.

Naturally, the day-to-day operations and ever-increasing work create great financial needs and at the Humane Society's animal sanctuary, you will find t-shirts with the society's logo, holdalls, collection boxes, a fundraising 'mail-back' brochure and a *Tail Waggin'* cookbook for sale in their shop-office-cum-video room.

Donation boxes can be found around the island at various hotels, the Epicurean supermarket and in the departure lounge of the airport. The society is extremely grateful for any contribution, no matter how small.

Alternatively, for just EC$ 40 (US$ 15) or more, you can become a (voting) general member of the Humane Society, and receive their quarterly newsletter, *Animal Tracks*. Simply send your name and address along with your cheques, made payable to 'Antigua and Barbuda Humane Society'; Mastercard and Visa are also accepted.

For further information contact: Karen Corbin, the Antigua and Barbuda Humane Society, PO Box 2052, St John's tel: (268) 461 4957 e-mail: abhumane@candw.ag

PAAWS

(Protect Antiguan Animals With a Smile)

PAAWS was officially formed in Antigua by Jenny Meston, on 13 March 1996, after she had already devoted all her spare time over the previous 15 years to helping stray and abandoned domestic animals. Her efforts were justly rewarded when only three months later her voluntary, non-profit making charity was recognised by the RSPCA, in June 1996, and subsequently made an association member on 1 November 1999. Monies raised from membership and donations are used towards medication, care, food and vet fees.

A large percentage of membership comes from visitors. Having noticed a donation box, or possibly been moved by the plight of a helpless cat or dog on the beach or in their hotel grounds, they have often called PAAWS for help and advice. Many such visitors, having returned home to the UK, Canada or the USA, continue to sponsor their rescued animal. Some even come back to Antigua to spend time with the pet they saved.

Jenny has strived to maintain a high profile for PAAWS and its goals in the community by working particularly with the youth in Antigua, and creating a higher awareness of animal welfare. There are regular PAAWS dog shows and other fun events involving local children and their dogs and puppies.

The dogs and cats they rescue are mostly from severe risk situations, suffering from acute thirst, lack of food, shock and often needing intensive care and isolation. All the animals are examined immediately by a vet, wormed and medicated and then given limitless time with individual care and love to socialise and prepare the pet before re-homing. Euthanasia is only used as a last resort, under veterinary

recommendation, in cases of physical distress beyond help. Potential new homes are carefully checked for safety and security, where the animal can roam freely within its confines.

To encourage such re-homing, not only are the animals now in first-class health but are given at least their first inoculations against any diseases. As a condition for adoption, new homes are required to ensure further inoculations, worming and neutering, where applicable, although financial help is sometimes given with costs. PAAWS successfully saved and safely re-homed 209 cats and dogs in 1996/97, 366 in 1997/98, 436 in 1998/99 and will far exceed this in future; they also have attended to bird problems and parrot rescue. Such sterling work has earned tremendous support from local businesses, restaurants and hotels, most of which promote the collecting boxes and participate in fundraising events (notably the Mango Bay Hotel).

In 1998, PAAWS had the privilege of attracting the attention of Lady Victoria Getty. As a regular visitor to Antigua, she became the patron in recognition of Jenny's Meston's efforts for these basically gentle and friendly animals.

Should you wish to become a member or make a donation, contact Jenny Meston, President, PAAWS, PO Box 819, St John's tel: (268) 461 6573 or Margaret Gould, Treasurer, tel: (268) 461 6217.

In the case of animal rescue, call either Jenny Meston, or Dr T. Brown on (268) 462 3060, or Dr F. Francis on (268) 460 8552.

Gloria and Nick Maley of Island Arts-PAAWS bird section, provide their Internet connection for PAAWS with saved and re-homed animal stories. See *A Letter from Sam*, and encrypted credit-card facility for donations at 1-by-1.com/PAAWS e-mail: PAAWS@1-by-1.com

The Environmental Awareness Group (EAG)

– protecting Antigua's paradise in a race against time

Established in 1989, the EAG is a non-governmental organisation, based in Antigua. With the motto, 'Education, conservation, participation, working to conserve our environment', they examine the effects of environmental problems, which are often not always obvious, but can have profound consequences.

Saving wilderness areas is essential not only for wildlife preservation but as the timeless stimulation to human imagination and creation. It can take years, even generations, to change long-accepted attitudes and habits. In this respect, the EAG exercise an excellent example of dedicated and committed work to

protect the islands and their inevitable fragilities, such as mangroves, rainforest sites, coral reefs, offshore islands (see page 222), and various threatened species of wildlife.

Working alongside community and other relevant groups to manage and conserve natural resources, they help to identify areas where a positive impact can be made for the improvement in the quality of life. They engage in mounting public displays at the Museum of Antigua and Barbuda, in promotions on Earth Day and World Environment Day, in the use of radio, television and newspaper articles, organise clean-up campaigns, tree planting ceremonies, poster competitions, and more. These all serve to heighten awareness of the fragile nature of the insular environment and to ease the planning for sustainable development.

Travellers can enhance this environment by holidaying without disturbing flora and fauna or harming coral reefs and learning about the twin-islands, by providing funds through donations and membership, and sharing expertise with the EAG and the Historical and Archaeological Society (HAS, see page 60).

Information gained through findings of rare species such as the native iguana, the Antiguan racer snake (*Alsophis antiguae*) (see Flora and fauna, page 98) and the beautiful West Indian whistling duck, could save them from extinction and its impact on the environment.

Rare or migrant bird and duck sightings are much appreciated, so please keep an eye out for such passerines, shore and sea birds wherever you go. The EAG would also be happy to receive any information on bats (particularly on Barbuda) regarding where there are large concentrations, caves, or where they are threatened. To assist with these findings and sightings, the EAG has various field guides,

West Indian whistling duck

EAG

descriptions and one of the largest libraries of environmental information in Antigua.

Do you fancy some light exercise in locations of environmental interest? The EAG has semi-monthly field trip walks with guides, usually the third or last weekend in the month, to which you are welcome. The EAG also conducts turtle watches for members only, but at a mere EC$ 40 annual membership, so why not join up and support a worthwhile cause, which also enables you to take advantage of such events?

They also look forward to welcoming you to their monthly meetings on the last Saturday at 5.15pm of every month at which guest speakers are invited to make presentations on various environmental topics. There are also various fundraising events throughout the year.

The Environmental Awareness Group tel: (268) 462 6236; e-mail: eag@candw.ag or please visit the EAG offices upstairs in the Museum of Antigua and Barbuda, Long Street, St John's
web site: www.homestead.com/eag-antigua/

Sailing

Antigua Sailing Week
– magical maritime Mardi Gras

From a fleet of only 24 rather elderly wooden boats competing in 1967, Antigua Sailing Week is now regarded as one of the top five sailing regattas in the world, number one in the Caribbean and the largest in the world on tonnage.

For those of you who may know nothing of this extraordinary event, it is seven days of rough-and-tumble yacht racing and seven nights of on-shore partying – a test of survival on both counts. The atmosphere is rich in Antiguan hospitality, keen competition and good sportsmanship.

Held around the coasts of Antigua each year in late April and early May, this is regatta time for ocean going yachts and the wandering skippers and crew who sail them. It is rather like a Nelson battle royal, fought on the borders of the Caribbean and the vast Atlantic with wheel and winch, instead of cutlass and cannon, out of which very few can win – but nobody really loses.

Thousands of visitors mill around English Harbour and the high grandstand vantage points of Antigua, not to race but just to be part of this aquatic carnival. Spectators flock to witness the racing fleets streaming past, multi-hued spinnakers billowing in front, unlike many other regattas where you merely see the boats disappearing out of the harbour to race, only reappearing hours later. Antigua Sailing Week is enjoyed by the many holidaymakers to the island; it is not just for the fit and under-forties, but very much for all the family, young and old alike. It is small wonder then, that so many people who have never been near a sailing boat in their lives come to Antigua to experience this magical maritime Mardi Gras.

Antigua Race Week competitors are in love with the sea and all those vessels capable of sailing on it. This is a mecca for sailors, where the trade winds are at a healthy average of 20 knots, making it perfect racing conditions for the hundreds of yachts which make their annual pilgrimage. Hundreds of non-racing spectator boats add to the colour and action as they follow the fleet during these five exhilarating days of racing.

Superb sailing conditions, keenly contested international standard courses, the island's beauty, friendly people and the after-race special social events continue to draw at least 5000 skippers and crew and around 250 boats to Race Week. As an event that is as important to the world's social climbing jet setters as it is amongst the worldwide sailing community it draws from over an astounding 35 countries, as far afield as Hong Kong. Antigua is regarded by sailing aficionados as the yachting capital, where local craftsmen are in demand the world over, particularly for varnishing, and where owners bring their boats for the perfectionist standard of work received.

Creating such a highly respected reputation, this successful nautical pageant draws yachts from luxury to bareboat, some of which travel enormous distances to compete. It is not all partying and races are considered a true challenge; the 16 different classes are conducted under International Yacht Racing Rules and the Caribbean Yachting Association Safety Regulations. Quality races, of between 16 and 28 miles, are exacting tests of hull, sail, stamina and seamanship. Under the auspices of the Antigua Hotels and Tourist Association, the all-volunteer Sailing Week committee start their own hard work for the next year's regatta, only the day after the last one finishes.

The notorious Lay Day is a supposed day of rest and recuperation for the serious sailors, but is also certainly a day for the serious merry-makers. The Antigua Yacht Club is responsible for this full day's programme of boisterous goings-on at the club's grounds in Falmouth Harbour. This is a much publicised day when at least 2000 people cram on to the decks, sidelines, hanging off boats and dinghies to watch the spectacle. After a day of more partying, eating, drinking and much laughter, it isn't only the sun which sinks below the horizon!

Aside from world-class yacht racing, this festive week features after-race parties at the different race-end venues, to which all visitors are welcome, plus many shore activities for all, including music, dancing, parties, contests, games, cultural shows, receptions and dinners, and finishes with the family favourite, Dockyard Day, on Saturday. Enjoy many amusing games such as walking the greasy pole out over the harbour and tug-of-war; listen to the steel band. Watch the maypole dancers and First Antiguan Cheerleaders, and take the children to the bouncy castle, before the presentation of prizes by the Minister of Tourism and other dignitaries.

Taking place from the old officer's quarters balcony, Nelson's Dockyard, the afternoon's activities are concluded at 6pm, when appreciative locals and visitors watch the Antigua and Barbuda Royal Police Band beat the retreat in front of the assembly on the balcony. The evening sees the Lord Nelson's Ball at the Admiral's Inn, a rather formal but fun affair, when the numerous winners are announced and the shining cups and trophies are presented against the backdrop of this historical naval building. This provides a fitting and stylish finale to a spectacular week, once experienced, seldom forgotten.

For further information contact Antigua Sailing Week tel: (268) 462 8872 fax: (268) 462 8873 web site: www.sailingweek.com

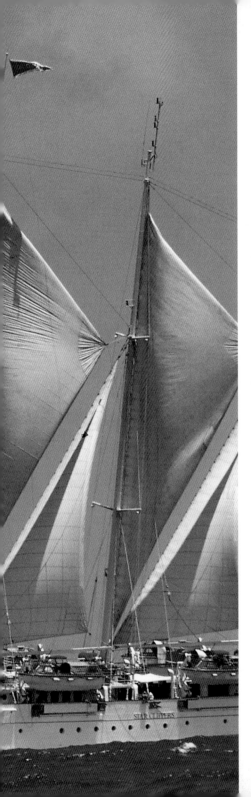

Antigua Classic Yacht Regatta

– the spirit of tradition lives on

> What shall we tell you? Tales, marvellous tales
> of ships and stars and isles ...
>> James Elroy Flecker

Varnished teak rails, topped by acres of billowing white sails of graceful traditional yachts majestically take to the seas proving that older yachts were built to last. The world's finest classic yachts, including schooners, gaffers and vessels of classic design, have converged on English Harbour since 1987, to compete in the Antigua Classic Yacht Regatta.

The short, simple but exciting races grant these great yachts full rein to demonstrate their power and strength, all starting and finishing outside Falmouth Harbour. The courses afford the many spectators, who have come from far and wide, easy viewing of such breathtaking scenery, inspiring some of the best and most beautiful photographic opportunities.

One of the foremost classic yacht regattas in the world, Classic Week takes place every April, conveniently just before the renowned Antigua Sailing Week. This celebration of traditional sailing vessels is a feast of elegance, terrific parties, with a wonderfully old-fashioned convivial atmosphere.

The beauty and aura of a bygone golden era has been further enhanced over the last few years, by the memorable 366-foot four masted Barquentine *Star Clipper*, which provides a dramatic backdrop whilst navigating its 36,000 square feet of sail, with the likes of tall ship *Mandalay*, around the course.

Skippered by Captain Uli Pruesse, one of the originators of the Antigua Classic Yacht Regatta

in 1988, *Star Clipper* initiated this tall ships class. Promoted by Captain Pruesse, this class will compete amongst themselves for the World Peace Cup, in tests of seamanship, small boat handling and presentation of the ship overall, ultimately bringing even more of these enchanting tall ships to Antigua.

However, not all the action takes place on the high seas; the day preceding the racing is host to the fabulous Concours d'Elegance. There is a wonderful party atmosphere accompanying the spectacular sight of over 50 classic yachts anchored stern-to-stern at the Antigua Yacht Club Marina, accompanied by a live commentary and music.

Complementing the historic atmosphere, Antigua Yacht Club keenly illustrates the heritage of traditional sail and its times with a Heritage Day Festival, which follows the last day of racing. The fun and the period costume often sported for the gig-racing attracts many families and spectators and takes place behind the glorious Admiral's Inn hotel in Nelson's Dockyard. This is also where a splendid tea party is held in the grounds, all quite reminiscent of a typical Henley-on-Thames, English summer's day. Finally a grand prize giving party completes the day.

Typical of those participating in past years have been the exquisitely restored 131-foot 'J Class' 1933 America's Cup yacht *Velsheda*, the gracious 1915 Herreshoff gaff schooner *Mariette*, the oldest competing boats, the *Marguerite T*, an authentic 1893 gaff-rigged Bristol Channel pilot cutter, the 1890 *Dunlin*, the hundred-year old *Irene*, and many other gracious, sleek competitors in the schooner, spirit of tradition, vintage and classic classes.

The celebration of traditional craftsmanship and sailing of the Antigua Classic Yacht Regatta is certainly guaranteed to provide a spectacular time, where competitors and spectators savour the infectious ambience of this grand marine event.

For further information contact the Antigua Yacht Club tel: (268) 460 1799 e-mail: classic@candw.ag web site: www.antiguaclassics.com

The Antigua Yacht Club

Established in 1967, the Antigua Yacht Club continues to uphold a valuable position within the sailing fraternity. Suitably situated by the marina in Falmouth, their premises encompass the Last Lemming bar and restaurant, above which is where you will find the club room and office (open five days a week), the dinghy shed and related facilities.

Originally called the English Harbour Yacht Club, it was founded to promote local yacht racing by a group of resident sailors, many of whom are still very active in the sailing community. Today the AYC acts as a national authority for the International Yacht Racing Union (IYRU), and is a member of the Caribbean Sailing Association (which is based in Antigua). It sponsors various events, including the Classic Yacht Regatta, and assists with Antigua Sailing Week.

Of particular note is the club's achievement to have successfully passed over 200 students between the ages of six and 18 years old in their Youth Sailing Programme. Having completed courses at the beginner, intermediate and advanced levels, such aspiring young sailors have been sent to compete in numerous international regattas. Taught mainly in optimists and lasers, many local and visiting yachtspeople have discovered that these 'students' are proficient enough on any size yacht and are sometimes used as extra crew for the Classic and Sailing Week Regattas. Indeed, Karl James, the dinghy programme co-ordinator, is Antigua's Olympic laser class representative.

Initially, the club organised weekly Sunfish races off Admiral's Inn but it was not long before the Thursday races were begun, complete with an after-race rum-punch party at the dockyard flagpole, ensuring that many sailors competed! The Thursday races have become a traditional event and are believed to be the Caribbean's longest running weekly race.

The AYC also organises a number of other sail-

ing events in which visiting yachts are welcome to participate. These include: an end-of-month Sunday race, the Carlisle Bay race, Hightide series, round-the-island race, featuring the popular Miss Round-the-Island contest, Queen's Cup and Independence Day race, the Guadeloupe race

The Jolly Harbour Yacht Club

Formed in 1992 and located in Jolly Harbour Marina, the club has major events in its annual racing calendar each year, including the Valentine's Regatta, the Antigua–Barbuda Cruising Race and the Annual Regatta (see Calendar of Events, page 70).

In addition, the Jolly Harbour Yacht Club schedules various events throughout the year including: full moon races, races to neighbouring islands (such as Guadeloupe) and races to various west coast beaches for an afternoon barbecue, followed by a return race to Jolly Harbour.

The Yacht Club has held Saturday afternoon races since its inception which have been enormously successful. Barring rare hurricane weather, avid members are on the water every Saturday afternoon at 2.30pm for the start of these weekly races. Visiting yachts are always welcome and encouraged to participate. Jolly Harbour Yacht Club members also actively participate in joint racing events scheduled by Antigua Yacht Club.

In 1998, the Yacht Club commenced a Youth Sailing programme for children aged eight to 16 years, with training in mini fish dinghies with an optimist rig. The Dogwatch Tavern is used as the Jolly Harbour Yacht Club's clubhouse, where burgees can either be purchased there or at the Yachting Caribbean office in Jolly Harbour's shopping centre (see page 192). New members are always welcome.

The Jolly Harbour Yacht Club
tel: Commodore Nick Maley (268) 562 0275
fax: (268) 461 6324
e-mail: nick@antiguatoday.com

and many more. The Caribbean Sailing Association rating system is used for handicapping and the club's fleet captain can assign a temporary rating should you not have one.

Antigua Yacht Club tel/fax: (268) 460 1799
e-mail: yachtclub@candw.ag

Nicholson's Charter Yacht Show

– power and panache

The historic southern end of the island is not only host to the famed springtime Antigua Sailing Week and Classic Yacht Regatta but also to the glamorous annual pre-Christmas, Nicholson's Charter Yacht Show. Like its cousin, Antigua Sailing Week, it was created from humble beginnings, nearly four decades ago.

Generally quoted as 'the largest charter yacht show in the world', it gathers the very best of the contemporary yachting fraternity, including hundreds of agents, press, marine and service related companies. Whilst only the brokers can personally visit the yachts, it is, nevertheless, a fabulous opportunity for any visitor to witness such a grand spectacle on the island.

This show is a superb presentation bringing together a class of the world's finest and most glamorous yachts normally associated with the likes of Monte Carlo, Cannes and Porto Cervo. Antigua boasts plenty of viewing space for more

than the 200 vessels normally registered, filling the dockyard and spilling into the Antigua Yacht Club Marina and Falmouth Harbour Marina, where the super yachts tend to dock. Here, the excellent marina complex with its comprehensive facilities, shops, bars and restaurants, coupled with the increased docking facilities, ensures Antigua maintains its worldwide reputation as a leading charter yacht destination.

There were very few yachts and certainly no yacht charter companies when the late Commander Vernon Nicholson RN (ret.) sailed from Cork, Ireland into Antigua with his family, on the beautiful schooner *Mollihawk*, over 50 years ago. With perfect weather conditions for sailing, they decided to settle in English Harbour, where the sea had been the main resource and a way of life since the Carib Indians arrived centuries ago.

Requests for cruises to nearby islands soon came, mainly from the well-heeled enclave on

the island, Mill Reef. The whole family became involved, including his sons, Desmond and Rodney, who fondly refer to those first charters as essentially for 'cruising, snoozing and boozing'! Business progressed and it was thought that if centuries ago this renowned hurricane haven was good enough for the Royal Navy, then it was certainly good enough for them to establish the first yacht charter company in the West Indies – followed by their own Charter Yacht Show in 1961.

More and more people are favouring a fully-crewed charter yacht holiday, with about 80 per cent of all Caribbean winter sailing charter holidays booked between August and October. Naturally charter cruises range somewhat in price, dependent on the size of the yacht, crew and amenities; although you should still expect the same standards of service, no matter what. Finding exactly what you and family or friends desire, with the multitude of different aspects involved, will necessitate liaising with a good charter broker or agent. They make it their business to know their yachts and crew intimately and to match them to your detailed requirements, tastes and budget.

Charter agents since 1949, Nicholson's specialise in charter management with a current fleet of about 75 luxury crewed yachts, sail and power, yacht services and yacht sales (see Appendix, page 319). Many famous yachts and ocean-going extravaganzas regularly attend the show, together with other top-class charter yachts, represented by such companies as Nicholson's, Fraser, Camper and Nicholson, Bob Saxon, Yachting Partners International (YPI), Caribbean Connections, Sun Yacht, Bounty, Nautor's Swan Charters, Merex Caribes and Ocean Marine to name only a few.

It's a veritable delight for the voyeurs of jet-set glitter, opulent yachts and the magnificent sight beheld here. Aside from the marine-related colour and action, ashore, the Royal Police Force Band often performs a tattoo, and the restaurants, bars, dockyard and marinas are a hive of activity.

For further information tel: (268) 460 1530 fax: (268) 460 1531 e-mail: nicholson@candw.ag

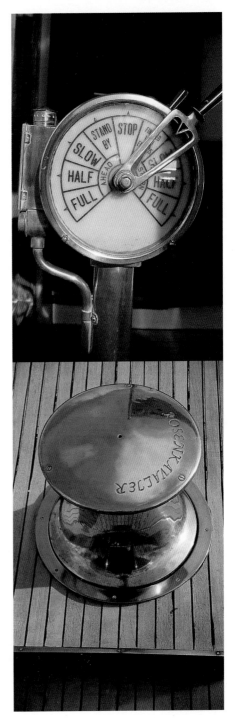

Model boat building
– small but perfect

In an age of computerised boat design, gadgets and turbo-technology, it is incredibly refreshing to know that the time-honoured, low-technology of building wooden model boats, as perfectly constructed as their full-size counterparts, still survives today, here in Antigua.

The biggest model boat competition of the year is the weekend before the Classic Yacht Regatta, in April, when the Department of Tourism holds its Annual Model Boat competition at Falmouth Harbour; there is normally another competition around Independence Day at the end of October.

It is a fantastic sight to see a myriad of coloured hulls and sails, set proudly atop their wooden stands at the water's edge, before the racing starts. The crowds obviously appreciate the dedication, time, effort and money spent on such works of art, further illustrated when the different sizes and classes of boats are set in the water and the action takes place.

Some of the island's most prolific model boat builders have been building boats for over 20 years, often having learnt from older members of the family. In the parish of St Paul's such skills were mainly handed down in this way, although the other area of Antigua known for model boatbuilding is The Point, Deep Water Harbour, where they produce completely different styles of boat and are so fast that, when competing with other model boats, they have their own class.

Using a good white pine (turpentine) tree, a species used centuries ago to build the huge wooden ocean-going boats, the builders choose one by the length and size of beam needed. Whilst in the old days a machete was used to cut this to size, they now sometimes use the more modern, quicker chainsaw, which also gives the advantage of creating two boats from the one piece of timber.

A guideline of the shape of the boat is drawn with a thick marker pen on the face of the timber. Then a cutlass is used to cut out that shape. This outline is always created completely 'blind' as the actual contours are in the designer's head. Then the process of planing begins. They always start from the deck down. The inside of the deck is chiselled out from the inside of the timber, to the required thickness the individual designer desires. Then the hull takes shape with the use of a cutlass, freehand and completely by eye, again to personal requirements.

At this point the boat's outline is ready to dry for a couple of months (or for those less patient, it can be baked in a brick oven). It is sanding time next and dependent on the designer, the keel, specific lead and weights, are determined. No two boats are the same; by their very nature they are all unique.

The deck is then sealed with epoxy and a remote control set up. Some owners have the more advanced battery controlled models with self-tacking, but when racing they are penalised for such advantages by having to finish in certain areas on the finishing line.

Whilst the normal mast and rigging would equal the length of the boat and beam, again this is created by personal choice and may alter slightly from boat to boat. The paint and filler used are exactly the same as on the expensive

full-scale yachts and therefore, relatively speaking, cost the same.

These model boat owners, designers, builders and captains inevitably have full-time jobs in the marine and yachting business so are well-catalogued in this area of the world, and can only dedicate themselves to such craftsmanship in their spare time. It takes at least four months to build a traditional classic racing model boat to such perfection, from timber to completion. These model boats are not small ornamental sizes – rather, three to six feet long and very seaworthy!

Further skill is required to be able to preset the rudder and sails to ensure victory according to each start and finish of a race. But unlike many other sports with such technicalities, competitors share their experiences and opinions relating to this and other factors such as the prevailing wind. There is great camaraderie.

Some builders use fibreglass, which is quicker and more advanced but also more expensive; however, it is said by the traditionalists that

such boats can seem cold. When the model boatbuilders have created something from a simple block of hewn wood, with their own minds and their own hands, they see something come alive before them.

Whilst the modern age clearly has many advantages, it is very sad when the price of progress is often the disappearance of the old traditional ways. The desire for hand-built items falls from favour, and demand diminishes to such an extent that yet another piece of heritage is buried.

Thankfully though, the guardians of this Antiguan heritage are young artisans who savour any time they can give to the artistry of building and racing their precious model boats.

Do take the opportunity of seeking them out and if you have the chance, don't miss one of their exciting and very different racing competitions!

For further information, or private commissions, you can contact the following: John Smith tel: (268) 460 3373; Vernon Harrigan tel: (268) 463 8156; Rusty tel: (268) 460 1196

THE ROYAL NAVAL TOT CLUB OF ANTIGUA AND BARBUDA

Unbeknown to many, even to those who have lived here for years, there is an almost clandestine ritual which takes place in a corner of the dockyard every evening.

Carrying on a naval tradition in a traditionally naval area of Antigua, the Tot Club meets every evening at 6pm sharp, for the traditional toasts of the officers and the lower deck of the Royal Navy.

The chairman, Michael Rose, was a chief petty officer and in the navy for 26 years. He was the initiator of this intriguing practice in Antigua, when looking after the Copper and Lumber Store Hotel during the summer of 1991 and having a tot of rum every evening, and thus the Tot Club began. The first few years of the club were somewhat chaotic, with people coming and going irregularly. It was then decided to form a membership.

The purpose of the club is mainly to carry on the revered naval tradition of a tot, with a gathering of like-minded people, in humour and attitude, as a signal to the end of the working day at 6pm, daily: to maintain the traditional toasts (if only a little modified) going back hundreds of years and now, of course, proposing the loyal toast to Her Majesty, the Queen; to promote and foster the element of a 'helping hand' and goodwill amongst themselves, in the English and Falmouth Harbour areas, all members being experienced in one field or another. It also handles many other voluntary projects.

The daily toasts, only ever taken with rum most similar to that issued to the Royal Navy, Pusser's Blue Label Rum, are (with a little humorous licence taken on some days): Monday – 'our ships at sea'; Tuesday – 'our friends' (was 'our men', meaning the hundreds of crew); Wednesday – 'ourselves' (as no one else is liable to consider themselves with our welfare); Thursday – a double toast – 'a bloody war and a sickly season' (traditionally said, but implying the death of one's immediate superior by one of the many diseases abounding at that time) and 'a bloody war and quick a promotion'; Friday – 'a willing foe and searoom'; Saturday – 'sweethearts and wives, may they never meet' (poetic licence and equality for women members 'lovers and husbands, may they never meet'); Sunday – 'absent friends and those at sea'. Following such traditional toasts and the loyal toast, there would also be a toast to historical events, in fact any kind of notable anniversary.

Typical annual events would include the club's official Christmas, Burns Night, Trafalgar Night and the Tot Club of Antigua and Barbuda layabouts pentathlon. Instead of the usual sports involved, this consists of pool, trivia, darts, 'liar' dice and golf, but all with a list of rules of course. Throughout the year, various parties are arranged at the slightest excuse, such as a toga party, a themed barbecue and so on.

Simply due to the numbers interested, there are overseas members at all times, but there is a limit of 15 full members. If somebody shows interest in joining, a verbal invitation is extended and they must join at the Copper and Lumber Store Hotel in Antigua.

A month's probationary period commences, during which time the potential member buys their own rum (only EC$ 5) from the club. There follows a minimum honorary membership period of three months, when new members can't hold office but can invite guests. If they are able to attend a minimum of four nights a week, they can then be elected to become a full member, but only when there are less than 15 full members, through somebody leaving the island or whatever. There are approximately 175 overseas members who must take a minimum of seven tots in a 14-day period.

For just EC$ 100 (US$ 40) you will obtain membership of any of the worldwide Tot clubs, even including such far-flung countries as New Zealand, plus the Tot Club t-shirt and the semi-annual newsletter. The latter is particularly designed to keep overseas members in touch with what's happening and listing all members, along with their addresses, telephone numbers and birthdays, so that other members may look them up when in their area.

Michael Rose, Chairman, The Royal Naval Tot Club of Antigua and Barbuda, PO Box W88, St John's tel: (268) 560 1946 fax: (268) 460 2616 e-mail: totclub@candw.ag

Sport and recreation

Active traveller

– land and leisure pursuits for sportspeople or spectators

Sport is something that does not matter, but is performed as if it did. In that contradiction lies its beauty.

Anon

Staying above water can be fun, competitive or relaxing, with as much action as you care for. Antiguans love sport and there is a wide variety of outdoor activities and sports including golf, tennis, horse riding, squash, netball, basketball, cycling, soccer, running, and more, as well as gyms and an excellent choice of health and beauty centres and spas.

CYCLING

Life is like riding a bicycle; you don't fall off unless you stop pedalling.

Claude Pepper.

Cycling is a booming sport. It is an excellent way to explore the island and its less accessible regions and you can even join in the road races and fun rides.

Bike Plus
St John's tel: (268) 462 2453/6050
e-mail: bikeplus@candw.ag
Adult mountain bikes can be rented (by the day only) and it is open six days a week.

Cycle Krazy
Popeshead and George Street, St John's
tel/fax: (268) 462 9253
Offering guided tours on mountain bikes by arrangement, with special rates for families. Tours, in groups of six or more, are accompanied by a 'following' support vehicle with refreshments. Alternatively, hire an adult mountain bike with safety helmet and locks (special

rates for more than three days), and plan your own adventure. Open Monday to Saturday. You can also contact any cycling club and the Antigua and Barbuda Amateur Cycling Association through them. Mountain bike races are organised to which visitors are welcome to view or participate.

Paradise Boat Sales, Rentals and Charters
Jolly Harbour
tel: (268) 460 7125 fax: (268) 462 6276
web site: www.paradiseboats.com
Despite the somewhat misleading name, they have mountain, cruiser and road bikes to rent by the day, week or longer. Also scooters (with

helmets supplied) and, of course, boats. Open seven days a week.

Tropikelly Trails
Fitches Creek tel: (268) 461 0383
fax: (268) 462 5464
Bike tours organised with guides who will point out the places of interest along the way. Mainly choosing routes away from the main roads, avoiding traffic, they often commence in St John's, with bike tours offered seven days a week and to suit various fitness levels; prices all inclusive of bike, helmet, guide and refreshments. Catering to both cruise ship passengers and hotel guests, bikes can also be rented to people wishing to organise their own tours.

GOLF

> One of the quickest ways to meet new people is to pick up the wrong ball on a golf course.
>
> Anon

Antigua is the perfect venue for both hacker and professional and there are golf courses to satisfy the increasing number of golfers who don't want to leave their clubs at home; golf, after all, is best enjoyed under sunny skies in balmy climates. Mark Twain once described the game as 'a good walk spoiled', and should you wish for an easier day, electric golf buggies are available.

Cedar Valley Golf Club

Cedar Valley tel: (268) 462 0161
fax: (268) 462 5635
An 18-hole, par 70 championship course of 6142 yards located close to St John's. Cedar Valley has been host to the Eastern Caribbean Golf Championships and is the venue for the annual Antigua Open which draws the Caribbean's top golfers. Part and full membership are available on this challenging, hilly course with breathtaking vistas. Monthly tournaments and excellent junior golf programme. Equipment and carts are available for rental and lessons can be arranged. Bar/restaurant, pro shop.

Jolly Harbour Golf Club

Jolly Harbour tel: (268) 480 6950
fax: (268) 480 6953
Designed by leading golf-course architect Karl Litton of Florida, this is an established par 71, 18-hole, 6001-yards championship golf course, one of the Caribbean's premier golfing venues. Adjacent to the Jolly Harbour Marina and surrounded by excellent shopping and beaches, it is set in lush tropical parkland. Easterly breezes cool you on the fairways which have been sculpted into a green hilly landscape, with seven lakes to make it more challenging. The club includes a driving range, clubhouse with restaurant, bar and locker rooms. Open to visitors on a daily fee basis, annual membership is also available. They also conduct tournaments and outings and offer golf-bag storage, rental shoes, clinics and private lessons with qualified golf professionals.

Dickenson Park Leisure Centre

Dickenson Bay tel: (268) 463 4653
fax: (268) 560 4653
For those less purist and wanting some good fun, try the extremely popular and challenging floodlit 18-hole miniature golf course within this friendly leisure centre. Incorporating the much-frequented Putters Bar and Grill, they also have a discotheque, video store, an Internet cyber café, a boutique and various shops. A great spot for families.

EXERCISE/FITNESS/GYMS

There are many first-class gyms in Antigua – weight training and workout enthusiasts needn't worry about putting on unwanted holiday weight – you will be able to keep yourself as toned and fit as you wish. Some hotels have gym facilities and there are a number of small local fitness centres dotted around the island. Below are listed the two largest professionally run centres, both with free weights, first-class weight, running and step machines, various studio keep fit/aerobic classes and changing, locker and shower facilities. Also listed are various related associations, federations and aspects covering a comprehensive range of fitnesses and disciplines.

National Fitness Centre

Campsite, St John's tel/fax: (268) 462 3681
Located near St John's just off the Old Parham Road this is the first professional gym established in Antigua; visitors are welcome to this supervised gym. Free weights and a full range of brand-name exercise and weight machines with trained instructors. Step and aerobic classes daily in the airy studio with certified instructors. Full changing room, locker and shower facilities; leotards, leggings and back support belts are often available for purchase, along with cold drinks and health preparations.

Antigua and Barbuda Aerobic and Fitness Association

Alexis Edwards tel: (268) 462 3827
fax: (268) 461 1758
Aerobics is a well-established form of energetic fitness worldwide and Antigua organises a huge annual aerobic championship. Governed by the world body, FISSA, Antiguans compete at high ranking world championships.

Antigua and Barbuda Bodybuilding and Weightlifting Federation

Bert Kirchner tel: (268) 464 6044
Bodybuilding has been popular here since the 1950s and over the years a number of body builders have been produced, winning titles both at home and abroad.

Antigua and Barbuda Boxing Association
President, Len Mussington
tel: (268) 461 3073 fax: (268) 460 5482
Woodberry Park tel/fax: (268) 462 0209
Antiguan Maurice Hope, undefeated British, Commonwealth and European light middle-weight champion of the late 1970s, is still very active in training local boxers at his gym and led the Antiguan boxing team at the Commonwealth Games in 1998. As interest in boxing on the island has grown tremendously in recent years, local coaches such as the Antiguan Lenior Gregory regularly train hopefuls. His boxing ring is just on the outskirts of St John's. Gregory organises regular 'Las Vegas' style outdoor matches which draw big crowds at Casino Riviera, particularly when there is a later showing of a live world boxing title.

Someone else who has seriously encouraged the sport is Warren Woodberry, who owns and runs Woodberry Park. Along with Graham White of Casino Riviera, he has promoted amateur, semi-professional and professional boxing here, offering the beneficial facilities of comprehensive training equipment and a full standard ring size. Situated on one of the main roads out of St John's, the Old Parham Road, his boxing evenings also draw big crowds. By now, plans to integrate Antigua into the heavyweight, middle and lightweight rating system and therefore into the international boxing scene should have succeeded, leading to international boxing matches being staged on the island.

Antigua and Barbuda Martial Arts Federation
General Secretary, Herbert Hood
tel/fax (local): 462 3780
e-mail: mabito@mailcity.com
Covering eight different schools of martial arts, from karate to jiu-jitsu, there is something for anyone interested in these ancient disciplines of mind, body and spirit. Keep up your training whilst on holiday by calling the federation (established since 1980) to ascertain the venue for your desired discipline, all within a one mile radius of St John's.

Yoga
Kathleen Sharpe tel: (268) 461 2484
Antigua offers a perfect environment to practise this gentle art of attaining physical fitness and mental tranquillity and visitors often join in the classes which are held on the island. The main local teacher, Kathleen Sharpe, holds excellent weekly classes to suit all levels. Held during the winter and summer semesters, which cover most of the year, classes are in the south of the island at Falmouth and in the north, near Crosbies.

HIKING, RUNNING, JOGGING AND WALKING

Antigua's rural countryside has a veritable lattice-work of tracks and footpaths worth exploring. Many of the most frequented lead to the different hilltops and fortifications (see Island Exploration, page 187). The Historical and Archaeological Society (HAS) frequently arranges interesting trips (see page 60), as does the Environmental Awareness Group (EAG) (see page 114).

You may wish to join the local runners, joggers and walkers early mornings and late afternoons as they follow their chosen road circuits. Because the roads can be narrow and hilly, take care to keep well to the edge of the road and face oncoming traffic. Alternatively, for something more organised and enormous fun, see Antigua Hash House Harriers, page 147.

There are still fascinating parts of Antigua not necessarily for the super-fit to explore on foot and guided tours are available.

The Hiking Company
tel: (268) 460 1151
With five years' experience of hiking in the southwestern district, Peter Todd has put his talents to use by sharing his knowledge with groups of six people (minimum) on day tours in this lush part of the island. These moderate hikes are suitable for children over six and anyone reasonably fit. With a taxi ride to meet up at either English Harbour, Wallings Dam or some other suitable point, you will be taken over trails through Fig Tree Drive to the crest behind John Hughes village, on to Rendezvous

Bay and beach for a two-hour gourmet picnic lunch and to relax and swim, and then walk along the cliffs to Dieppe Bay. The hikes are organised with flexibility and total freedom in mind, commencing at 9am and finishing by 5pm, or according to group preference.

Tropikelly Trails
tel: (268) 461 0383 fax: (268) 462 5464
Fully insured escorted hiking tours take place at 8am and 3pm, commencing in the rain forest area at Wallings Reservoir, Fig Tree Drive. A steady climb takes you to the top of these southern hills for panoramic views of Antigua, and neighbouring islands on a clear day. Each hiker is supplied with water in a convenient carrying flask and snacks.

HORSE RACING

Antiguan style fun is to spend an afternoon at the Cassada Gardens' race track, near the airport, with the Antigua Turf Club. This may

not be Belmont or Ascot, but the meetings, run by the horse owners, are raw and exciting. Races are for thoroughbreds, many of which have been imported, and locally bred horses. A colourful and interesting time can be spent here whilst taking in the electric atmosphere and enjoying terrific food and drink from the local ladies who freshly cook chicken, meatballs, salt-fish cakes and other delicacies at their stalls. Races are generally run on Sundays and most holidays, and usually start at about 2pm, continuing until the light fades. Keep an eye out for announcements in the papers, on the radio, television or call the contact below.

Antigua Turf Club
Norma Prudhon tel: (268) 460 1093
fax: (268) 460 1524

HORSE RIDING

This is another very popular recreation, but this time on four legs! Some hotels have a string of local horses and operators outside their gates for gentle beach saunters but people who wish for a professional, more organised ride are also catered for. Formed nearly five years ago, the Caribbean Equestrian Association, of which Antigua is an active member, presents Inter-Caribbean shows in Antigua and the Antigua Horse Society also organises shows, gymkhanas and fundraising events.

Spring Hill Riding Club
Falmouth tel/fax: (268) 460 1333 or (local) 460 7787 e-mail: eastonj@candw.ag
Home of the Antigua Horse Society (AHS), this is a superb Caribbean horse riding stable, set amongst beautiful countryside and near the sea. Accepted by the Fédération Equestre Internationale (FEI), this equestrian centre represented Antigua for the first time in 1999 and competed at elementary dressage level, in spite of being a developing country and the smallest nation of the 55 countries participating in this prestigious global FEI dressage event. The AHS and Caribbean Equestrian Association also

SUN, SEA AND CONTRACT BRIDGE

The game played today called contract bridge, the most popular card game in the world, is derived from the old English game of whist. Most players are passionate about the game and if you are within this category then you will be pleased to know that there is a flourishing and enthusiastic Antigua and Barbuda Contract Bridge Association.

Rubber bridge is played at 5.30pm on Mondays, Tuesdays, Thursdays and Fridays at the Bridge Club on Factory Road, one of the main roads leading out of St John's. A weekly pairs tournament is held at 6.00pm on Wednesdays and a teams of four competition, when master points are awarded, is played on Saturdays at 5.00pm. Visitors are welcome to play in the tournaments or in the rubber bridge sessions as well as the Annual Antigua and Barbuda Open Independence Bridge Tournament at the end of October, plus the Inter Regional Tournament, usually held on the first weekend in November. Members of the World Bridge Federation and the Caribbean and Central America Bridge Federation, players here take part in regional tournaments. This is a pleasant way to while away a few hours from the sun and sea and an excellent way to meet new friends.

Antigua and Barbuda Contract Bridge Association Al James tel: (268) 462 1459 fax: (268) 462 1444 e-mail: jamesp@candw.ag

hold Inter-Caribbean show-jumping competitions here.

Horse-riding lessons, both in a class and individual, and hacks, are taken by professionally trained instructors. It is very reasonably priced for such quality horses, tack, facilities, supervision and surroundings. There is a menage and jumping arena. Complete beginners and children are just as welcome as are those wishing to improve their riding skills and enjoy Antigua from the saddle.

General beach and trail riding

Reliable Stables tel: (268) 461 4086
St James's Club tel: (268) 460 5000
Sun Fire Riding Academy tel: (268) 723 4794
Wadadli Riding Stable tel: (268) 461 2721

MOTOR RACING

Not traditionally what you would expect to find in the Caribbean, but yes, Antigua has race meets. Whilst still in their relative infancy, the races are mainly referred to as 'drag' or 'sprint' racing, where the quarter-mile, 1320-feet long strip can accommodate cars up to a 10-second quarter-mile capacity.

With one official drag race a month, usually on a Sunday, involving specially imported sports cars, Japanese and European with some American, it draws thousands of eager spectators. Viewing is superb on the immaculately kept grounds of the John I IV and V Recreational Centre, where crowds either congregate at track level, around the food and drink tents, or on the slopes and high on the ridge, where there are also various food and drink stalls, overlooking the track and far into the distance. It is a fun day, just a short ride from town, where even members of the public may participate in some of the races with their regular everyday saloon cars. The competition is likely to increase with safety rules in operation. Overseas participants are encouraged to join in this burgeoning, exciting sport.

The John I IV and V Recreational Centre
All Saints' Road, PO Box 1330, St John's.
Antigua and Barbuda Autosports Inc.

For further information contact the chairman, Paul Ryan tel: (268) 462 5760 e-mail: ryanp@candw.ag

TENNIS AND SQUASH

Most of the tennis courts, many floodlit for night play, are part of hotel amenities, reserved for guests. This is fine if your hotel has courts; otherwise, a call to a hotel that has them should result in a reservation. Most hotels have a weekly guest tournament and clinics and many have their own tennis professional for instruction. Antigua also has first-rate glass-backed squash courts.

One of the highlights of the sporting calendar here is Antigua Tennis Week. Hosted by Curtain Bluff Hotel, Grand Slam sports legends such as Fred Stolle, Ross Case, Owen Davidson, Kathy Rinaldi and other impressive international competitors lend their expertise and participate in the tennis clinics and pro-amateur tournaments. Having celebrated its 25th anniversary in 1999, this annual event takes place in May.

BBR Sportive Ltd
Jolly Harbour tel: (268) 462 6260
fax: (268) 460 8182
The Jolly Harbour Sports Centre has four floodlit tennis courts, two clay and two artificial grass. Tennis equipment for hire and a full range of facilities including showers, locker rooms, bar and restaurant, plus a 25-metre swimming pool and a half basketball court. Reservations are necessary for these plus the international glass-backed squash court with full range of facilities. Rental equipment and short- and long-term memberships are available. All major sporting events can be viewed via satellite television.

Temo Sports
English Harbour tel: (268) 463 6376
fax: (268) 460 1781
Established and well-known, this complex is located adjacent to the yacht club in Falmouth. Their much-booked range of sports includes tennis on floodlit synthetic grass courts and two excellent glass-backed squash courts with full facilities. Equipment can be rented or bought from the shop; court reservations are recommended. Very sociable year-round bar and restaurant.

The Antigua Hash House Harriers

Now this has something for everyone! You can sightsee, meet locals, get some exercise and have a great social time all in one go – a wonderful year-round fortnightly event for runners, joggers, walkers or even strollers, of all ages and fitness levels, including families.

This is certainly a tremendous opportunity for those keen on photography, exploring areas of the island even the Antiguans often wouldn't get to, meeting people of all ages from all walks of life and from many parts of the globe.

Developed by expatriates in Kuala Lumpur, Malaysia in the 1930s for fun and fellowship, this non-competitive exercise has spread to total over 500 Hash chapters around the world. It started in Antigua in 1991 and at times attracts over 100 people. On Saturday afternoons, when the heat of the day has subsided, the 'hashers' meet at a previously planned rural venue, which could be anywhere right across the island.

With two blasts of the hunting horn and a few words from the Hash Master, the two groups of hashers, led by a leader, gently move out in the quest to follow the correct five to seven mile trail through the countryside – and back to base! (Anyone not able to join in the walk can stay with the 'groupies', who 'guard camp'). Previously chosen 'hares' will have already marked routes, one for the walkers and one for the runners (the 'hounds'), with flour or shredded paper trails. Some are the real paths and some are hoax. The former is comfortingly confirmed when the sound of a horn or whistle and the call 'On, on' is heard, and everyone follows accordingly.

After an hour or so of enjoying all the sights and sounds en route, the desire for quenching your thirst and staving off hunger pangs is satisfied when the afternoon ends with food you may have brought for the barbecue, and drinks (although you may, of course, choose to leave and eat at your hotel or elsewhere). As darkness falls the generator is started and a chain of lights appears, strung up over poles or romantically draped over a tree or bushes. The coolers full of ice, beer, wine and soft drinks start to dissipate in this most friendly scene, as the barbecue sizzles with your supper. This is certainly a fun and worthwhile day!

Contact the Hash Master, Laurie Parke on (268) 560 2518 (after working hours), or Kim Chapman, the honorary secretary, on (268) 461 9392 (after working hours). Alternatively, look at the noticeboard at O'Grady's Bar, Redcliffe Street St John's tel: (268) 462 5392. The Hash Harriers meet here at 6pm on alternate Fridays for a very sociable gathering, and to plan the next route. You are most welcome to join in.

The best of health

Antigua offers reliable, professional health centres, massage parlours and practitioners for sheer indulgence, or for when you should be unfortunate enough to pull a muscle or ache from over extending yourself in any of the sports mentioned in the Active Traveller section. Whilst there are too many recommended establishments across the island to include here, some of the most popular or well known are listed below. Antigua also boasts first-rate medical, dental and eye-care specialists and a number of excellent health-food shops and naturopathic centres (see Appendix, page 319).

COSMETIC AND SPECIALIST DENTISTRY

**Dr SenGupta, BDS and Associates,
Implant, Cosmetic and General Dental Clinic**
Woods Centre tel: (268) 462 9312
fax: (268) 462 9314
This practice offers first-class dental care and service with the latest technological advances in dentistry, all at reasonable prices. Whether you wish for cosmetic dentistry, dental implants or orthodontics, or are unfortunate enough to require emergency dental care whilst on holiday, you can receive professional treatment in sophisticated, state-of-the-art surroundings. Along with visiting specialists, Dr SenGupta and his team offer a clinic with four surgeries, a recovery room, a sterilisation room and teaching facility, on a par with any dental practice in the US and Europe.

HEALTH AND BEAUTY SALONS AND SPAS

Akparo
Nelson's Dockyard tel: (local) 460 5705
fax: (268) 460 5704
Well-established hairdressers, Patricia O'Grady and Akame Shimizu run this Feng-Shui designed salon, with colleagues who all specialise in taking care of you. All hairdressing needs are provided, including shiatsu head massage, colouring, perming and hair treatments and personalised beauty care – facials with skin analysis, manicures, pedicures, waxing, body scrubs, eyebrow shaping and colouring and eyelash tinting as well as Swedish massage for total body, back or head and shoulders. Akparo offers the finest products and a philosophy based on listening to your body as well as your tastes.

Blue Waters
Soldier Bay tel: (268) 462 0290
fax: (268) 462 0293
A comprehensive hair and beauty salon, spa and gymnasium situated within this beautifully redesigned hotel of great repute, where no expense has been spared to create the very best available. Be pampered by qualified therapists offering manicures, pedicures and massages in this elegant salon, or relax in the steam and sauna rooms.

Equilibrium
St John's tel/fax: (268) 462 7919
Air-conditioned health spa at Gambles Medical Centre, on the edge of St John's, near Woods Mall. Fully qualified therapists offer passive exercise on therapeutic massage beds, a toning table exercise system, bodyslim electrotherapy treatment, plus bodywraps, body scrubs, holistic massages, electrolysis, waxing, facial toning and facials.

Esthetiques Plus
Creekside, Valley Road, PO Box 2527, St John's
tel: (268) 562 2098
Purpose-built air-conditioned premises situated a 10–15 minute drive from St John's. Friendly, experienced therapists offer facials, massages, manicure, pedicure and waxing, body wraps, body sloughing for women and men in a relaxed environment. Steam room and sauna. Complimentary tea and juice. Open seven days a week, Monday to Saturday 9am–9pm, Sunday 11am–6pm.

Pillar Rock Spa Health and Seawater and Holistic Centre

Pillar Rock, near the Royal Antiguan Hotel
tel: (268) 463 0444 fax: (268) 480 4240
Offering an unusual range of holistic and thalassotherapy services including reiki, shiatsu and Swedish massage, plus reflexology, combined with aromatic and musical treatment; sea water therapy, consisting of sea water showers, massages, sea scrubs and special private sea water whirlpool room; unique oxygen and ozone therapy for all disorders; sauna and steam bath; ear-candling. The herbalist prepares her own herbal remedies and they sell herbal and homeopathic formulas, vitamins, minerals, teas, weight-control products plus essential oil blends and soap. Open by appointment 1–6pm, Saturday 9am–3pm, closed Wednesdays and Sundays.

Strands

Woods Centre, PO Box W1001
tel: (268) 462 9465
Large air-conditioned hair and beauty salon conveniently situated at this popular mall just outside St John's. Wide range of hair services including cuts, relaxers, colouring, perms, highlights, styling; therapeutic foot spa; manicure, pedicure, facials, waxing, body massages, paraffin treatment. Complimentary tea and coffee. Fully trained cosmotologists. Open Monday to Saturday 8.30am to 8.30pm (last appointment 6pm); Tuesday 10am to 7pm.

Tree House

English Harbour tel: (268) 460 3434
fax: (268) 460 3200
Conveniently located between English Harbour and Falmouth, the renowned and long-established Tree House is a complete body shop for men and women. Hairdressing, manicure, pedicure and massage; Swedish therapy, shiatsu, lomi lomi, sports and deep tissue massage, trigger points therapy, plus chiropractic and reflexology in a relaxed and tranquil environment.

PERSONAL THERAPY

The Traditional Chinese Medicine Clinic

PO Box W888, Woods Centre, Anchorage Road, St John's
tel: (268) 463 8834/8877
After working in a hospital in China for 20 years, Dr Zhenhua Tang moved to Antigua and opened his now well-established clinic specialising in traditional Chinese treatments such as acupuncture and massage along with herbal medicines. Situated ten minutes' drive out of St John's near Dickenson Bay. Open 9am–5pm daily.

Yoga School

Falmouth tel: (268) 461 2484
Extremely experienced practitioner for lymphatic drainage massage and shiatsu-plus therapy (see Active Traveller, page 141).

Water world

One of the most attractive aspects of Antigua and Barbuda is that the numerous beaches make the sea easily accessible to you – in the water, under the water (see Diving, page 157) or participating in a sport skimming along the top. The water is always clear, clean and warm even during Caribbean winter.

Watersports are why many come here and are high on the 'to do' lists of visitors. Whether your intention is to pursue familiar water activities or explore new areas of interest, Antigua can offer a tempting selection of year-round participant water activities, with professional tuition, the best equipment and high safety standards.

Depending on the hotel you may be staying in, and its location, an abundance of watersports is available and, in some cases, to non-guests for a fee, often as a 'half' or 'one day' package; in addition, there are a number of privately run watersports facilities.

DEEP SEA/SPORT FISHING

Get hooked! Antigua's fleet of sports fishing boats has been modernised and expanded to offer a wide choice of deep sea fishing options, with experienced crew and full safety equipment for this rapidly growing sport. A day's sports fishing is becoming one of the island's greatest attractions. Depending on the season, fine catches can be made of tuna, wahoo, kingfish and dorado, although the relatively constant water temperatures give almost year-round fishing opportunities. Big game anglers (men, women and juniors), have been attracted by this for many years, to the Antigua and Barbuda Sports Fishing Club Tournament held every Whit weekend and other sports fishing events here.

Antigua and Barbuda Sportfishing Club
President, Francis Nunes Jr,
tel: (268) 462 0649/1961 fax: (268) 462 3119

Missa Ferdie
tel: (268) 462 1440/460 1503 fax: (268) 462 1788
e-mail: shoulj@candw.ag
A fine 38-foot phoenix sports fisherman with twin 415hp diesel engines, extensive safety equipment and fully equipped with a wide range of the finest gear available. Charming, prize-winning crew available for full- and half-day charters, taking a maximum of six people. Fishing trips include an open bar; picnics, day and business trips can also be arranged.

Overdraft
tel: (268) 462 1961/464 4954
fax: (268) 462 3119
web site:
www.antiguafishing.com
A fully equipped 40-foot fibreglass sport fishing boat with diesel powered engine, available for picnic charters and any other pleasure cruise you may desire, plus experienced fishing skipper.

Offwind Boat Charters
tel: (268) 460 9210
fax: (268) 462 7686
Based at Jolly Harbour for about five years, they can arrange deep sea fishing, sailing and power boat charters. You can choose your destination for fun days, overnight and private charters with crew.

SWIMMING

Splash out! As you are spoilt for choice with Antigua's famed ring of beaches around both islands (see page 213), you will find that swimming here can be almost as natural as walking. Where you are staying is likely to be on, or near, warm, relaxing waters for swimming and most hotels have a swimming pool. Should

you wish to really test yourself, BBR Sportive at Jolly Harbour Beach and Golf Resort also has a 25-metre pool designed to meet the highest competition standards and accommodate swimming events.

WATERSPORTS

Jolly Harbour Watersports

Jolly Harbour tel: (268) 462 7771/3

Located on this stunning, long white beach, next to the Driftwood Beach Bar, their beach recreation facilities include windsurfing, water bicycles, waterskiing, para-sailing, sausage runs, sunfish dinghies, jet skis, wave runners and ocean kayaks.

Long Bay Hotel

Long Bay tel: (268) 463 2005

fax: (268) 463 2439

A comprehensive selection of watersports is available to non-residents for various fees. These include scuba diving, waterskiing and tubing, snorkelling, picnic snorkelling trips, inshore fishing and deep sea fishing and yacht charter. There is instruction available for any watersport.

Mango Bay Hotel and Beach Club

Long Bay tel: (268) 460 6646

fax: (268) 460 8400

A stylish all-inclusive resort offering non-resident guests a day pass for all drinks, meals, pool and beach, including watersports facilities when not fully booked.

Pappy Water Sports

Dickenson Bay

tel/fax: (268) 463 5487

Long established watersports operation, having been situated next to The Beach Bar Restaurant on Dickenson Bay for over 15 years. A wide range of facilities including jetskiing, waterskiing, scurf and knee boarding, banana boats, snorkelling trips to Paradise reef, windsurfing, parasailing, sunfish sailing, kayaks, and deep sea fishing. Lessons available. Also rental of sunbeds and umbrellas.

Rex Blue Heron

Johnson's Point

tel: (268) 462 8564

fax: (268) 462 8005

Located on the tranquil west coast, this all-inclusive resort offers non-resident guests full use of all their watersports facilities for a rental fee per sport. These include snorkelling, pedalboats, sunfish sailing, windsurfing, waterskiing, with lessons also available in the last three categories.

Sandals

Dickenson Bay tel: (268) 462 0267

fax: (268) 462 4135

This well-known couples all-inclusive resort,

situated on Dickenson Bay, offers various passes to non-residents. Enjoy their dining, bar and entertainment facilities as well as their watersports, including waterskiing, kayaks, aqua cycles, hobie waves and snorkelling.

Seasports

Dickenson Bay tel: (268) 462 3355
fax: (268) 463 0722
A complete watersports facility, established since 1980. Situated between Sandals and Warri Pier, activities include waterskiing, parasailing, jet skis, jet bikes, kayaks, snorkelling, sunfish sailing and windsurfing. Cold drinks and sunbeds are available for a relaxing day on the beach.

Sunsail Club Colonna

Hodges Bay tel: (268) 462 6263
fax: (268) 462 6430
With a flotilla of sailing yachts for teaching and enjoyment, non-residents can purchase a full- or half-day pass for use of restaurant, bar, pool and all watersports facilities, including waterskiing, kayaks, snorkelling, windsurfing, dinghy sailing and Sunfast 20s yachts.

WINDSURFING AND BODYSURFING

Ride the waves! Whether you're a first time or experienced 'boarder', you'll find Antigua's coastal waters and conditions make it a windsurfers' paradise. Dickenson Bay is where beginners and intermediates can learn and experience safe windsurfing; Dutchman's Bay serves expert windsurfers, as well as giving beginners calmer water inside the reef. On the eastern side of the island, Half Moon Bay offers good wave sailing. The water is clear and waves break in about 20 feet of water. In the middle of the bay the body surfing is brilliant, but at the far end the water is really calm – perfect for the children. A few miles south is Willoughby Bay, about three miles across with waves breaking on both sides. The St James's Club is located on the southern side of the bay and has good waves on its outside waters. However, only advanced sailors should try the waves there because it gets pretty 'gnarly'. Even the local experts have been caught in the froth at this spot. If you like surfing, Galley Bay has brilliant waves that break November–March, and Turtle Bay is great for surfers.

Diving and snorkelling

The warm waters and reef encrusted coastline of Antigua and Barbuda invite you to a veritable dive odyssey, where you can be transported to a world of mysterious fascination, colours and marine life. The coral reef habitat is one of the most dense and diverse on the planet, even rivalling the Amazonian rainforest in complexity and number of species. Here, Antigua's marine world is amongst the most beautiful in the world within which you can discover a new sense of freedom, peace and exhilaration.

In the 1950s scuba diving as a sport attracted only a few thousand people. Today, that figure has increased to several million. There is no age limit in scuba diving; the basic requisites being good health and a keen curiosity to explore the unknown and wonderful space of beauty which the marine world promises. Adherence to certain rules underwater is required to avoid serious consequences and, therefore, professional instruction and guidance in this sport are imperative.

Dive operations in Antigua can provide PADI, NAUI, NASDA and SSI certification, catering for the more advanced with programmes of several days' duration, night dives and beginners' afternoon resort courses. A resort course provides basic training in a condensed form (about three hours), with a minimum of academic knowledge and normally including one confined water session and one scuba dive. Proper instruction from a recognised dive instructor is a must. Certified divers should present their certification card to enable them to rent the necessary equipment or to participate in an organised dive.

Both Antigua and Barbuda are virtually surrounded by coral reefs and shipwrecks and so have dozens of unspoilt dive sites to suit all levels of proficiency. Please remember, the delicate balance of the reef structures surrounding the islands are in jeopardy. Nature unwittingly does its own damage by silting up reefs and tearing away fine coral structures through tropical storms; but humankind is also responsible for a more conscious destruction by removing coral, sponges and other 'souvenirs', clumsy diving, spear fishing and pollution. Whilst there is the protection of the National Parks Authority to help preserve the flourishing reef life for most of Antigua's spectacular sites, their efforts cannot be successful if others are destroying their progress. Unfortunately, it is even possible to kill some of these marvels with a simple touch.

Divers entering the underwater world of Antigua and Barbuda will find an exceptional variety of sponge and coral formations, for the most part in healthy condition, together with almost every species of fish indigenous to the tropical western Atlantic. Divers have been known to see eagle rays, lobster, barracuda, turtles, tiger groupers, parrot fish, nurse sharks (harmless) and a myriad of small colourful reef fish (there are almost 400 species of Caribbean reef fish). You will find shallow reefs, fringing and barrier, drop offs (the south coast), caverns, walls and wrecks. Water temperature is an inviting average of 80°F, and visibility is 50 to 100 feet.

DIVE SITES

North/northeast

Dive expeditions off this rugged coast feature reef, canyon and cliff diving, and 'walk-in' diving is possible, along with wrecks, at Green Island, Nonsuch Bay to the east. Many sites are only 10–15 minutes' boat ride away, as is Bird Channel, in between Little Bird and Great Bird islands to the north, also an area where the wreck of the 310-foot *Jetias* has lain since 1817, and now lies in just 25 feet of water. This freighter is surrounded by elkhorn coral and is home to many reef fish. Other fascinating wrecks include the 90-year-old three-masted merchant ship *Andes* which burnt and sank in

20 feet of water at the entrance of Deep Bay, and a 90-foot tug which lies in 50 feet of water in St John's Harbour. The engine room is home to a large moray eel.

The reefs in this North Sound area of Antigua may be shallow but have some interesting diving, especially Salt Fish Tail Reef and Horseshoe Reef, featuring damsels, angels, trumpet fish, rock beauties and the occasional grouper.

About 10 miles north, a long ride but well worth it as it is less visited and fished, is the Ariadne Shoal, a knoll with depths of 40 to 70 feet. You will see a variety of hard and soft corals, nurse sharks, schools of blackjack fish, barracuda, hog fish and a very friendly turtle called Pickles.

Southwest

Off the leeward coast, Cades Reef stretches for over two miles, with smooth waters and a wide variety of hard and soft corals. It has numerous dive sites and exceptional visibility to admire its abundance of reef life, especially staghorn coral, large grey angels, groupers and parrot fish. Sites include Monks Head, so called due to its proliferation of fringes of coral topped with sand resembling a tonsure, which has depths from 20 to 50 feet and where you will find conch, stingrays and possibly rare eels and the Chimney. Here there is a small cave at 60 feet, with sponge-filled gullies descending to 80 feet, home to large parrot fish, lobsters, eels and harmless nurse sharks.

Sandy Island Reef is full of piscine life – swim along the reef among star and pillar coral and dive to a white sand bottom at 50 feet. Named after HMS *Weymouth*, wrecked here in 1745, is Weymouth Reef, home also to the slaver, *Nancy*, and possibly two or three other ships.

On the west coast are three sites of particular note: the Knoll, featuring a spectacular coral head covered with gorgonians and soft coral rising from 50 feet to just 25 feet below the surface and Thunderhead – a wreck strewn reef at 35 feet, allowing exploration of the gently sloping hard coral for artefacts. The Ridge is a coral-head honeycomb haven for reef fish, nurse

sharks, some turtles and with a wall dive, from 25 to 60 feet.

South

This world of strange beauty and vibrant colours presented to many first-time divers is so enchanting and exotic that it often becomes the highlight of their holiday, and even for the more experienced diver who can reap the benefits of deeper dives and take in the history of diving around such areas as English Harbour (Nelson's Dockyard) in the south. Home of the British Fleet from 1700 to the 1850s, a trail of artefacts is still to be uncovered and wrecks can also be explored.

The Pillars of Hercules, so called because of the unique pillar formation above the site at the entrance to Nelson's Dockyard, offers perhaps the greatest cross section of underwater reef life in these waters – it often has visibility in excess of 100 feet. This shallow dive site has large French angels, parrot fish, rock beauties, queen trigger fish, trumpet fish, grouper and hind, goatfish and grunts. Maurice, a five-foot green moray, awaits feeding as do snapper and other small creatures such as cleaner shrimp, jawfish and sandtile fish. Visits of schools of bluetang, barracuda, and turtles are common and occasionally dolphins swim on by.

Snapper Hole is a wall which starts at 45 feet and drops to a white sand bottom at 80 feet. Here you will encounter schools of grunts, large southern stingrays, occasional spotted eagle rays, and a ledge at 60 feet with many deep fissures where lobster and moray eels are seen.

Amongst other endless possibilities for the experienced diver in this area are the great sites of Sunken Rock and Cape Shirley. The former, with depths to well over 120 feet, is a pinnacle awash off Indian Creek, and offers a trail through a deep cleft leading to the rock itself, for the most part vertical, with coral overhangs of magnificent gorgonians in many flamboyant colours, together with brilliant sponges – classic opportunities for photographers. This is where you will find the larger fish, amberjacks,

grouper, barracuda, turtles, spotted eagle rays, stingrays and the occasional dolphin. The latter, Cape Shirley, reaches the height of dive excitement for some, where giant boulders have found a resting place to become the foundation for every sort of hard and soft corals. They leave a trail of valleys and caves, drop offs with coral overhangs and fissures, finishing at 110 feet with a sandy bottom. Here you can see the unexpected around any corner. Large grouper, parrot fish, rays, turtles and spade fish abound.

Barbuda

Encircled by reefs, this gentle sister-island shouldn't be missed for its incredible number of sunken wrecks; ships which were often lured onto Barbuda's coral outcrops over 200 years ago and foundered at their peril. Shallow, crystal clear waters can be found around Barbuda and are superb for snorkelling.

Of course, should you desire a particular dive agenda, timing or arrangements for a private group, most dive companies can tailor-make a trip to your requirements. Night diving gives some superb diving experiences. Many exotic creatures, not seen during the daytime, come out at night and provide the diver with a whole new array of subjects. Tube anenomes rise out and spread their tentacles like delicate flowers. Basket starfish which remain furled up in a tight ball during daylight spread their radar antenna-like arms to catch drifting plankton. Many fish which are difficult to approach during the day can be found quietly sleeping on the sea floor at night.

SNORKELLING

There is no simpler or more inexpensive way than snorkelling to investigate the many jewels which lie below the shallow, warm waters of this twin-island state. Many bays provide excellent opportunities: the two-mile long stretch of Cades Reef off the west coast; Great Bird Island on the northeast coast; the reefs along Boon Channel and Sandy Island in the north. On the east coast there is Green Island in Nonsuch Bay (which you may visit by powerboat, yacht or the boat service from Harmony Hall), where Tenpound Bay and the reef south of Ricketts Harbour provide wonderful snorkelling. First-class opportunities can also be found in the south at Horseshoe Reef in Willoughby Bay. Off English Harbour there are the Pillars of Hercules and Berkeley Point (accessible without a boat), and Falmouth gives you Bishops Reef off Pigeon Beach and Windward Beach.

Many dive operations also offer accompanied, interesting snorkelling trips. However, the legendary transparency and luminosity of such waters may encourage you to take a course in diving.

Like the many divers and snorkellers who flock here from around the world, you can discover that the wonder and adventure of the islands doesn't necessarily end at the water's edge, but also begins there!

Aquanaut, St James's Club, Mamora Bay tel: (268) 460 5000 ext. 208 fax: (268) 460 3015

Deep Bay Divers, Historic Redcliffe Quay, St John's tel/fax: (268) 463 8000 e-mail: deepbaydivers@candw.ag

Dive Antigua, Rex Halcyon Hotel, Dickenson Bay tel: (268) 462 3483 fax: (268) 462 7787 e-mail: birkj@candw.ag web site: www.diveantigua.com

Dockyard Divers, Nelson's Dockyard tel: (268) 460 1178/729 3040 fax: (268) 460 1179 e-mail: dockdivers@candw.ag web site: www.dockyard-divers.com

Jolly Dive, Jolly Harbour Marina tel/fax: (268) 462 8305 e-mail: divemaster@kokomocat.com web site: www.kokomocat.com

Long Bay Dive Shop, Long Bay tel: (268) 463 2005 fax: (268) 463 2439 e-mail: hotel@longbay.antigua.com

Octopus Divers, English Harbour tel: (268) 460 6286 fax: (268) 460 7671 e-mail: octopus-divers@candw.ag web site: octopusdivers.com

Day cruising tours

– nautical … but nice!

The romance and thrill of sail is still very much evident and really no visit to Antigua and Barbuda is complete unless you take to the sea.

You neither have to be an accomplished sailor nor charter a yacht, for all this, and more, is arranged for you on one of the all-inclusive day sailing tours. Everything is well organised for a fabulous day, or evening, sail, with plenty of good food and drink, companions, snorkelling gear, relaxation or fun and frolic.

There is something truly special and adventurous about skimming along the water's surface, flying before a good wind with the sails stretched to their limits, and a glass of rum punch in your hand. As well as being an effortless way to improve your tan, you can see the islands from offshore, whilst being pampered by the constant cooling breezes.

Even the most determined landlubber will love one of these day cruises, whether on a glass bottom boat, speedboat, on a speedy 'cat', or a traditional two-masted schooner. So – how about a few hours under sail, cruising around the beautiful coastline of Antigua?

JOLLY ROGER PIRATE CRUISES

This legendary two-masted 'tall ship' schooner pirate ship has been the scene of uncountable hours of fun for nearly 20 years and it is exceptionally popular with locals and visitors. At 108 feet long and 22 feet on the beam, with hull and deck of solid Swedish pine, she was built in 1944 as the last wooden sailing ship built for the Swedish Navy, for ocean going routes, and has circumnavigated the world three times!

She sails complete with cannons, pirate ensign, red sails, open bar and with plenty of space for sunbathing and dancing. Half the seating is under shade and there's a large, quiet

lounge, wash-rooms and changing facilities. She also has all the modern safety devices on board, including ship-to-shore radio.

Children love the idea of a pirate ship and families are especially welcome. Trained lifeguards are aboard at all times, so parents can relax.

Superb buffet food is offered on the exciting and varied lunch and evening cruises. As well as the ubiquitous rum punch, they also offer top quality premium label whisky, gin and vodka plus good wines.

When the ship is anchored in a secluded cove on a day cruise, you have the choice of sunbathing or beachcombing on one of our spectacular beaches, or swimming and snorkelling from a special fully-equipped barge, and rope-swinging and 'walking the plank' on deck for the more adventurous.

The entertainment on the return day trip cruise features a hilarious Pirate Wedding and the lighthearted Limbo competition. All the while you can dance 'upstairs' on the poop deck and during the last hour's lively 'West Indian Jump Up'. The spacious sun deck has an awning for shade, if desired. Be as active or inactive as you wish.

TIAMI CATAMARAN CRUISES

They promise to make you feel pampered and indulged aboard one of their immaculate sailing or power catamarans with smooth sailing and personal service, from the champagne and orange juice to the excellent snorkelling.

Enjoy one of the best days of your holiday with a crew of professional, experienced, polite and friendly Antiguans.

One of these crafts is a custom-built state-of-the-art power catamaran, *Excellence*, which will take you on a circumnavigation of the island or a trip to Barbuda in the fastest time and to untouched tropical scenes further away than the regularly visited spots.

The daily lunch cruises include unlimited drinks and a delicious grilled lunch of steak, chicken, fish or lobster (when available), served while at anchor. Swim in the calm turquoise water, snorkel with our certified dive instructor

over an undewater marine park teeming with tropical fish, or just soak up the sun, ending the day with total satisfaction.

All crew are first aid trained and safety is their number one priority. *Tiami* has won prestigious awards including Princess Cruise Lines 1999 C.R.U.I.S.E. Shore Excursion of the season, Thomson's Gold Award and Thomson's Safety Award.

Tiami Cruises excel with private charters, sunset and moonlight cruises with options for specialised catering, live music, water sports, beach barbecues and games to add an extra special touch to birthdays, weddings, anniversaries, private parties and other special occasions.

WADADLI CATS

With three well-established catamarans and five successful cruises to choose from, state-of-the-art 66-foot long catamaran *Spirit of Antigua* guarantees the fastest sailing speeds, perfect for those who can be slightly 'queasy' when sailing, as this assures less rolling and helps avoid sea sickness. Such exhilarating, fast travelling also allows for more time to enjoy the best beaches and snorkelling sites and relax over your al fresco buffet lunch.

It's the only 'cat' with fresh water showers, to sail with a spinnaker, convenient stern ladders and a large roofed area. It is fully equipped with comfortable covered lounge areas, deck awnings for shade, snorkelling gear, safety equipment and an open bar and delicious buffet.

Both catamarans are available for private charters, whether for a sunset cruise, Barbuda day trip, moonlight cruise or another of your choice.

Their scheduled cruises are: the Bird Island cruise, the Cades Reef cruise, the triple destination cruise, a 60-mile circumnavigation of Antigua cruise and the Sunset cruise.

KOKOMO CAT

A 61-foot catamaran, built in 1994 to American Bureau of Shipping standards, the twin-hull configuration allows this boat to sail at a very respectable 16 knots, whilst ensuring a smooth, stable and enjoyable passage. It is available for private custom charters but also offers a comprehensive and wide selection of full-day cruises.

On all but the Sunset cocktail cruise the *Kokomo Cat* will pick up passengers at Jolly Harbour/Jolly Beach, Hawksbill, Deep Bay, Dickenson Bay and Sunsail Colonna Beach Club. All cruises are inclusive of an open bar, and include an excellent Caribbean lunch on the full-day cruises.

Their five cruises include the snorkel/sailing/Island safari, the sportif/snorkel cruise, the romantic sunset cocktail cruise, the circumnavigate Antigua cruise, just as Lord Nelson circumnavigated Antigua in 1784, and the triple destination Sunday cruise.

'JUST SAILING'

Specialising in custom charters and small private groups, 'Just Sailing' offer two sailing craft. The first, *Heatwave*, is the only trimaran in Antigua. At 33-feet long, it has huge sunbathing platforms which can be used whilst sailing and operates out of Jolly Beach, Coco Bay, Rex Blue Heron, The Royal Antiguan and other west coast hotels. Enjoy a three hour sail, including free rum punch, along the scenic Caribbean coastline, cruising from St John's to Johnson's Point. Available for private charter groups of 16–20 people.

The second is the beautifully presented sailing yacht *Augustine*, a 42-foot sailing sloop. This is for those who wish to experience a day of cruising pleasure on board a yacht with only their choice of friends or family, whilst being pampered by the professional crew. For an individual touch, add an overnight charter to your holiday, with a romantic dinner under the stars.

TREASURE ISLAND CRUISES

The large, luxury Caribbean Queen is the only vessel with a live steel band and treasure hunt. All cruises not only serve a super West Indian buffet lunch but also morning and afternoon snacks of fruit and local pastries, plus a display and sampling of a local dish.

Free pick-ups are arranged for their four cruises, inclusive of snorkelling gear, open bar, on-board galley for snacks and buffet lunch, and a friendly, experienced crew. The spacious sun deck has an awning for shade, if desired. Be as active or inactive as you want.

Four cruises are offered: the Bird Island special, the Cades Reef special, the triple destination and the circumnavigation special.

ANTIGUA YACHT CHARTERS

Based in Nelson's Dockyard, they specialise in advice and bookings on a wide range of day charter options, including day sailing, sports cruising and deep sea fishing.

BELUGA

A strikingly designed 45-foot trimaran based at Mango Bay on the east side of Antigua, which will gently sail you to Bird or Green Island for a barbecue, snorkel or sunset cruise. Ideal for small groups or private parties.

COASTLINE SAFARI CRUISES

A new powered catamaran party boat, fully insured and equipped to US coastguard specifications, and carrying up to 65 passengers on its 50-foot long double decks. Specialising in full day all-inclusive trips to Barbuda, full-day circumnavigation and triple destination cruises with music, full bar and buffet lunch, plus a dinner cruise, they also welcome private charters. This company has the advantage of offering unique sea and land day trips, being associated with Estate Safari. Therefore, should you fancy both experiences, it is possible to start with a 'coastline' tour and finish your day on land with Estate Safari (see page 212).

ECO SEA TOURS

Flexible half- and full-day tours by sea are provided to Historic Nelson's Dockyard, Great Bird National Park and the isle of Barbuda. Their custom-made 41-foot rib has a seating capacity of 25 passengers and offers various refreshments (depending on type and length of tour), with personal service and first-class equipment.

FIRST TRI CRUISES

Snorkelling and sailing cruises are organised aboard a 35-foot trimaran which generally operates out of the west coast but which also offers private charters island-wide. Sail along the southern coast to clear, shallow waters, perfect for snorkelling. Drinks and snacks are included.

FRANCO'S GLASS-BOTTOM BOAT CALYPSO CRUISE

Established for over 20 years, they offer calypso glass-bottom snorkel cruises to the extensive Cades Reef on the west coast. All refreshments and open bar are included, plus snorkel equipment enabling you to enjoy the best of Antigua's underwater life and scenery. Private charters can be arranged.

LE BISTRO SPEEDBOAT CHARTERS

Ride their fast, safe Wellcraft 'Scarab' Supersport or 'Puma' Tecnoyacht for a great day-long excursion around the island visiting bays and offshore islands. Both Le Bistro boats are fully equipped to strict US coastguard standards, equipped with GPS state of the art navigational system and cellular telephones. The captain gives a detailed commentary along with sophisticated cuisine, wine and sound systems. They also offer excursions to Barbuda and both boats are available for private charters.

LII LY SPEED

A 40-foot boat, tailored for a sophisticated sail, with a maximum of eight people, European multi-lingual staff will take you for excellent snorkelling, swimming and relaxing. Known as the 'gourmet sailor', it offers French food, wine and champagne to the gentle sounds of classical music. Successful through regular recommendations, it is available for the day, half day, sunset, dinner under the stars, or any special request and private charter.

MIGUEL'S HOLIDAY ADVENTURE

Celebrating 25 years of operating his ferry-like boat all-inclusive picnic charters, Miguel takes his many regular and repeat guests on the short five-minute ride to Prickly Pear island, just off the north coast. Over this time, he has fashioned this islet almost as his own private enclave. He has built a covered area to offer shade and a suitable dining and bar area for his extensive West Indian seafood buffet, including freshly cooked lobster. You have a relaxing full day to swim, snorkel or laze on the beach on which he also provides beach chairs and umbrellas.

SHORTY'S FUN CRUISE TO GREAT BIRD ISLAND

Renowned calypso artist and entertainer, 'King Short Shirt', has been offering two all-inclusive cruises on his well-established glass-bottom boat for over 27 years. Accompanied by his singing and calypso music, join the all-inclusive full-day trip to Great Bird Island. You can walk or hike across this small nature reserve and enjoy the calm waters or relax on the beach. Whilst snorkelling, pick up your own conch, which they then tenderise as your personal 'catch of the day' and give you the splendid pink shell as a souvenir (sensitive to the fragile marine ecosystem, Shorty abides by his maxim of 'leaving the babies and the ladies', regarding both conch and lobster). There is a full bar and an 'all-you-can-eat' extensive and varied Antigua style local buffet, including steak, barbecue chicken, fresh lobster and seafood. Pick-ups are available from some hotels.

Jolly Roger **Pirate Cruises** tel: (268) 462 2064 fax: (268) 462 2065
Tiami **Catamaran Cruises** tel: (268) 462 2064 fax: (268) 462 2065
Wadadli Cats tel: (268) 462 4792 fax: (268) 462 3661
Kokomo Cat **Cruises** tel/fax: (268) 462 7245
Treasure Island Cruises tel: 461 8675/8698 fax: 461 8698
Antigua Yacht Charters tel: (268) 463 7101 fax: (268) 463 8744
Beluga tel/fax: (268) 463 3361
Coastline Safari **Cruises** tel: (268) 463 4713 fax: (268) 480 8478
'Just Sailing' tel: (268) 462 2855/464 0928
Eco Sea Tours tel: (268) 462 3355 fax: (268) 463 0722
First Tri Cruises tel/fax: (268) 462 7645
Franco's tel: 462 6025 (local calls only)
Le Bistro Speed Boat Charters tel: (268) 462 3881 fax: (268) 461 2996
Lilly Speed tel: 464 3736 fax: 460 1827 (local calls only)
Miguel's Holiday Adventure tel: 461 0361
Shorty's Fun Cruise to Bird Island tel/fax: (268) 462 6326

Island exploration

The 108 square miles of limestone coral and volcanic remains, responsible for the palm fringed beaches for which Antigua is so renowned, also embody much more of interest, when you are tiring of the sea and sun. You will soon find that appreciation of the island comes from absorbing the intriguing sights with an exploratory drive – in itself an education in island life.

As you flew into the island, you may have already seen the gracious hills and gentle contours which inspired Columbus to name the island in honour of Santa Maria de la Antigua.

Whilst some of the sweeping bays host the modern day bastions of the twentieth century tourism industry, albeit strategically placed, inland you will experience a landscape full of colour and activity, Of course, its long, multifaceted history, merely adds to the mystery which unfolds before you, as you travel around the island. Admirable restoration and identification of all the sugar mills, forts and estate houses have been underway and the most remarkable testimony to this lies in the major attraction of the eighteenth century Nelson's Dockyard, in English Harbour (see page 205).

Antigua's little sister island, Barbuda (see page 297), lies just 26 miles off the north coast and is famed for its marine life and miles of pinkish coral sand. This remote and quite stunning island is also one of the largest, rare nesting and breeding sites in the world of the frigate bird (see page 108).

Whether by walking, bus, taxi, rental vehicle or in a friend's car, you will discover in Antigua quiet country back roads, untouched villages, small harbours, pineapple groves, banana trees, beautiful churches, the outline of the giant remains of various historical and military structures, rugged beauty and isolation, tropical forests and exotic flowers, all virtually unchanged for over 300 years. But it helps if you know where to look. An introduction to island life has been compiled over the following pages.

Tis the sense of majesty, and beauty, and repose, a blended holiness of earth and sky.
William Wordsworth

St John's and area

St John's, the Capital, is esteem'd the most regular Town in the West Indies, and has the most comodious Harbour of any, belonging to our English Leeward Islands.

Stated on an eighteenth-century map of St John's

St John's, situated on the northwestern tip of the island, with its foundation dating back to the late seventeenth century, is the economic base and capital of the island. Located in a sheltered cove, it was the official headquarters of the Leeward Islands group and is one of the oldest trading ports in the Caribbean. The sailing clippers of yesteryear have been replaced today by sleek cruise ships visiting this important tourist destination.

The main shopping and commercial area of St John's is still largely confined within the limits of the original bustling eighteenth-century town, with its broad avenues and narrow cross streets. In many aspects, save for present day vehicles, much is unchanged and its old world charm is retained in the many eighteenth and nineteenth century buildings and the highly individual and colourful wooden buildings and private homes.

The lively, vibrant town centre, with most of its tourist activity centred around its two waterfront developments, Heritage Quay and Historic Redcliffe Quay (see Shopping, page 229), protects its West Indian village atmosphere and is easy to walk around.

CENOTAPH High Street

The War Memorial to Antiguans who died serving in the First World War was unveiled in 1919. Remembrance Day is still celebrated annually with a service for those who gave their lives during the wars of 1914–18 and 1939–45.

St John's Cathedral

THE COURT HOUSE
Long and Market Streets

This neo-classical building is the oldest still in use in St John's today and was designed by Peter Harrison, a Yorkshireman born in 1716. It was constructed in 1747 from yellow freestone quarried from Long, Guiana and Pelican Islands, off Antigua's northeastern coast, and finished in 1750. The Court of Justice was on the ground floor, with the Council and Assembly upstairs, where, through the centuries, many laws were enacted and amended. Damaged by the 1843 earthquake, it was restored two years later, when the upper floor was strengthened with large Victorian cast-iron pillars. The building was finally renovated by the British government after the earthquake of 1974. Today this historic building serves as the Museum of Antigua and Barbuda (see page 176).

THE EBENEZER METHODIST CHURCH
Redcliffe and St Mary's Streets

This impressive building, completed in 1839, was badly damaged in the 1843 earthquake, repaired, and damaged again by the 1974 earthquake, after which it was demolished and rebuilt. Repaired and strengthened in 1982, this was declared a historic building. Methodism was brought to Antigua in 1760 by the plantation owner and Speaker of the House of Assembly, Nathaniel Gilbert, after hearing the preaching of John Wesley in England. The first chapel, built in 1786, became too small, and the present Ebenezer church was built to replace it.

FORT JAMES

This is located off Fort Road, at the promontory of Fort James beach, about two miles northwest of St John's and is one of the oldest of the nation's fortifications, with surviving remains over 300 years old. The first section was completed in 1706, during the reign of Queen Anne, on top of an earlier fort at the entrance to St John's Harbour, on a promontory defending this and the northwestern part of the island. Most of the buildings seen today date from 1739 and by 1773 there were barracks for

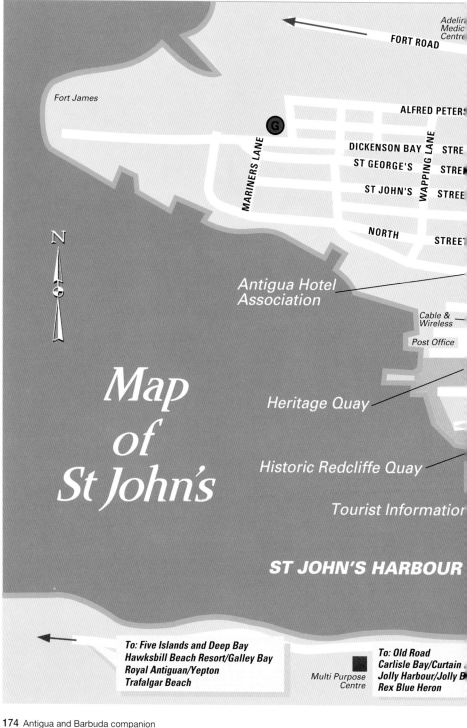

Map
of
St John's

ST JOHN'S HARBOUR

To: Five Islands and Deep Bay
Hawksbill Beach Resort/Galley Bay
Royal Antiguan/Yepton
Trafalgar Beach

To: Old Road
Carlisle Bay/Curtain
Jolly Harbour/Jolly B
Rex Blue Heron

Multi Purpose
Centre

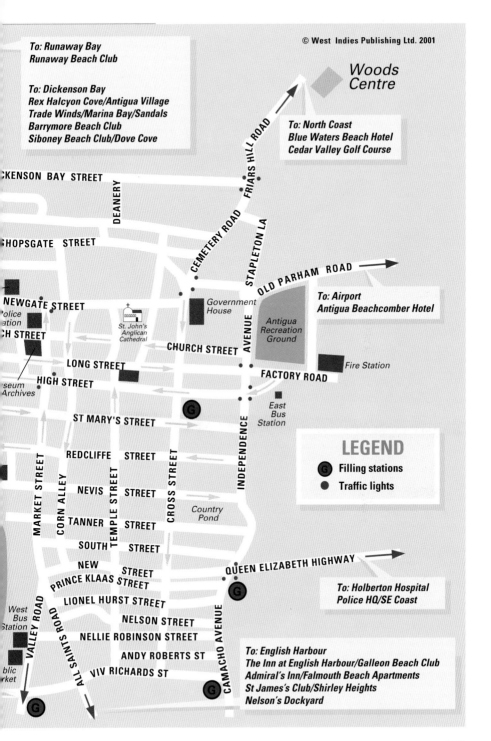

To: Runaway Bay
Runaway Beach Club

To: Dickenson Bay
Rex Halcyon Cove/Antigua Village
Trade Winds/Marina Bay/Sandals
Barrymore Beach Club
Siboney Beach Club/Dove Cove

© West Indies Publishing Ltd. 2001

Woods Centre

To: North Coast
Blue Waters Beach Hotel
Cedar Valley Golf Course

CKENSON BAY STREET

DEANERY

SHOPSGATE STREET

FRIARS HILL ROAD

CEMETERY ROAD

STAPLETON LA

OLD PARHAM ROAD

NEWGATE STREET

Police Station

CH STREET

St. John's Anglican Cathedral

Government House

AVENUE

Antigua Recreation Ground

To: Airport
Antigua Beachcomber Hotel

CHURCH STREET

LONG STREET

HIGH STREET

seum Archives

FACTORY ROAD

Fire Station

ST MARY'S STREET

East Bus Station

REDCLIFFE STREET

MARKET STREET

CORN ALLEY

NEVIS STREET

TEMPLE STREET

CROSS STREET

INDEPENDENCE

TANNER STREET

SOUTH STREET

Country Pond

NEW STREET

PRINCE KLAAS STREET

QUEEN ELIZABETH HIGHWAY

LIONEL HURST STREET

West Bus Station

VALLEY ROAD

NELSON STREET

NELLIE ROBINSON STREET

ANDY ROBERTS ST

ALL SAINTS ROAD

VIV RICHARDS ST

CAMACHO AVENUE

blic rket

To: Holberton Hospital
Police HQ/SE Coast

To: English Harbour
The Inn at English Harbour/Galleon Beach Club
Admiral's Inn/Falmouth Beach Apartments
St James's Club/Shirley Heights
Nelson's Dockyard

LEGEND

G Filling stations
● Traffic lights

GOVERNMENT HOUSE/ THE GOVERNOR-GENERAL'S RESIDENCE

Set in three acres and originally a private house in 1750, merchant Thomas Kerby let it to St John's Anglican church in the 1780s, whereby it served as the original clergy house connected with the cathedral. The British government bought it in 1807 and the house became the official residence and office of the Governor-General of Antigua and Barbuda. Known as Government House, 35 governors have lived here.

Situated opposite the Antigua Recreation Ground on Independence Avenue, it has an unconventional architectural history. It is an elegant Georgian colonial building, which features many tropical adaptations of Georgian architecture, such as the imposing 'fan light' archways connecting the rooms and includes many features peculiar to Antigua. As the needs of the crown's representative evolved, the house went through extensive alterations and additions which have resulted in the imposing facade

with its two-storey colonnade.

The house with its interior dating from c.1800 is currently being sympathetically and sumptuously restored to its former glory with extensive, fine restoration work to both the building and furnishings. Following considerable colour testing, it has been faithfully redecorated using original colour schemes with gold leaf accent. A project of this magnitude takes much time and resources, and funding is urgently required; donations are therefore appreciated. As a wonderful example of heritage tourism, visitors are welcome by prior arrangement and guided tours are being planned. Tel: (268) 462 0003.

about 75 men, with 36 mounted guns. When the foundation stone was laid in 1739, It was engraved with full Masonic honours an extraordinary event for a military fortress. In the nineteenth century a gun was fired at sunrise and sunset and salutes fired for visiting warships. Now there are ten cannons (not in use) with five-and-a-half inch bores. Each two-and-a-half ton cannon, capable of penetrating timber five feet two inches thick from a 100-yard range with a double shot of four-pound charge, was handled by a team of eleven men and a powder man. There is also a small detached kitchen to be seen, complete with seventeenth-century open range fireplace.

INDUSTRIAL SCHOOL FOR THE BLIND
All Saint's Road

Visitors can buy a wide variety of basketry, straw hats and other useful items such as trays made by these talented people and watch them in their workshop located just behind the main public market, tel: (268) 462 0663.

MUSEUM OF ANTIGUA AND BARBUDA
Long Street and Market Streets

This is another of those 'don't miss' attractions of the island. The museum's displays interestingly interpret the story of the islands from their geological birth through political independence to the present day. There are lively

NATIONAL ARCHIVES
Rappaport Centre, Factory Road

This houses documents concerning the life and history of Antigua including the famed, unique Codrington Papers (see page 300). Visitors can browse through information relating to education, the government and the Antiguan people through family records. Its opening hours are Monday to Thursday 8am to 4.30pm, Friday 8am to 3.00pm, tel: (268) 462 3946/7.

POLICE STATION
Newgate Street

This was originally used as a munitions depot and arsenal from the mid-1700s, when St John's superseded Falmouth Harbour in importance in the defence of Antigua, until 1933. East of this was the old guardhouse, built in 1754. Adjoining it is a long stone building with grated windows, which served as Antigua's first jail until 1831 and is now the charge room of the present police station. Deserving close inspection, the iron railings enclosing the courtyard facing Church Street were actually created from musket barrels, some with bayonets still attached.

displays of ancient tools and artifacts (some dating back to pre-Columbian times), shells, flora and fauna, the island's naval history, plantation history and slavery. There is a replica of a typical Arawak hut, an intriguing model of St John's cathedral and interactive exhibits. Upstairs there are six large royal portraits and an interesting permanent exhibition, 'Exploring the ecosystems of Antigua and Barbuda through local sites', which gives an insight into Antigua's natural history. Additonally, there is a hands-on section, as well as quizzes and games for the children, an extensive library and research centre, plus a marvellous gift, craft, book and local souvenir shop.

It is also here that the Historical and Archaeological Society (HAS) (see page 60) and the Environmental Awareness Group (EAG) (see page 114) are housed. The museum is open every day except Sunday. Admission is free, but a minimum donation of US$ 2.00 is most appreciated, and goes towards upkeep, tel: (268) 462 4930/1469.

DO YOU WONDER IF YOU MAY HAVE ANTIGUAN ANCESTRY?

The Museum of Antigua and Barbuda allows visitors to explore its computer records to seek out possible family history. There has also been exhaustive research to create a database of 1200 monument inscriptions recorded from tombs around the island. Many people have been surprised in their quest to find some Antiguan links!

PUBLIC LIBRARY Market Street

The Antigua Library Society was instituted in July 1930 and, following the earthquake in 1974 which destroyed the original library, the present public library has been sitting atop the haberdashery store, Lolita's, about half way down Market Street, since 1978. As a growing number of residents and visitors use the now rather cramped library, there are plans for a major new construction adjacent to the easily accessible National Archives building. The new two-storey central public library will have a capacity for over 72,000 volumes and provide seating for 160 people, tel: (268) 462 0229.

PUBLIC MARKET
Southern far end of Market Street

This is a good place to sample the unusual fruits and vegetables grown on Antigua, as well as Seaview Farm pottery, basketry and a myriad of other items of interest. It is particularly lively on Fridays and Saturdays when you can feel the unchanged atmosphere of bygone days, and locals and merchants ply their trade. Early risers will see it at its best, but a stroll at any time is worth it.

ST JOHN'S CATHEDRAL
between Long and Newgate Streets

Whether approaching from the sea, driving into town or walking around, visitors cannot miss the silvery cupolas of the twin towers belonging to this huge grey church, positioned on a hill top at the northeastern end of the main area of St John's. The mother church of the Anglican diocese of Antigua, it is regarded as one of Antigua's national monuments and possibly the most imposing Anglican cathedral in the West Indies. The original wooden building of 1683 as ordered by the governor, Sir Christopher Codrington, was said to be 'devoid of beauty and comfort' and was replaced by an English brick building around 1789, 'washed a light yellow colour and cruciform in shape'. Destroyed by an earthquake in 1843, it was rebuilt in freestone and three years later was opened for services and consecrated on 25 July, 1848 (having been elevated to the status of a cathedral in August 1842).

The classic interior is completely encased in pitch pine, intended to secure it against hurricanes and earthquakes, being described as a 'church within a church'. Some interesting memorial stones and many other objects of interest lie in this peaceful oasis, designed by architect J. Fuller of Bath, England. White painted, tall bronze figures of St John the Baptist and St John the Divine, said to have been taken from one of Napoleon's ships, stand atop the pillars of the iron south gates, themselves dating from 1789. Having withstood the test of time and survived many great hurricanes, fires and a significant earthquake in 1974, thankfully, this stunning baroque-style, twin-towered structure, still majestically dominates the capital's skyline.

St John's Cathedral

V. C. BIRD MONUMENT
between the Post Office and the old Administration Building

This bronze bust of Sir Vere Cornwall Bird was unveiled in 1987. As the first Chief Minister, Premier and Prime Minister of Antigua and Barbuda he was also known as the 'liberator and father of the nation'. Revered for all the immense milestones he achieved for 'my people', he died in June 1999.

WESTERBY MEMORIAL
Lower High Street

Erected in 1892, this attractive Victorian styled monument in the form of a drinking fountain, commemorates the work of Moravian missionary Bishop George Wall Westerby. It is the original historic point of arrival and departure of all visitors to Antigua.

St John's Cathedral

The arrival of H Excellency Sir E B Sweet-Escott K C M G Governor and Commander in Chief of the Leewards Islands

WALKING TOUR OF HISTORIC ST JOHN'S –
the colourful legend lives on

There's no better way to get to know a city than to walk around it; the history and culture are there at your feet, not to mention shopping and dining.

The Historical and Archaeological (see page 60) Society of Antigua and Barbuda, a non-profit making organisation dedicated to the preservation of the town's historic fabric, has produced an absolutely fascinating guide to historic St John's. After much research and planning, they now offer this superb, enjoyable way to familiarise visitors not only with the general layout of the capital, but also to glean little known facts and anecdotes of its landmarks, buildings, churches, monuments, streets, merchants, trade, architecture, and their history.

St John's remains much the same as it was when conceived around 1700 and has been praised for its broad avenues and grid layout, which can be seen on an original map drawing in the Museum, dated MDCCLXXXVIII (1788). The major thoroughfares run east to west, with smaller cross streets north to south. Such streets still carry fascinating names of a bygone era: Temple, Corn Alley, Popeshead, Newgate Street, Thames Street, and so on.

Many of the original structures, with present day businesses operating, are over 200 years old and stand proud, having withstood the ravages of hurricanes, earthquakes, fires and the wrecking crew. Particularly severe fires in 1769 and 1841 destroyed many fine dwellings and upon being rebuilt, existing structures are reckoned to be approximately 150 years old. Enough survives today to give a strong sense of old world charm and elegance which lingers in the architecture: Georgian, Romantic, Victorian, vernacular and international, all bearing special features such as verandahs, hurricane shutters,

lattice work, fretwork and Demerara windows to name a few.

You will truly be captivated by the colourful wooden buildings and amazed that so many of today's stores, restaurants and outlets in St John's, carefully refurbished to retain their original features, have so much absorbing history.

The recommended guide to this beautiful and proud city which slopes gently to the sea is available from the Museum of Antigua and Barbuda (see page 176). It encompasses 34 points of interest, a corresponding map and a description of the various architectural designs to be seen. Proceeds from the sale of this leaflet help finance the work of the Historical and Archaeological Society of Antigua and Barbuda.

Police Barracks, St. John, Antigua, B, W, I.

THE COURT HOUSE
Saint Johns Antigua.

Historic Redcliffe Quay

Whether you want to shop for the latest European fashions at duty-free prices or just stroll around an area rich in historical and architectural interest, Historic Redcliffe Quay offers something for everybody contemplating a day out in Antigua.

You will find duty-free shops stocking international brand name goods at unbeatable prices, located within some of the best examples of restored seventeenth- and eighteenth-century buildings in classical 'Georgian' West Indian architectural style. The restored waterfront area, which once formed the heart of the bustling coffee and sugar trade with seventeenth-century Europe, now offers duty-free shopping along an attractive boardwalk and marina with docking for pleasure craft from around the world. Read on for some intriguing background information and highlights.

From the earliest days of adventuring on the Spanish Main, Europeans recognised the strategic importance of the tiny chain of islands fringing the Caribbean Sea, popularly known as the West Indies. Antigua, which is the most northeasterly or windwardly of the island chain, with all its bays and safe anchorages, soon became recognised as strategically crucial to controlling the Spanish treasure shipments that were financing the latest war or royal campaign in Europe.

Old Road and Falmouth Harbour on the south side of Antigua were colonised initially and, whilst Parham in the east was the first town, an Act of Parliament was proposed in 1668, and approved, to build a town in the northwest to be called St John's. From its inception St John's was a harbour town, widely regarded as the business and trading centre of the Caribbean, and life revolved around the docks and quays as in any other trading port of its time.

However, over the next two centuries, life was far from easy, as a brief delve into the historical archives of Antigua show. In 1668, shortly after work on St John's was commenced, the French invaded and razed the town. Soon after, a hurricane again destroyed the humble dwellings, and in 1793, 'nearly all the inhabitants of St John's were ill with yellow fever, many died'. In 1841, a 'dreadful fire' again destroyed much of the rebuilt city, particularly Historic Redcliffe Quay's warehouses, shops, houses and livery stables. These were swiftly rebuilt in mahogany and other timbers from regional islands and as far afield as Canada. Then, in 1863, there was a fire in a Portuguese rum shop caused by 'throwing up rum', when 10 houses were destroyed.

Benefiting from the stationing of British ships and ships from other military garrisons, St John's boasted important trading items of the time, including cotton, sugar, indigo, molasses, ginger, coffee, tobacco, sheep skins and lumber. Much of the trading in these items was done by a large contingent of Scottish immigrants. Probably recently freed indentured labourers fleeing the poverty and oppression of Scotland and the Highland clearances, they set up their 'Scotch Shops' to the north of Historic Redcliffe Quay, in 'Scotch Row', now Market Street. Ever since that time, St John's has been at the heart of what is a fascinating period steeped in tales, dramas and adventures.

Today it is still possible to catch a flavour of those bygone years with a visit to Historic Redcliffe Quay, situated at the end of Redcliffe Street on the pleasant waterfront in St John's. The street was named after the church of St Mary Redcliffe, in Bristol, England. The section today called Historic Redcliffe Quay runs down to the slipway and boardwalk, backs onto what historically was a very busy quay and overspills onto Lower Nevis Street, named after Ben Nevis in Scotland. The history of Historic Redcliffe Quay is exceptionally intriguing and also important in that to a large extent it reflects the history of Antigua itself.

Originally comprising over two acres of

beautifully restored old warehouses, taverns, and docks, these now house some of the most interesting shops and finest restaurants and bars in Antigua. As you wander through the tropical gardens and grand old buildings, not all that physically different from bygone eras, it is easy to imagine yourself transported back to those early days, when tall ships unloaded their precious cargoes of supplies into the warehouses that were awaiting deliveries for the sugar and cotton estates and other nearby islands.

In the mid-eighteenth century, Historic Redcliffe Quay was owned by the Kerr family, also of Scottish descent. Charles Kerr was a good businessman, who could turn his hand to most trades. He was appointed chief victualler to the navy in 1781, supplying preserved food and ship's rations, as well as drinking water for the long voyages back to England. He was also a ship broker, buying and selling vessels to the navy and local merchants. His island connections made him an invaluable contact for recruiting local labour when extra hands were needed for the unloading of barges or the transatlantic voyage back to Europe. Additionally, he ran a small shipyard where ships could be repaired or even built on Historic Redcliffe Quay. Thus, Historic Redcliffe Quay became a bustling waterfront docking, trading and storage area. Ships' rations were stored in large warehouses and lumber and staves were piled high on the waterside for repairs and building of crafts. Barrels made in the on-site cooperage were used to store pickled beef, ships biscuits, drinking water, and of course rum – all the vital rations for the journey across the Atlantic. Charles Kerr, who, according to his tombstone, died in 1795, is buried in St John's cathedral churchyard.

Historic Redcliffe Quay was also known as Pickett's Wharf, when owned by a direct descendant of Captain Pickett who, in the reign of Queen Anne, shot dead the governor of the island, Daniel Parke, who had arrived four years earlier in 1706. Governor Parke was a controversial character typical of the time, who appointed John Ham, a known pirate, as captain of a privateer. He was also known to roam the streets of St John's at night in heavy disguise, 'to gather opinion of himself'.

The Pickett family owned a substantial part of the area; what is now the Gazebo emporium, was once a Pickett warehouse for the storing of sheepskins and tamarind (a fruit introduced from India used as a base in curries, condiments and soap manufacture). Nearby is the Redcliffe Tavern housed in an eighteenth-century warehouse used to store lumber for ship repair and at one time a hardware store owned by the Brown family. Hosting a fine collection of carefully restored historic machinery from around the island, cleverly integrated into its interior, the tavern is an extremely popular spot for breakfast, lunch and dinner.

For many years before slavery was abolished in 1834, the area behind Historic Redcliffe Quay, and all the way along to Deep Water Harbour, was lined with many slave holding compounds or barracoons. This barracoon area of Redcliffe and Nevis Streets was used not only for the holding of slaves for Antiguan plantation owners, but as a transit station for slaves to be shipped to other islands within the Caribbean or the United States. For a while the wharf at Historic Redcliffe Quay was known as 'Barbuda Wharf'. The Codrington family had leased all of the island of Barbuda for slave breeding and growing sugar cane, so much of the shipping of provisions and products supplied by the Barbuda slaves for Codrington's five estates in Antigua arrived here.

A barracoon sign can still be seen over the doorway of the side entrance to the Coates Cottage art gallery and shop in Nevis Street. It was Charles Kerr who transferred this barracoon to the Antiguan Robert Coates in the late 1700s and when Coates left for England in 1807 to pursue his acting career (appearing regularly at the Royal Theatre, Bath, Somerset), he passed it onto his son Coxie. Confirming the cottage's historical stature, it was the son who then built the present structure. You may see ruins of sugar mills but never a barracoon. The delightful Coates Cottage is one of the oldest

surviving buildings in the entire Caribbean.

Next door, on the corner of Lower Nevis Street, and the small road to Redcliffe Street, is a restored building on the site of the original bargaining house for slaves. They were led from here through a still existing doorway and arch at the back of the Coates Cottage garden, to the harbour in Historic Redcliffe Quay, where there were further auctions and branding of the slaves. After the slavery era, the site became the Freemasons' Lodge, their meeting place in the early 1900s.

Opposite Coates Cottage, at this edge of Historic Redcliffe Quay, was the artisan area of St John's. Here, from the 1800s to the mid-1900s, tinsmiths, washerwomen, blacksmiths and so forth plied their trade. About this latter date, the quay also served as the off-loading stage for Pan American seaplanes prior to the opening of the airport.

But for a century or so after the abolition of slavery, Redcliffe and Nevis Streets merged in character with the more typical streets in St John's, filled with merchants' shops and grog shops. There were no pavements, so everyone had to fight for a right of way through barrow men, carriages, gigs and horsemen, cattle, sheep, goats and mules.

Having been for so many years the most significant trading point in Antigua and as a major landing jetty for tenders, which took cargo from the sailing ships anchored some three miles out, a severe decline set in after World War II and the area was left to decay. This was compounded when the deep water harbour at the mouth of the St John's harbour was dredged and the outer reef removed. The largest bulk carriers were now able to dock at these berths and the smaller Historic Redcliffe Quay docks and their associated warehousing were used less and less. After this long period, the area became derelict and abandoned. An ominous silence fell over an area accustomed to the bustle of grog shops and the excited trading and bargaining of an active port.

Fortunately these buildings, mostly from the mid-1800s as you see them today, remained largely undisturbed. As recently as ten years ago, the area was recognised as being of significant historical and architectural importance and purchased with the aim of restoring Historic Redcliffe Quay to its past glory. The old buildings and docks were refurbished over a period of several years so that today when you visit you will see one of the finest and most extensive examples of traditional eighteenth- and nineteenth-century West Indian architecture in the Caribbean.

In testimony to this, the area was awarded the prestigious American Express Preservation Award for the 'protection and enhancement of the Caribbean's cultural and architectural heritage', calling Historic Redcliffe Quay 'a model of conservation of eighteenth- and nineteenth-century vernacular buildings'.

Today Historic Redcliffe Quay is an excellent example of the fusion of combining environmental aspects with commercial reality and where the history and tradition of its origins have been honoured and preserved. It offers the best in contemporary shops and some of the most popular restaurants, bars and entertainment in Antigua.

Elsewhere on the island

AITON PLACE

Surrounded by lush gardens and tropical birds, this is the home and studio of international artist, Star Wars veteran and Emmy nominee, Nick Maley, the 'Yoda guy'. His elegant residence houses a large collection of original art and prints, relics of Nick's film work, rare memorabilia and on a 'by chance or appointment' basis, you can usually gain access Monday, Tuesday, Wednesday and Friday 9.30am–4.30pm. For a unique experience, on two afternoons weekly, Nick and his wife, Gloria, open their doors for 'Tales of Star Wars and other movies' – two hours of cocktails and insights into the crazy world of film making told by the maestro himself; tel: (268) 461 6324 for times and reservations. **Aiton Place is located about four miles north of St John's behind the Hodges Bay Club.**

FIG TREE DRIVE AND AREA

An exceptionally popular and picturesque drive through the lush vegetation of the rain forest, which includes wild mango, guava, orange, coconut and banana trees. Along the scenic southwest Caribbean coast to Old Road, Fig Tree Drive climbs up and down hillsides and inland roughly to the centre of the island, affording breathtaking views. Travelling this way, you will pass Wallings Dam (see page 197) and the Culture Shoppe, a delightful local spot for local crafts, fruit and refreshments, run by the charming and helpful proprietress, Elaine. Hidden behind the verdant hills on the northern side, around the middle of this country stretch, is Body Ponds. This is a series of bamboo and palm fringed picturesque dams, flanked by meadows of lemon grass and pasture, which thread their way through the valley, creating an ethereal beauty – a totally unexpected delight. Also reached via Bendals

Shirley Heights and English Harbour stretching to Falmouth and Monk's Hill

and the remote village of Sawcolts, with its ancient church, this is an area of rural tranquillity, which has defied the march of time and where you could happily explore and roam for hours.

This scenic country drive will take you near the village of Swetes, where you will come out opposite the pink Tyrells Church (see page 190) and the main road to English Harbour (or the north). At weekends, fruit and vegetable vendors sell their produce from stalls set up outside their homes.

Fig Tree Drive is located on the west coast at Old Road by Carlisle Bay, or to travel in reverse is reached from the road between All Saints and Liberta opposite Tyrells Church, to come out on the west coast.

FORT BARRINGTON

This is situated atop Goat Hill, on the promontory at the northern beach side of Deep Bay. An

Below: Fig Tree Drive
Following page: Body Ponds area

imposing signal station, Fort Barrington reported ships' movements to Rat Island via flag and light signals, and saw the heaviest military action in Antigua's history. It was captured by the French in 1666 and recaptured by England the following year, when it was named after Admiral Barrington who had captured St Lucia from the French a year before. The present fortifications were built in 1779 and a short, easy walk up this prominent hill guarantees sweeping views of the entrance to St John's harbour, and excellent sightings of St Kitts and Nevis are possible, set against the backdrop of the stunning sunsets here.

Fort Barrington is located via Five Islands, near the Royal Antiguan Resort.

INDIAN TOWN AND DEVIL'S BRIDGE

This has been a National Park since the 1950s and the site of an archaeological excavation, situated at the extreme eastern point of the island on the road to Long Bay. It possibly was the site of an Arawak settlement. Here Atlantic breakers sweep in at the end of a 3000-mile fetch from Africa, producing enormous swells and energy. Over the centuries these powerful foaming breakers have carved out a natural limestone arch called Devil's Bridge and created blowholes through which geysers of spouting surf crash with spectacular results.

Indian Town and Devil's Bridge are located on the extreme eastern tip of the island, past Betty's Hope and Willikies village, near the end of the road towards Long Bay.

MEGALITHS, GREENCASTLE HILL

For the adventuresome a relatively easy climb to the 565-foot high rounded grassy hilltop, the remains of an isolated volcano, will reveal many interesting megaliths and magnificent panoramic views, including the remaining southwestern volcanic mass and the island's interior plain. Situated at the northern end of this southwestern mountainous region, these extremely unusual geological formations, some say, were scenes of religious ceremonies and phallic worship. Others say that the remains of the upright stone circles suggest the hill was once an astronomical outlay for the measurement of time. Nearby, under a stone plaque bearing the inscription, 'He loved the people of these islands', are the ashes of the much loved former governor of the Leeward Islands (1947–49), Lord Baldwin. An Amerindian site exists not far from Tomb Rock.

Greencastle Hill is located about three miles due south of St John's between the villages of Jennings and Emmanuel.

OLDEST HOUSE

Keep an eye out when travelling through Hodges Bay for this house located on the main road, at the north side from St John's. Antigua's oldest occupied house is reputed to be the old great house of Hodge's Estate and possesses a typical seventeenth-century open hearth kitchen. It is not open to the public and is located in Hodges Bay, past the Colonna Beach Club.

ORANGE VALLEY NATURE PARK

Here lies 30 acres of hiking tracks, walking trails and a wide variety of flora and fauna species. Including all those of Antigua, the tree and plant species are labelled with both their local and botanical name. Most of the fauna is tame and hand reared by the indefatigable Hugh Pigott, who created this wonderful project. Enjoying many visitors, he and his hardworking wife and family also take schoolchildren on educational trips and church and nature related groups often like to camp in the safety and peace of this environment. With suitable visitor facilities, Pigott's dream is yours to discover, tel: (268) 462 0592.

It is located in the west, seven miles from St John's, by Darkwood Beach.

OUR LADY OF PERPETUAL HELP, TYRELLS CHURCH

This striking pink church cannot be missed whether travelling from Fig Tree Drive, or on the main road to English Harbour. The parish

Perfect for Families
Harmony Hall

Enjoy a full day here with much to do and see in stunning surroundings on their six and a half waterfront acres overlooking gorgeous Nonsuch Bay. A beautiful retreat with the historic Brown's Bay Mill Great House within the heart of this location on the east coast of the island and offering great alfresco dining, with an eclectic Italian and Caribbean cuisine. This old style cut-stone plantation house, dating back to 1843, houses a sugar mill bar with tower look-out, swimming pool and airy villas. There is also a comprehensive gift and craft shop and an Art Gallery with a collection of paintings, sculptures and pottery by top Caribbean and international artists. New exhibitions featured once a month. A peaceful and romantic setting which is often the choice for weddings and celebrations. Great boat trips from their dinghy dock can be easily arranged to uninhabited Green Island at a reasonable price. This one-stop wonder is recommended by *The Sunday Times*, *Bon Appetit*, *Travel & Leisure*, *Condé Nast Traveller*, *Caribbean Travel & Life* and all major travel guides. Tel: (268) 460 4120. **Located on the road to Half Moon Bay, through Freetown village, continuing towards Brown's Bay.**

JOLLY HARBOUR
– A COMPLETE RESORT AND MARINE COMMUNITY
'THE VENICE OF THE CARIBBEAN'

The original archaeological site here revealed the earliest settlement on the island, dating from 1775 BC. Now, spread over 500 acres and home to Jolly Harbour, the area accommodates the largest marina, golf and beach resort in the Caribbean. The development is certainly worth a visit (perhaps en route to beaches on the west coast or whilst travelling to Old Road and Fig Tree Drive), for all its amenities and facilities and the impressive Mediterranean styled architecture. With berthing for about 160 yachts, the atmosphere is reminiscent of the Mediterranean coastline.

Located in the centre of the resort is the shopping centre amidst tropical gardens on the marina waterfront. Boutiques, art galleries, bars, restaurants, supermarkets, stores, and a bank are all conveniently situated here. Car rentals, deep sea fishing and charters can also be booked at the various stores.

The comprehensive Jolly Harbour watersports shop is next to the Driftwood (see Active Traveller, page 153) Beach Bar on the stunning, long sweep of beach and has every conceivable form of water 'toy' and equipment for active beach days.

Overlooking the marina is the BBR Sports Centre with a 25-metre swimming pool, four tennis courts (both clay and Astroturf), a glass-backed squash court, a half basketball court. (See Active Traveller, page 145 for further information.) The popular bar and restaurant have regular major sports satellite transmissions and night-time entertainment.

Beside the car park at BBR you can't fail to see the helicopter of Caribbean Helicopters. Their office is situated at the entrance to BBR for fantastic aerial sightseeing tours of various durations which are well worth the experience for amazingly picturesque routes, panoramas and unrivalled photographic opportunities.

The championship 18-hole, par 71 golf course is located adjacent to the Super Yacht Terminal. Much frequented by visitors with its cool easterly breezes, hills and seven lakes, the club also includes a driving range, and is open to the general public on a daily fee basis. (See Active Traveller, page 140 for further information.)

Jolly Harbour Marina (see Appendix, page 319) is Antigua's only full-service marina and boatyard, including a Super Yacht Terminal. Through the Jolly Harbour Yacht Club (see page 129), all visiting yachtsmen and women are welcome to participate in the race on Saturdays or crew on the Club's racing yachts.

Due to its obvious appeal and opportunities for property purchasers, Jolly Harbour regularly offers a variety of villas, some with private mooring, and land for sale at affordable prices; fully equipped villa rentals are also available.

Jolly Harbour is on the main road out of St John's, on the west coast, just after Bolan's village.

of this Roman Catholic church in Tyrells covers the southern half of the island. Foreign missionaries from all over the world minister in the diocese which embraces two mission stations in the villages of Sea View Farm and Willikies.

It is located between All Saints and Liberta villages.

PARHAM/ST PETER'S ANGLICAN CHURCH

Parham was the earliest British settlement and the first town in Antigua in the seventeenth century, becoming the centre of seaborne trade. The harbour and town got their name from the ancestral home of Antigua's first governor, Lord William Willoughby of Parham, Captain General and Chief Governor of Barbados, Antigua and the rest of the Leeward Caribbee islands, who was granted land in Antigua in 1663. The economy of the area, however, predates the British by some 2,500 years. Archaeological finds provide evidence that sea-faring Amerindians lived around Parham and the North Sound.

As the island's first port, with its natural harbour, Parham Town exported the refined products of some 20 sugar estates in the area. It contained many thriving commercial and civic buildings until 1920, when with sugar seriously in decline, it ceased to be a port of entry. Today on Market Street, imposing Georgian remnants can still be seen and it is home to an impressive stock of Antiguan heritage. A road connects this village with the main road traversing the island.

Parham is notable for its spectacular church, St Peter's, which has been described as 'the finest church in the British West Indies'. One of the most distinctive churches in the region, it was rebuilt in the 1840s after the original wooden church, built in 1711, had burnt down and its replacement of 1754 was dismantled. It has a unique octagonal shape of beautiful proportions with a fascinating ribbed wooden ceiling and richly decorated stucco plaster work.

Designed by the famous British architect of the mid-1800s, Thomas Weekes, the very neat keystone work and excellent smoothness in the wall joints was the responsibility of the head

You cannot fail to see sugar mills dotted around the landscape, remnants of Antigua's 'king sugar' colonial days. Some are in ruins but you will still see the solid walls of these historic structures still intact. By 1705, Antigua was mainly planted with sugar cane (hence the lack of woodlands, cut down by Europeans in pursuit of more agricultural land to meet sugar demands) and 170 mills for crushing cane were constructed. The Museum of Antigua and Barbuda in St John's has recorded these along with their current status (there are still 114 documented mills on the island), but of course, the jewel in this particular crown, can be seen at Betty's Hope (see page 198).

mason who was a black Antiguan. Despite an earthquake in 1843 which damaged the structure, it still remains a masterpiece of ecclesiastical Georgian style, built in the Palladian manner.

Plans are afoot for extensive improvement and development of the Parham area. Meanwhile, for a 'Walking tour of Parham', available as an interpretive guide to the area, contact the Parham Co-operative office in the village which is located in Parham, in the northeast.

POTWORKS RESERVOIR AND DAMS

This is reputed to be the largest expanse of freshwater in the Eastern Caribbean, a mile long and half a mile wide, covering 320 acres and, when originally built, had a capacity of approximately one thousand million gallons of water when full. This large reservoir, held by two dams, is a welcome and surprising sight as you drive in the direction of Harmony Hall, Half Moon Bay or the Bethesda route to English Harbour. There is

Following pages:
Left: Our Lady of Perpetual Help, Tyrells Church
Right: Parham

forest walks, of varying lengths, with lookouts, shelters and picnic sites, reached by a nature trail from John Hughes Village. About half a mile along the trail, the awesome wide-stepped spillway of the dam appears, almost as if it were a spectacular folly. A magnificent example of Victorian industrial architecture and workmanship, it is an extraordinary sight in such surroundings, with its rounded capping and small round tower. Started in 1890 and completed ten years later, this incredible overflow system was designed to hold 13 million gallons of water. The tunnels for the water pipe were dug through solid rock at least 50–60 feet underground – an unexplained marvel. In 1945 a small additional dam was finished, creating the Fig Tree reservoir, and together these two dams occupy 268 acres.

Most of us are aware of the importance of trees to the environment and even nearly 90 years ago there was a reforestation project to help increase rainfall in that area. As a result, today, the increased forest of trees reaching up to 80 feet high from those original tree seeds planted, have afforded Antigua the priceless benefit of receiving 25 per cent more rain annually. Call the EAC (see page 114) to enquire about guided nature walks.

This is located in the southwest parish of St Mary, in the meandering, picturesque Fig Tree Drive.

> Beauty is Nature's coin, must not be hoarded,
> But must be current, and the good thereof
> Consists in mutual and partaken bliss.
> John Milton 1608–74

also some interesting birdwatching around the western edge of the reservoir.

The reservoir is located inland, in the southeast.

ST GEORGE'S ANGLICAN CHURCH

This ancient church dating back to 1687 was built on land granted to Daniel Fitch (the area is still known as Fitches Creek), and was the first parish church of St Peter's. Remodelled in 1735 and given its present name, its setting is particularly lovely with views overlooking Fitches Creek Bay on one side and Parham on the other. **It is located in the northeast.**

WALLINGS FOREST AND RESERVOIR

One of Antigua's most beautiful and valuable conservation areas, the Wallings forest is the largest remaining tract and the best example of the moist evergreen forests which covered the island before the Europeans started clearing them three centuries ago.

There are fine mixed evergreen deciduous

Betty's Hope

– Antigua's pioneer sugar estate, founded c.1650

As you flew over the island upon your arrival or whilst driving around you may have noticed sugar mill towers dotted throughout the countryside. Whilst difficult to visualise the life, times and workings of such wind generated mills, there is now a superb chance to understand and appreciate sugar and rum production by making a worthwhile visit to the historical site of Betty's Hope estate. Established in 1674 by Christopher Codrington (who named the estate for his daughter), the key feature of this historic site is its twin windmills, located amidst gently rolling hills in the northeastern limestone area.

Betty's Hope was chosen for restoration and preservation because of its historical importance. This was a unique opportunity to establish a major West Indian heritage monument of international standards, dedicated to all who toiled on this land and to their lives on a sugar plantation. In 1985, the Betty's Hope Project was established through collaboration among the Department of Tourism, the Ministry of Economic Development and the Historical and Archaeological Society. In 1989, the Betty's Hope Trust, a non-profit making organisation, was formed.

Now a centre for archaeological excavations (under the guidance of Antiguan Dr Reginald Murphy), research and interpretation of the Antiguan sugar era, it boasts the restored seventeenth-century north mill, the only functional and authentic windmill in the Caribbean. Inside it stands the magnificently renovated crushing machinery made in the early 1800s by Fletcher and Company of England and recently restored by the Whiting Iron Works of New York. Watch for the 'Turn her in … turn her out' viewings, when the sails are turned into the wind, cane fed into the crushing rollers and the juice flows from the reconditioned machinery, just as it worked over 300 years ago.

The initial restoration was a fantastic Herculean achievement and certainly a unique archaeological experience for Antigua's first local archaeologist, Dr Reginald Murphy, who founded and tirelessly presided over the project.

The fascinating story of Betty's Hope is told at the visitors' centre (open Tuesday to Saturday 10am–4pm) mainly through the archives of the Codrington family of Gloucestershire, England, who, arriving from Barbados, introduced large-scale sugar production to Antigua and owned Betty's Hope for almost 300 years. These enlightening documents illustrate how sugar and rum were produced during the colonial period by generations of Antiguans, with the introduction of efficient large-scale sugar cultivation and the then innovative methods of processing sugar.

Betty's Hope was renowned for its skilled Antiguan labourers and craftsmen; by 1720 an estimated 80 per cent of the population of 23,000 in Antigua were slaves, many of whom were on the Codrington estates, at the time totalling 1689 acres. This particular sugar plantation continued to prosper after emancipation in 1834 and was a popular place to work.

This is a tremendous opportunity for you to gain another perspective of Antiguan society. Admire the fabulous country views, learn about the dominant 'king sugar' era and let your imagination soar as its steps into the past, tel: (268) 462 1469 (Antigua and Barbuda Museum).

Betty's Hope is located just south of Pares village, in the parish of St Peter.

Antigua and Barbuda National Parks Authority

The National Parks Authority (NPA) is responsible for 12 square miles of land encompassing the exquisite coastline in the southern and most historical part of Antigua, from Mamora Bay to Carlisle Bay.

It is within this remarkable area, just half an hour's drive from St John's, which represents 10 per cent of Antigua's total land area, where you could happily spend an hour, an afternoon, a day, or much more – and still have wondrous things to discover and savour.

Within this national treasure of Antigua, you are presented with an unforgettably rich tapestry of history, beaches, country lanes, villages, shopping, nightlife, dining, stunning views, military fortifications, marinas, nature trails, sporting activities. The list goes on.

And yet, the integrity of the park has not been lost to commercialism, high-rise buildings and waste, but preserved with a unique blend of the atmosphere of bygone days without the clichés, whilst still offering all the amenities and advantages of the modern age. Immense sensitivity has been utilised in creating this ever-evolving environment, with its thriving local community life and without nature, humankind or structures having to be penalised, or worse, irrevocably lost.

PLACES TO VISIT

Nelson's Dockyard

Located in the heart of this most spectacular National Park is Nelson's Dockyard. Deserving a chapter to itself (see page 205), it is the only existing example of a Georgian naval dockyard in the world today and fitting testimony not only to Admiral Horatio Nelson but also to the Royal Navy, which used the site in the eighteenth and ninteenth centuries. Beautifully restored, today the old naval vessels have been replaced by stunning yachts. This historic site warrants at least one visit.

Fort Berkeley and Nature Trail

It is from the western end of the dockyard's marina, by the dinghy dock and jetty, behind the Copper and Lumber Store hotel, where you can start on a marked nature trail to Fort Berkeley and en route take advantage of superb opportunities for photography. Construction of this 25-gun fort began in 1704 on a spit of extending land, to protect the entrance to English Harbour as the first line of defence, and this is self evident when you walk along the easily accessible route, suitable for all the family, young and old.

Keep an eye out for three or four volcanic 'bombs', seen on the downward slope of the footpath. These rocks were hurled from a now extinct volcano when the island was formed 34 million years ago.

On the left, and built in 1811, is the bomb-proof powder magazine which held 300 barrels of gunpowder and incorporated a cooperage and shifting room. The guard house next door has been accurately and interestingly restored, illustrating the use of smaller stones required to extend the wall height after a previous hurricane had blown the roof off.

A 25-ton, 24-pounder cannon, within the battlements at the end of this peninsula, was made in Scotland in 1805 and shows the cypher of King George III. It took eleven men,

Officers
Quarters at
the Blockhouse

plus a powderman to handle this cannon, which had a range of 15 miles with an eight-pound charge.

In the nineteenth century, a strong chain and timber boom was drawn across the entrance of the harbour to stop intruders entering Nelson's Dockyard. A cannon, fixed upright in the rock, used for fastening the boom, may still be seen at Fort Berkeley.

From here you will be able to see clearly Clarence House, Antigua Slipway, Freeman's Bay, Charlotte Peninsula, the Pillars of Hercules; above to the left overlooking Galleon Beach is the Dow's Hill Interpretation Centre, and high up to the right, the renowned Shirley Heights.

Clarence House

Instead of turning off the main road from Falmouth to the right, signposted English and Falmouth Harbours, drive straight on as if heading for Shirley Heights, and around a couple of bends, you will see on the right, the gracious Clarence House (c.1787).

Prince William Henry, Duke of Clarence (often referred to as the 'sailor king', when he later became King William IV, 1765–1837), who was in command of HMS *Pegasus*, built his home using English stonemasons, opposite the dockyard to escape the heat and bustle. It later became the country residence of the governors of the Leeward Islands and, in 1960, was used for the honeymoon of Princess Margaret. This Georgian house, now the official residence of the governor general of Antigua, was severely damaged by hurricane Luis in 1995 and is now the subject of a historical research project as part of the archaeological contributions to the general restoration process.

Dow's Hill Interpretation Centre

Carrying on up a little higher, you will see signs for the multimedia presentation and the many facilities of Dow's Hill Interpretation Centre. This is arguably where you should start your exploration, as no visit is really complete without the help of the knowledgeable tour guides here and a viewing of the captivating multi-

media show. Comfortable seating in air-conditioned surroundings prepares you for a first-class professional show. The dialogue is in the charming fashion of a little boy asking his father about his homeland from its first settlers through to the present day. Everyone comes away not only having enjoyed the 15-minute show but more knowledgeable about Antigua's culture, heritage, history, nature and people. There is wheelchair access.

It is at this vast green area centrally located on a hill originally owned by a dockyard employee (Archibald Dow, who became a naval officer), where you will enjoy two of the finest panoramic views of the southern end of the island. You can take in a 360-degree view of Nelson's Dockyard National Park either from the extensive grounds of the centre itself, or atop the fine observation platform, the Belvedere, with informative placards, built on what was the eighteenth-century residence of the General Commanding Officer. There is also a café and excellent gift shop.

The Blockhouse

Further on up the hill, you will enter the large military complex of Shirley Heights (see page 202) and the various ruins of this extensive fortress. This is an interesting insight into British naval history and a very pleasant stroll as you meander from one fortification to another. A fork in the road, to the left will take you past the military fortifications of the stronghold blockhouse, dating back to 1787, including the majestic arches of the blockhouse officers' quarters, and onto a circular area with the still-standing powder magazine where the ammunition was stored. Showing the cypher of King George III, the breech of a 1780-built, 32-pound cannon lies pointing to Indian Creek.

Tremendous views can be enjoyed from the vantage point of Blockhouse Hill atop Cape Shirley, situated 450 feet above the Atlantic Ocean.

Blockhouse officers' quarters

To the right of the fork and on up the road, you will pass the remains of the officers' quarters with the parade grounds to the side. Built in

1793 for 75 men, you can still admire its long row of arches.

Military cemetery

Directly opposite, on the other side of this road, you will see to the right, two stone pillars forming the entrance to the military cemetery, situated on the hillside. Apart from five dominant graves, there is an obelisk in memory of the officers and men of the 54th Regiment, West Norfolk, who died on service in the West Indies between 1845 and 1851.

In recent years, this has benefited from a major clearing and cleaning up operation, with money donated by the British government. Visiting sailors from British ships, HMS *Argyle* and HMS *Boxer* painted the rails around the obelisk and the graves; a bright sign graces this important spot.

Shirley Heights

Just over the crest at the end of the road, the spectacular Shirley Heights lookout will be in sight, sitting high above the whole National Park area. Famed for its party-time six hours of non-stop musical entertainment on Sundays (and Thursdays, when the atmosphere is a little more restrained), with steel band music, barbecue, jump-up and ambience, the breathtaking views from here are legendary. Falmouth Harbour lies clearly in the distance under the protection of the fort at Monk's Hill, which is evident by its flat top at the extreme right. At this most southerly tip of Antigua, the island of Montserrat can easily be seen and on a particularly clear day, Guadeloupe as well.

Fortified by General Shirley, Governor of the Leeward Islands in the 1780s, to defend the precious cargoes in the harbour below, its barracks, arched walkways, batteries, cisterns and powder magazines are scattered all over these heights. The lookout gun battery was one of the main signal stations from which the dockyard was warned of approaching ships – now its handsomely restored restaurant (once the ordnance building where shot was stored) and bar is the regular gathering place for visitors

Pillars of Hercules/Charlotte Peninsula/Carpenter Rock

At the end of the point marking the east entrance to the harbour, below Shirley Heights, is the well-known enormous pillar-like landmark and extraordinary geological formation, the Pillars of Hercules. This is also part of the unique Charlotte Peninsula, so called as behind these famed pillars lie the ruins of the upper and lower Forts Charlotte (c.1700–1830), named after Queen Charlotte, wife of King George III.

Stunning beaches and the spectacular Charlotte Reef entice visiting yachtspeople and locals, and for those in the know, the little-known Carpenter Rock over the hill is also an amazingly unusual site. Beautiful ocean-facing rock formations create intriguing rock pools and is generally a wild, open space. Ruins of the habitation of the c.1750 Carpenter family of settlers can still be seen amongst the bush – all preciously preserved from human resettlement and development by Friends of English Harbour amongst others.

Monk's Hill and Fort George

In the 1680s, this 699-foot table hill, owned by Nathaniel Monk, was chosen as the perfect site for a substantial fort and retreat to protect the main town of Falmouth from the French. The ruins can be reached from the villages of Liberta and Table Hill Gordon, or from behind Falmouth, and afford a stupendous bird's-eye view of the entire National Parks area.

Over the ensuing years, buildings were continually added to the fort which carries a stone inscription to King George II and the west magazine, built in 1731 still to be found. Three years later, 33 guns were mounted, the sight of which succeeded in driving the French on to Montserrat and the fort never saw a battle.

The fort's eight acres are surrounded by a wall of unusually coloured green stone, only found in the vicinity of Liberta. You enter through

an arch and several ruins may be seen, notably the powder magazines, the huge water cistern and original gun sites.

Many famous British regiments served here as well as the excellent black West Indies regiments. Due to its commanding position, the fort was not merely a defence and last place of refuge but was utilised as a station for relaying signals from Shirley Heights and English Harbour to St John's and other outlying forts around Antigua's coastline.

The superlative beauty and wonders of the Park's woodlands, singing birds, plants, fruit and flowers play vital roles for both animal and humankind, and its natural features ensure a heritage precinct. As Parks Commissioner, Ann-Marie Martin succinctly sums up, 'this all points to the need for respect for the natural world, not only from an aesthetic point of view, but for the ecological and historical aspects of our country'; hence, a government mandate that approval be sought from the National Park Authority (NPA) before any development can proceed in this area.

Every effort is being made to preserve, nurture and cherish such natural resources and visitors are urged to respect this by taking picnic litter home or using the park's rubbish bins. Any help is appreciated in ensuring that having survived the last two centuries, the presently unspoilt National Park will still be here to welcome the future generations of Antiguans, Barbudans and visitors from overseas.

Nelson's Dockyard National Park
tel: (268) 460 1379 fax: (268) 460 1516
Dow's Hill Historical Centre
tel: (268) 460 2777
Dockyard Museum tel: (268) 460 8181
Shirley Heights tel: (268) 460 1785

Nelson's Dockyard
– harbouring history

> The dockyard presents a fine and noble appearance; and ... everything seems to be conducted in the best possible manner; while the yard itself is kept so beautifully clean, that a walk through it affords real pleasure.
>
> Mrs Lanaghan, *Antigua and The Antiguans*
> (1844)

Nelson's Dockyard is the only existing example of a Georgian naval dockyard in the world today. A visit is essential for an informative and romantic step back in time, for adventure and relaxation.

Interestingly, English Harbour was set up as a naval yard on the initiative of the Antiguans themselves at the suggestion of two British naval captains. The Antiguan Assembly was anxious to provide local facilities to cater for the basic needs of warships when they could be spared from the 1000-mile patrol of the valuable British West Indian sugar islands.

Its formidable land-locked basins formed within the old volcano cone, and its one narrow passage to the sea, made it a hurricane haven for ships as far back as 1671. The British began to use it as a royal dockyard in 1725 when St Helena, located on the eastern side of the harbour (where Antigua Slipway is today), was allocated funds for construction. In 1743 Commodore Charles Knowles established the dockyard at its present site and developed it extensively. The dockyard's main use was as a careening station. By being able to repair, vic-

---

THE SHIPS

The first recorded ship to use the harbour was a yacht which arrived having survived a hurricane at sea in 1671. The *Dover Castle*, chartered by Charles II, was for the use of the first governor of the Leeward Islands, carrying him on official visits to the islands and for chasing pirates.

Warships sheltered in English Harbour from hurricanes in the latter part of the seventeenth century, and for undergoing refits. The most frequently seen vessels were frigates of about 28 guns, brig-sloops of 18 guns, schooners of four guns and cutters. The average sized ship gun fired a round shot of 22 pounds whose range was about a mile. The largest sized ship reputed to use the harbour was the captured French ship-of-the-line *Foudroyant*, 180-feet long with 80 guns.

Nelson's frigate, HMS *Boreas*, was 128-feet long by 34-feet and drew 16 feet of water and had a complement of about 200 men.

The deep waters so close to the shore of the harbour afforded the perfect conditions necessary for careening ships. These huge ships were careened by hauling down the masts so that the bottom came above water for the purpose of repair and painting. They were then hauled down the opposite side to effect repairs on the other side of the keel.

Ships also came for general refits, for provisions and supplies, sail repair, to order new sails or boats, and to take on loads of shot from the ordnance wharf. Captured enemy ships were brought into the harbour to be renamed, converted for naval use, and old ships called for the last time, to be broken up.

tual and water ships in the West Indies, sparing the expense and dangers of having to sail to the northern American colonies, it afforded Britain the means to keep a fleet of ships continuously in the Caribbean. A survey of 1774 outlined the present layout and most of the buildings seen today were built between 1785 and 1792.

Commanding the Northern Division of the Leeward Island Station was Horatio Nelson, then aged 26, with headquarters in English Harbour. Captain Nelson, as he was then, and his ship, the 28-gun frigate HMS *Boreas*, arrived here in July 1784 and stayed until 1787. During his time here, Prince William Henry, later King William IV, was captain of the frigate HMS *Pegasus* and built Clarence House overlooking

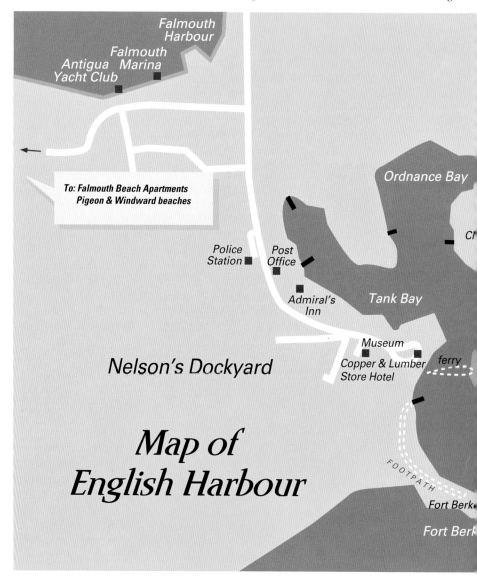

Falmouth
Harbour
Falmouth
Antigua Marina
Yacht Club

Ordnance Bay

Cl

To: Falmouth Beach Apartments
Pigeon & Windward beaches

Police
Station   Post
Office

Admiral's
Inn

Tank Bay

Museum

Nelson's Dockyard

Copper & Lumber   ferry
Store Hotel

Map of
English Harbour

FOOTPATH

Fort Berk

Fort Berl

the yard (see page 201); he was best man at Nelson's wedding on the island of Nevis.

English Harbour's importance was accentuated by the loss of the American colonies after the revolution. During the wars with the French (1792–1815), the royal dockyard reached its zenith. The dockyard was never attacked because it was so well protected by military fortifications,

In the 1750s, ships at anchor had the delight of black 'bum-boat' women who would undress and place their clothes over their produce in wooden tubs and swim out to the warships, pushing their tubs before them. On arrival at the gangway they would dry off, dress, proceed to sell their wares. Then these enterprising women would undress again and swim back with their clothes in their, hopefully empty, tubs as before!

especially those in the surrounding hills, now known as Shirley Heights (see page 202), after governor-general Shirley.

After the battle of Waterloo in 1815, peace reigned over the warring nations and gradually English Harbour lost its importance; however, it was still maintained for another 75 years as a coaling station for smaller ships and until 1878 for the Royal Mail Packet Company with Antigua mail. The industrial revolution contributed to its decline as did the coming of steam-powered ships. Such gradual disuse resulted in the Royal Navy closing it completely in 1889. Thus there is cause to be eternally grateful that the fine old buildings were left unaltered by such actions to eventually become the fine national monument enjoyed by all today.

Throughout the dockyard's history many famous people have visited. Following Admiral Rodney, Nelson and King William IV, Prince George (later to become George V, in 1910), visited the yard in 1833 when he served as a sub-lieutenant on the corvette HMS *Canada*. In more recent times, the list of those interested in the restoration of the dockyard must be headed by Queen Elizabeth II, who visited in 1964, 1966 and 1977 and Lady Churchill launched an appeal for restoration in 1955.

In one year alone, 1960, the following notables visited: Princess Margaret on her honeymoon, Sir Winston (Nelson was his idol) and

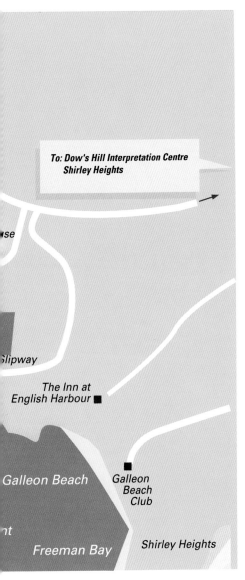

To: Dow's Hill Interpretation Centre
Shirley Heights

se

Slipway

The Inn at
English Harbour ■

Galleon Beach   Galleon
                   Beach
                   Club

nt

Freeman Bay   Shirley Heights

Lady Churchill arrived on Aristotle Onassis' yacht, the then Princess Royal, Maria Callas, Lord Avon, Lord Beaverbrook, Lord Hailes, Sir Grantley Adams, Marian Anderson and the US Ambassador John Hay Whitney.

The first attempts at restoration were made by Governor Sir Reginald St Johnston who founded the dockyard and Shirley Heights restoration fund. The officers' quarters were repaired and the first guide book was published. Another governor, Kenneth Blackburne, created the Friends of English Harbour, formed in 1951, which breathed new life into the dockyard, and, after much preservation and restoration work, it was officially reopened in 1961.

Now this Georgian naval dockyard is part of Antigua's first national park, under the Antigua and Barbuda National Parks Authority (see page 199). A mandate was established to preserve, manage and develop (with much aid from Canada) the natural resources and heritage of English Harbour, making it Antigua's most thriving and prized historical possession.

When Admiral Horatio Nelson was at the dockyard, he had six pails of sea water thrown over his head every morning, drank one quart of goat's milk every day and night, and said he was, 'woefully pinched by mosquitoes', even though he slept under a net. When he left English Harbour to sail back to England, he was so ill that he had a barrel of rum shipped aboard, for him to be preserved in, should he die.

English Harbour was known as the 'grave of Englishmen' as there was no shade, too much drink and too many women!

Copper and Lumber Store Hotel

Today this historic maritime monument provides one of the best examples of adaptive use found in the Caribbean; meaning that the harbour and many of the buildings are being used in ways that approximate the purpose for which they were originally built. The harbour is used for private sailing yachts that are based here, instead of repairing old naval vessels, and for those anchoring here while making ocean voyages. History has come round full circle.

The Annual Charter Yacht Show (now named Nicholson's Charter Yacht Show) was started in the 1950s (see page 130) and a three-day Lord Nelson Regatta was held in 1968 from which Antigua Sailing Week (see page 119) developed. The Classic Yacht Regatta (see page 123) is also held here, preceding Sailing Week.

With tourism now providing Antigua with a major source of revenue and employment, the dockyard authorities have taken on a new dimension. The development of tourism, craft industries (many with Antiguan ownership) and maritime activities has thus created employment and attracted thousands of overseas visitors to what is now also a hub of lively activity.

Do tear yourself away from Antigua's beau-tiful beaches to spend time in this unique area, dotted with fascinating eighteenth-century forts and military installations. The intriguing walled-in dockyard, where you are free to roam at leisure and take full advantage of all its facil-ities, including a bank with cashpoints, is just a 30-minute drive from St John's. Large informa-tive signs are in front of each structure describ-ing its original use and any other interesting pieces of information. Alternatively, friendly, local guides give daily tours explaining the vari-ous historic buildings and their highlights, right up to present day activities.

This setting, straight out of a historical novel, includes other restored buildings trans-formed into inns, restaurants, bars, boutiques, gift shops and an enlightening museum (see below). The harmonious, glorious scene is fringed by stunning yachts moored here, an attraction in themselves.

Such living history will help visitors to see 'Antigua's Living Park' as the author H.W. Coleridge saw it in 1825, when he called it, 'the prettiest little harbour I have ever seen, a com-bination of tropical beauty and English style and spirit.'

THE MUSEUM OF NELSON'S DOCKYARD

Housed within the naval officers' house, heralded by the distinctive bust of Nelson, is where the history of the English Harbour area is narrated. As its research director, the indefatigable historian Desmond Nicholson, comments, 'a museum is a place where you get an interpretation of a certain subject, of research and enquiry, not just a place where you go and see arti-facts.' True, museums can conjure up visions of dusty, slightly boring places to have a quick walk round and leave. This is not so here. Under Desmond Nicholson's painstaking research and passion for reviving the rich and varied history here, this is a place which will fascinate you and capture your imagination with interpretive displays and interactive exhibits.

Completely upgraded, the museum tells the actual story of the dockyard divided into five periods (from pre-Amerindian set-tlement, c.900 AD, to the present day), its natural and rich history, the conditions and way of daily life, the toil and sweat of the workers and its purpose through the cen-turies. There is also a gift shop and research library with an extensive naval his-tory database available. Admission is free.

SOME OF THE BUILDINGS
OF PARTICULAR INTEREST

The Admiral's Inn

This was built in 1788 with bricks that came over on English ships as ballast. Originally the naval engineer's office, and pitch and tar store, with a cellar for the barrels of strong pitch and Stockholm tar it was restored in 1961 as a delightfully attractive inn, with superb outdoor dining at the water's edge, next to the huge capped pillars of the former boathouse, where careening took place. Carvings of names of ships which called at the yard may be inspected on the present bar top at the inn, the most notable being HMS *Canada*, which arrived in 1884, with Sub-lieutenant Prince George, who later became King George V.

The Copper and Lumber Store

The original sheet copper and lumber store of the nineteenth century, was built in 1789. The upper quarters were for the seamen whose ships were being careened. It is now a gracious and romantic small hotel, retaining its Georgian architecture. The entrance boasts a traveller's palm, planted by HM Queen Elizabeth II. Further on is the unique arched courtyard.

The Capstan House

The remaining low walls mark the area of the old capstan house. The three restored capstans were turned by men, kept in time by a fiddler playing sea shanties. This is where ships were hoved, and the ships' masts hauled down by ropes attached to the capstans for careening.

The Naval Officers' House

Presided over by an antique bust of Nelson, the elegant two-storey house, built in 1855, was originally constructed as a residence for the naval officer in charge and the storekeeper. (See also Nelson's Dockyard Museum, page 210.) Beside the house is the sandbox tree, over 200 years old, whose pods were used to hold sand, which was substituted for blotting paper on desks. Behind can be found the ancient old stone kitchens.

Do you fancy a quick bite and a cool drink? There are wonderful bars and restaurants in Nelson's Dockyard, and there is also a bakery, situated in the original kitchens behind the museum. Using fresh ingedients, the dockyard bakery bakes everything on the premises daily. As well as unsurpassed homemade bread, rolls and croissants, they specialise in buns, turnovers, pastries, local cakes and irresistible meat and vegetable pasties. Take one of these and a cold drink, or freshly ground coffee, and sit under the enormous, 200-year old sandbox tree outside.

Here today you will still see bakers busy at work producing their oven fresh pastries and bread; hot and cold drinks are also for sale.

The Officers' Quarters Building

Started in 1801, the building was finished in 1821. Level with the ground are twelve 16-feet by 20-feet water cisterns with a total capacity to catch 1000 tons of rain water. Officers from the ships lived here on the upper floors during the hurricane months which now house an art gallery and various shops.

The Pay Office

Built in 1807, this accommodated the offices of the commissioner, master shipwright, master attendant and store-keeper. It is now a very pretty small two-storey building with shops below.

The Saw Pit and Saw Pit Cabin

This is the oldest part of the dockyard visible today, having been built in 1769. Planks and other lumber were sawn by hand here having been rolled up the sloping platform. Tools and records were kept in the saw pit cabin next door.

Off-road sightseeing tours

For something different, and to take you off the beaten track, there are excellent tours available in four-wheel drive vehicles. Such day trips enable you to go beyond the normal sightseeing routes and see Antigua from a totally new perspective. Wear comfortable clothes, sensible shoes and take swimming gear.

BO-TOURS

Multilingual trained guides escort you on their off-road safaris to areas only accessible by their sturdy four-wheel drive vehicles. Drive through the tropical rainforest area of Fig Tree Drive, stopping at Wallings forest and reservoir, with its spillway and dam, a magnificent example of Victorian industrial architecture. Other points of interest include Devil's Bridge at Indian Town Point, Fort George at Monk's Hill, the twin sugar mills of Betty's Hope, a Caribbean lunch in a village restaurant and a beach stop. The price is inclusive of guides, entrance fees, lunch and drinks. This professional company also specialises in multilingual guided island tours.

ESTATE SAFARI TOURS

Established for five years, relax in one of their four-wheel drive Nissan Patrol vehicles and see Antigua from a historic angle, exploring places you didn't know existed. Friendly, knowledgeable guides show you the island's hidden highlights and spectacular views. Day tours include snacks, drinks, lunch and swimming. Should you wish to combine land and sea, then you can start your trip on land and finish on the powered catamaran *Coastline Safari* (see page 165).

ISLAND SAFARI

Step into one of the custom built, safari rigged Land Rover Jeeps and prepare yourself for an adventurous and fascinating tour of the island, taking you to some of the most interesting places. Places which are inaccessible to tour buses but are no problem with four-wheeled vehicles. These Land Rovers are specially equipped with Bob Cat seats and belts and each vehicle is protected by padded roll bars. Be picked up to join this 'off-road' expedition to the southern and western side of the island. Their fully trained and experienced guides will give you a chance to stop at some magnificent locations on the island. Lunch with a glass of wine, soft drinks and rum punch are included along the way.

TROPIKELLY TRAILS

Comfortable Mitsubishi Pajeros take you to the lesser known, quieter parts of the island and beautiful, historic sights which not many have the opportunity to see, including old forts, plantation houses and sugar mills. Fully insured with passenger liability, their multilingual guides escort you to the unusual and spectacular, from sea level to the highest point on the island. They provide a shaded, water's edge picnic-style lunch and the day finishes with a swim.

Bo-Tours tel: (268) 462 6632
fax: (268) 462 5336
Estate Safari tel: (268) 463 4713
fax: (268) 480 8478
Island Safari tel: (268) 562 5337
fax: (268) 462 2065
Tropikelly Trails tel: (268) 461 0383
fax: (268) 462 5464

Beaches
– barefoot beachcombing

To see a World in a grain of sand,
And a Heaven in a wild flower,
Hold infinity in the palm of your hand,
And Eternity in an hour

William Blake

If you hadn't already realised, you have found the best island in the Caribbean on which to beachcomb. Antigua is famed for its legendary 365 gleaming beaches, fronted by warm, crystal-clear waters. While it is doubtful they have ever actually been counted, there could even be more.

Antigua has been unusually blessed with a fine blend of both coral and volcanic formations. Created eons ago, this resulted in a long, scalloped coastline all around the island, each bay and beach, brimming full of deliciously white, pink or tan shaded sand.

Cut by reefs and coves, they afford the luxuries of privacy, tranquillity and beauty. Ideal for sunbathing, picnics, barbecues or simply practising the West Indian art of 'liming' – just doing nothing in particular but enjoying hedonistic bliss by doing whatever it is in an easy, unhurried way. The waters are clean, clear and perfect for rejuvenating the body and cleansing the soul.

The formation of Barbuda is, in total contrast, mainly made up of coral. Whilst relatively flat and featureless, it is particularly renowned for an abundance of very long, sweeping, pristine, pinky-white sand beaches with the calmest sea, competing with the sky for the clearest blue. On the southwestern shore these stretch for uninterrupted miles, protected by barrier reefs, whilst the eastern beaches, on the Atlantic side, have somewhat rougher waters, although they are excellent for beachcombing. Reached by a very short flight or boat, to fully enjoy this totally uncommercialised island an organised trip is recommended (see page 302).

Remember, it is unlawful to take away any coral, even dead coral, as it is an endangered species and forms part of the ocean's ecosystem. Don't concern yourselves with sharks or barracudas, they are way beyond the reefs and present no danger. On the remote beaches around underwater rocky areas, keep your eyes open for black spiky sea urchins which sting badly if you step on them. They can easily be seen through the clear waters.

If staying at a hotel, the chances are you are probably only a short walk from a superb beach just outside your door. However, it is certainly recommended you take the time to explore other beaches. All are public. Some appeal to local tastes and others tend to cater to those of visitors. You're welcome to use the beach at a different hotel for a change of scenery; however, hotel amenities such as beach loungers are probably for their residents' use (unless on a really deserted beach, you can often hire a lounger for the day for a few US dollars). Take a packed lunch, a beach towel, sun cream, swimwear and snorkelling gear for those sparkling turquoise waters.

Categorising Antigua's beaches poses the same sort of problem as counting grains of sand, so to simplify matters the following covers those which are definitely accessible and on the tourist map, coupled with a few which are 'off the beaten track'. Beaches at the northern end of the island are described first of all and then others in an anti-clockwise direction round the island. Before commencing your beach-bound 'tour', please be responsible for your rubbish. Bring a bag and take it away with you – even if everyone else may not have followed this example!

DICKENSON BAY

Almost at the top of the island, it is the most well-known and active beach. This is a striking half-mile stretch of 'Caribbean' beach, backed by several of the larger hotels. If the rest of the island seems sleepy, you will usually find some action here. By day, it's sunbathing, reading, draping recuperating bodies over beach bars or water-skiing, parasailing, jet skiing, snorkelling, diving or horse-riding. At sundown, it's a great place for a romantic stroll and a 'happy hour' drink; as darkness falls, music fills the air as the restaurants and bars come to life. One of the major hotels on this bay, the all inclusive Sandals (see Appendix, page 318 for contact details), offers various full, half and evening passes for non-residents to enjoy their dining, bar, watersports and entertainment facilities.

RUNAWAY BEACH

This is just around the corner, to the south and adjacent to Dickenson Bay, past Corbisson Point and is a fine bay with gently sloping sand into the safe, cool waters. It is ideal for families and children. On the beachfront here sits the Lobster Pot restaurant and bar and at the far end of this long sweep of beach is the lively Lashings Sports bar and café.

FORT BAY, FORT JAMES

You get to it by continuing southwards, to the western side of the mouth of St John's Harbour. Antiguans favour this long beach closest to St John's, named after King James II, who reigned at the time when the fort was first built. Sometimes there can be strong undercurrents; however, the large cordoned area is safe for swimming. Miller's Beach Bar and Restaurant offers sunlounger facilities at a nominal cost.

DEEP BAY, FIVE ISLANDS

Going through St John's, out onto the road skirting the harbour and the peninsula will eventually bring you to the Royal Antiguan Resort. The building is not typically Caribbean, but the beach beyond definitely is. The fortunate part of progress is that you can now drive, park and walk to enjoy this excellent beach, with beach bar and amenities.

GALLEY BAY

A peaceful ribbon of beach, well-known among surfers for the excellent wave breaks which build around the point during the winter months. Such westward facing beaches can become quite rough if groundswells are running, but when not to swim is quite obvious.

HAWKSBILL BEACH

Further on round the Five Island peninsula, the Hawksbill main beach, in front of the hotel complex, offers the advantage of a poolside bar and restaurant. A stretch away, are their other three crescent-shaped beaches, becoming by human nature, progressively quieter and less formal, to the point of clothing optional on the fourth and last beach, with its fine sand and coral reefs perfect for snorkelling out to the Hawkshead rock.

HERMITAGE BAY

This remote, long stretch of beach is reached from the main road at Jennings village, via a long track which partly runs alongside the north of the Jolly Beach complex. Worth the trip, you can then enjoy two beaches for the one ride, as having reached the lovely Hermitage Bay, a sharpish turn to the left will take you onto the even more isolated Pearns beach. This is a good area for exploring and beachcombing.

JOLLY BEACH

The signposted public beach access is just after the main entrance of the Jolly Beach Hotel. It is one of the loveliest, longest white sand sweeps of beach on the island with safe bathing. For those staying in the nearby villas or just passing through, you can use the extensive watersports facilities available, next to the Driftwood Beach Bar. Whilst this bay is largely occupied by the all-inclusive Jolly Beach Hotel, you can purchase a half-day or full-day pass. This would enable you to enjoy all the facilities (food, drink and entertainment included) which the hotel has to offer (see Appendix, page 317). If you are ready for some serious partying and have a huge

Opposite: Darkwood; pages 216–17: Carlisle Bay

appetite, the passes are very good value! Next door is the marina complex – a good interlude on your trip around the island (see page 192).

VALLEY CHURCH BAY

About a mile farther south, just opposite Valley Church, is a short track leading to an opening where fishermen pull up their catch and so can be strewn with general flotsam and jetsam. However, to the right is a lovely secluded sweep of unpopulated, natural beach, stretching to a rocky peninsula and bordered by trees and bush. Its typically Caribbean warm, calm waters are a favourite haunt of many local pelicans.

FFRYES BEACH

Very popular with locals and visitors alike, this is a long, sweeping bay backed by a deep grassy, sandy area, well shaded and perfect for barbecues, games and offering plenty of parking space. It can be reached by a prominent track, with landmark sugar mill, off the main road just before Darkwood beach.

DARKWOOD

This is another fabulous and very scenic beach. By the roadside on this southwestern section of the coast, it is an island and tourist favourite and certainly one of the most photographed beaches in the Caribbean. Still unspoilt, with Montserrat in the distance, it has no hotels (but a good local bar/restaurant), and its picturesque multihued waters have the barest touch of caressing surf.

TURNER'S BEACH AND JOHNSON'S POINT

Continuing on, the road curves and you come to the long stretch of spectacular white sand beaches of Crab Hill Bay. Although not all readily accessible, you can still find spots where you can drive down to the serenely empty expanses, also with fine views of Montserrat, and calm waters with cordoned swimming area of the Rex Blue Heron hotel. Two excellent beach bars, both renowned for lobster, sit at either end of this stunning wide bay. There are interesting walks to nearby fort ruins from the far end at Johnson's Point.

MORRIS BAY

This is situated down the coast a short way from Turners, right alongside the plush Curtain Bluff hotel. Simply pull off the road into the grove of coconut palms at the back of the beach. The water on this side is often just a little cooler and crystal clear for a refreshing dip and a beach walk to dry off.

CARLISLE BAY

This is situated just at the beginning of the lush, tropical rainforest drive of Fig Tree Drive and is a very glamorous, uncluttered wide sweep of bay with only small local dwellings nearby and a hotel behind. It is perfect as a film set, a television commercial or a swimwear fashion shoot!

RENDEZVOUS BAY AND DOIGS BEACH

These two quiet beaches are only accessible by four-wheel drive or by various footpaths – but well worth the trek necessary to reach them.

PIGEON BEACH

When sightseeing around the English Harbour area, you may enjoy a trip to this ribbon of beach, often quiet, sometimes busy in season. At Falmouth Harbour, take the road behind the Antigua Yacht Club, pass Falmouth Beach Apartments and take the short uphill dirt track road. Turn sharp left on the bend and drive down the hill and around to the right. Gentle graduating waters, as well as a good beach bar, await you.

WINDWARD BEACH

This can be found along the same road to Pigeon; just carry on to this often deserted white sand beach, favoured by the yachting community.

GALLEON BEACH

En route to Shirley Heights, past Clarence House, a steep road to the right takes you to the beach of the Inn at English Harbour and Galleon Beach Club. A nautical air pervades with yachts at anchor in the bay. Galleon is a beautifully main-

Opposite above: Pigeon Beach; below: Dickenson Bay

English sailors used to be called 'limeys', because they ate limes to ward off scurvy. When their ships were in port they had ample time to lounge around, thus the local verb 'to lime' came to mean 'hang out'. (L. Rose Limited – manufacturers of Roses's Lime Juice today – started importing lime juice from the West Indies in the 1860s. Trade thrived because merchant ships were compelled to carry limes to prevent scurvy.)

tained property with lawns leading onto the palm fringed beach and offers the convenient facilities of a first-class Italian restaurant and great bar.

ST JAMES'S CLUB

With a security entrance to provide their guests a certain amount of seclusion and decorum, you may certainly take advantage of this luxurious enclave by purchasing a half- or full-day pass, for the usual facilities offered at similar all-inclusive hotels (see page 318 for contact details). The beach inside the lagoon is somewhat artificial and very calm whilst the Atlantic windward beach is natural, windswept and protected from the ocean by Mamora Reef.

HALF MOON BAY

Despite its popularity, it is too large to ever be overcrowded. At the very end sits the Half Moon Club (presently closed). Most of this mile-long striking crescent-shaped bay is left in its natural state, to be explored to the fullest. In the centre of the beach, on all but the quietest of days, the waves roll in providing excellent body surfing. To the eastern end the sea is quieter, safer for small children and pleasant for snorkelling amid underwater crevices of rock and coral. The Half Moon Bay National Park, as it is officially named, is a perfect place to lie in the sun, take a walk, frolic in the ocean or play beach cricket, frisbee or volleyball. There is plenty of room. The

Travel Channel (USA) recently voted this beach as the number one in the list of the world's ultimate beaches. At the entrance to the car park, you will find a highly recommended beach bar and restaurant, and a riding stable.

BROWN'S BAY AND GREEN ISLAND

This is a perfect break in your journey. There is a small beach here, plus one at nearby Harmony Hall (see page 191), with its gift shop, art gallery, swimming pool, grassy slopes, bar and excellent outdoor dining overlooking the splendid Nonsuch Bay, most suitable for all the family. This one-stop sojourn also offers short boat rides from its tiny beach and jetty to uninhabited Green Island (see page 225, Antigua's Outer Islands) with its three wonderful beaches and terrific swimming conditions.

LONG BAY

This sits at the end of the road, if you head through Willikies and beyond, passing Devil's Bridge to your right. On your left is the Allegro Resort Pineapple Beach, a popular all-inclusive resort which offers day passes to non-residents. Long Bay enjoys still waters and superb bathing. Just a short swim to the reef, to which the bay owes its protection, will give some fine snorkelling. A good beach for families with young children, it is well worth packing a picnic. To your right is delightful Long Bay Hotel, with superb bathing, beach and snorkelling plus excellent beachside lunches and a great old-fashioned Caribbean bar. The stylishly colourful resort of Mango Bay sits between both these hotels, on the bluff. As a non-resident, you can take advantage of a fully inclusive day pass (see Appendix, page 317 for all contact details).

DUTCHMAN'S BAY

This is situated back up to the north, close to the airport. As well as having a good reef protected beach, it is the home to Windsurfing Antigua. All the local windsurfing enthusiasts hang out here and when the wind is blowing, the action is fast and colourful, especially during the Windsurfing championship competition.

> The parrotfish scrapes minute chunks off the coral reef's edge, digests and grounds it into the sand and in a year, excretion from this one parrotfish will have contributed a ton of sand towards its immediate marine habitat and the beach underfoot! No wonder William Blake, in the nineteenth century said, 'to see a world in a grain of sand'.

JABBERWOCK BEACH

This natural, non-commercialised beach has been chosen as a sponsored programme by Cable & Wireless who, with the aid of the AH&TA (Antigua Hotels and Tourist Association) and the Antigua and Barbuda Defence Force, will design and construct public changing rooms, showers and toilets, parking and picnic seating facilities. Special shady trees will be planted, the area will be well lit, and beautification of the immediate surroundings and consistent upkeep will be maintained. As Jabberwock is one of Antigua's main nesting sites for the rare and endangered Hawksbill turtle, Cable & Wireless are also sponsoring the Hawksbill Sea Turtle Research Project. This will ensure that the ecosystem here is protected for the turtles, whilst still improving the beach for the general public and visitors.

Most of these beaches have hotels, restaurants, cafés or bars on them or nearby, but you are always advised to travel with a bottle of water and maybe a snack in case you become dehydrated between these stopping off places. With over 365 beach gems studded around the coastline, it is not possible to mention them all but the explorers amongst you will relish the adventure of finding your own little piece of paradise.

Take nothing but photographs, leave nothing but footprints, kill nothing but time.

Anon

Antigua's outer island jewels

> How pleasant it would be to pass one's life in such quiet abodes
>
> Charles Darwin

Unusual for most Caribbean islands, Antigua is blessed with numerous, unique outer islands, notably on the highly indented, eastern or windward side. Sheltered by reefs and cooled by gentle trade winds, it is possible to visit many of these uninhabited, secluded havens whether cruising around Antigua or on one of the numerous all-inclusive day trips offered by day sailing tour companies (see page 162). Apart from stunning views, it is quite something whilst on these islands to realise that looking due east across the Atlantic Ocean, the next landfall is Africa!

NORTH SOUND ISLANDS

North Sound encompasses a marine environment and group of 15 islands, totalling about 1000 acres, off the northeast coast of Antigua, one of the last true Antiguan wildernesses for all to enjoy. Whilst most are tiny coral outcrops or small limestone islands, the larger ones are frequently on visitors' agendas.

As attested to by the many local fishermen, the North Sound area is one of the richest in marine and terrestrial wildlife in Antigua. Its surrounding mangroves and coral reefs provide a habitat, spawning and nursery ground for an abundant inshore marine ecosystem; up to 80 per cent of the seafood caught by fishermen spend some part of their lives in a mangrove.

There are numerous interesting Amerindian archaeological sites (both archaic and ceramic) scattered across the islands, notably Guiana and Crump Islands, plus at least seven shipwrecks in the waters of North Sound.

A Nature Haven

As an impressive natural environment, significant attributes of the area include Antigua's largest reef system, the largest lobster spawning area, beautiful beaches, the largest stretch of mangroves in the Lesser Antilles, the largest concentration of seagrasses, the largest tracts of native dry forests and the largest, most important seabird nesting and feeding area for the many internationally and locally threatened and endangered seabird species.

Antigua's only snake (see also page 98), the rare endemic Antiguan racer snake (*Alsophis antiguae*), finds refuge on Bird Island. Threatened sea turtles live and nest in the North Sound, including the hawksbill, leatherback, green and loggerhead turtles (see page 103) and the waters are a sanctuary and breeding ground of the Nassau Grouper.

GREAT BIRD ISLAND

One of the largest of the North Sound islands is the very popular Great Bird Island – visited by some 20,000 tourists annually who generally regard it as a 'desert island' dream. Whilst this is better known for its superb beaches and closely surrounding coral reefs than any wildlife, you will see the exotic red billed tropic birds (*Phaeton astherus*), sometimes the brown pelican (*Pelecanus occidentalis*) and the magnificent frigate or man o' war bird (*Fregata magnificens* – see page 108). Bird Island is a sanctuary for the afore-mentioned, precious (and harmless) racer snake, driven off mainland Antigua in the 1890s by the introduction of the mongoose.

As the world's rarest snake (indeed one of the world's rarest animals), in obvious need of protection, and with the impact of constant visitors, a conservation project began on Bird Island in October 1995, developed by the Environmental Awareness Group (see page 114).

This very attractive, gentle one-metre long *Alsophis antiguae* grass snake has a population of just about 100, confined to the island's area of only 0.083 square kilometres. Although safe from the mongoose which initially decimated it, it was subsequently threatened by black rats

(*Rattus rattus*), inadvertently introduced to the island by swimming ashore from passing boats and ships. You'll be relieved to learn that these have since been arduously and completely eradicated!

In September 1997, the EAG erected an informative welcome sign on the beach, designed to create greater awareness of the ecological importance of this particularly high-profile offshore island. Conducting regular clean-up operations, they have also helped to create a fascinating Bird Island trail guide. This short but very interesting marked route has a path to the top with panoramic views over the other islets and the northeast coast of Antigua. Students from St Joseph's Academy, St John's, who kindly volunteered to develop the trail and produce its descriptive guide, were suitably rewarded at that time, by being finalists in the prestigious *Island Magazine* eco-tourism award for their sterling efforts.

You can easily visit this enchanting outer island and enjoy swimming, snorkelling, walking, exploring, picnics and drinks through one of the day sailing tour companies (see page 162).

GUIANA ISLAND

As evidenced by findings of their flint flaked tools and ground conch-shell adzes (chisels) at several of their sites, Siboney Indians from South America first settled here about 3000 BC, followed by the peaceful agricultural and pottery making Arawak Indians (after the birth of Christ) who left ceramic remains on their sites.

The last major occupiers of Guiana Island were of manufacturing ilk, the Europeans and Africans who grew cotton and ground provisions. They all thrived particularly due to the abundant supply of marine resources.

In 1998, however, there was a ground breaking ceremony for a major hotel and leisure development. During 2000, public access to this island was not possible and this will presumably remain the situation until either the first phase is completed or other plans are formulated.

Prior to this, it was the indefatigable Mr and Mrs 'Taffy' Bufton, originally from Wales, who were the sole caretakers of the island (with no piped water, electricity, phone or radio) for over 30 years. They stoically preserved its ecological integrity, protecting and feeding the resident fallow deer, as well as the rare West Indian tree duck, the fulvous whistling duck, and the locally rare tropical mocking bird.

OTHER NORTH SOUND ISLANDS

Some of these other outer islands include Maiden Island, with its scrubby vegetation and fringing mangroves, used by local families for generations as a perfect camping ground, particularly at Easter and Crump Island, with a convenient dock and again with extensive mangroves, typical low lying vegetation, but no particular beaches; Hell's Gate Island, so named for its majestic limestone arch looking out towards the Atlantic Ocean, has a spectacular blowhole on the leeward side, forming fascinating ponds in its vicinity. Sturdy

shoes are needed to walk to this island across the small beach. The group of Galley Islands, Rabbit and Red Head Islands have incredible surrounding reefs and superb fishing. Exchange Island is a very beautiful island with tiny beaches.

The future

A management area of North Sound is gradually being developed, aiming to conserve the unique wildlife of the North Sound by raising awareness and managing the area sustainably. This group of islands' coral reefs, mangroves and sea grasses are an invaluable natural resource, which in turn contribute substantially to Antigua's economic well-being and as such it is understandably vital that great amounts of the natural environment should be retained in a healthy state.

LONG ISLAND

Further north, above the North Sound islands, is this large, private island – an exclusive resort and enclave of magnificent private villas. Visiting yachtsmen and women can enjoy the beaches here, as all in Antigua are public. Whilst the island's facilities are not available to non-residents, lunch and dinner reservations are welcome. A pleasant, 10-minute ferry ride takes you across the channel from the Jumby Bay dock at the Beachcomber hotel. Caring enormously for its environment, the island's residents put great effort into the turtle sanctuary situated on Pasture Bay (see page 104).

GREEN ISLAND

Still on the east coast, but much further south is Antigua's easternmost point, Green Island. An idyllic, uninhabited island, on the outer edge of tranquil Nonsuch Bay, it is protected from the open Atlantic Ocean by extensive reefs. With very similar vegetation to other offshore islands, it is, however, not so easy to walk through. There is a rough, rocky path up to the highest point, and sturdy shoes would be recommended. Nevertheless, the sheltered turquoise waters, snorkelling, lovely beaches and abundant seabirds attract yachtsmen and women and those seeking some peace.

Whilst leased by the luxurious Mill Reef Club, the beaches are public like all the others in Antigua and Green Island is included on some itineraries of the day sail companies (see page 162).

For those bird lovers, here are some of the birds seen in North Sound: night heron; blue heron; broadwinged hawk; sparrow hawk; osprey; frigate or man o' war bird; West Indian whistling duck; white-cheeked pin-tail; sooty tern; roseate tern; least tern bridled tern; brown noddy; laughing gull; red bill tropic bird; brown pelican; white crowned pigeon; zenaida dove; mangrove cuckoo; grey kingbird (a flycatcher); Caribbean elaenia; black whiskered vireo; kingfisher.

If not with your own or a chartered boat, the other easy and convenient access is via the boat service from Harmony Hall (see page 191). This comprehensive sightseeing, wining and dining spot offers an economical and refreshing 10-minute ride from their dinghy dock to Green Island, along with coolers and food if desired.

Should you wish to learn more about Antigua's ecology, wildlife and environment, do not hesitate to call the EAG (see also page 114) on (268) 462 6236; e-mail eag@candw.ag or visit the EAG upstairs at the Museum, Long Street, St John's.

Shopping

HERITAGE QUAY
DUTY FREE
HOPPING COMPLEX

UND LEVELS

NTRE	#1	EUROPEAN IMPORTS	#12
STORE	#2	JCM JEWELLERS (ANTIGUA) LTD	#13
SHOP	#3	SWISS AMERICAN NATIONAL BANK	#14
OOZE	#4	KRIZIA	#15
	#5	SWISS AMERICAN BANK	#16
	#6	WEST INDIES ICE COMPANY	#17
	#7	LITTLE SWITZERLAND	#18
A) LTD	#8	LA PARFUMERIE	#60/70
SPLAY	#9	GUCCI	#100
	#10	EMERALD DEVELOPMENT AGENCY	#110
	#11		

PER LEVELS

	#34	HERITAGE SPORTS	#46
	#35	SADDLERS	#47
	#36	JOANETTE BOUTIQUE	#48
	#37	SWISS AMERICAN BANK	#49
	#38	SUNSEAKERS	#51
	#39	NAF NAF INTERNATIONAL	#52
	#40	LAND SHOP	#53
ENT	#41	BENNETON	#54
	#42	PICKS OF PARADISE	#55A
	#43	TROPIC WEAR	#55B
	#44	LAUREEN'S BOUTIQUE	#71
	#45		

Shopping arcadia

How quick come the reasons for approving
what we like!

Persuasion, Jane Austen

Most people wouldn't think to end their holiday without some memento, be it inexpensive souvenirs for themselves and friends or a luxury item of crystal or jewellery. Many hotels have boutiques or shops catering to the basic needs of their guests, sometimes along with beachwear, and beach vendors are always in sight for that local piece of jewellery, t-shirts, sarongs and even bottles of natural aloe for soothing sunburn.

However, Antigua's small capital, St John's, has a surprisingly comprehensive selection of stores with internationally famous brands and first-rate local merchandise, sufficient to arouse the interest of even the most jaded shopper (see What to buy, page 45).

Moreoever, a stroll around St John's is a wonderful way to pass a morning or an afternoon, and is more than a shopping trip. It's a step back into Antiguan history and worth more than one trip even if you buy nothing. Fortunately, any redevelopment has, so far, not eaten into or dramatically changed the traditional integrity of St John's. There still remain many original wooden private residences dotted throughout the main streets in town and most building facades

have stayed intact so that the whole area still retains that fascinating display of colourings: aqua, green, ochre, yellow and blue buildings, still a delight to the eye of the beholder (see also Walking Tour of St John's, page 181).

There are small, bustling local shops lining most streets: the delightful spectacle of Historic Redcliffe Quay (see page 183), with its waterfront duty-free stores, brightly painted shops and restaurants, resonant of their eighteenth- and nineteenth-century history as warehouses and slave barracoons, and, of course, the plethora of famous names and exotic wares available at the duty-free haven of the extensive Heritage Quay.

Attractively laid out on the waterfront of St John's, Heritage Quay is one of the most prestigious duty-free shopping complexes in the Caribbean. At this modern pedestrian network, laid out on two floors, goods bought here can be taken away immediately, unlike some other islands where duty-free purchases have to be delivered to the airport or port. All you need is your passport (for proof of identification) and airline ticket (or cruise-ship pass); simply pay and take your merchandise away with you.

In St John's, you could easily spend a whole day browsing, from one complex and street to another, enjoying the village atmosphere and all that this colourful, friendly town has to offer. There are many cafés, bars and restaurants in which to peacefully take your ease with a cool drink or lunch and gather energy for the next bout of shopping. Don't forget to investigate the wares of all the traders in the Vendors Shopping Mall, between the two quays, in Thames Street.

For a really colourful, lively Caribbean atmosphere, make an early start at the Public Market at the end of Market Street in central St

Historic Redcliffe Quay

John's. Only a few minutes' walk from the very centre of town, you will find every variety of tropical fruits and vegetables, spices, plus some straw-work and local pottery. You are advised not to offend the local vendors by taking pictures without the courtesy of asking them first, as a rebuke will only disappoint you.

Parking in St John's can be difficult, particularly when cruise ships are in, but possible; just be sure to take notice of the parking restrictions, as well as the one-way-street signs.

In the north of the island is the large, modern, air-conditioned Woods Centre, just ten minutes from St John's. A first-class bookshop, First Editions, is based here, along with a variety of shops including a 'dollar' store, photographic store, baby store, music store, video store, dry cleaner's, fashion store, home furnishings store, electrical store, a beauty salon, pharmacy, a post office, and an enormous supermarket, the Epicurean, which stocks the widest range of goods and delicacies.

On the west coast, about 20 minutes from St John's, is the very attractive Jolly Harbour Shopping complex. Situated alongside the active Jolly Harbour Marina (see page 192), it has more than 40 stores and includes restaurants, bars, a bakery and sports complex.

English Harbour (see Antigua National Parks Authority, page 199) not only lures visitors with its yachts and historic buildings but has an attractive range of boutiques, shops, cafés, restaurants and bars situated at the Falmouth Marina complex, adjacent to the main road, and at the majestic Nelson's Dockyard.

Fashion is exceptionally well catered for with cool and casual clothing appropriate for the nature of Antigua's climate plus designs and fabrics suitable for wearing when you return home. Fashion stores, boutiques and shops across the island have an extensive array of lightweight attire by renowned local designers and from around the world, including the latest and most famous names and labels.

The island is a treasure trove of art, crafts, pottery and handicrafts (see page 235). Many visitors are attracted by the wealth of locally designed and handmade items available. Those interested in local art and culture would do well to seek out the shops and stores selling them, much of them reflecting Antigua's tropical colours, nature and environment, often combined with African, European and Amerindian influences.

Whilst most shops operate between 8am to 4pm during the week (possibly with a one-hour lunch break at midday), some are open to 5pm, especially on Fridays, and in the season, even to 9pm. Saturdays are generally the same timings for visitor related shops, but others may only be open for half a day, as well as the traditional half day on Thursday. On Sunday, some of the shops in Heritage and Historic Redcliffe Quays will open if a cruise ship is in the harbour.

Upon leaving the island, there is a last minute chance to browse and purchase local and luxury duty-free goods at the airport.

Prices are normally quoted in EC (Eastern Caribbean) dollars, but the larger outlets may display both EC and US prices, so check before buying. Credit cards are almost universally accepted and US currency is normally accepted at shops, but do check with out-of-town venues.

Whoever says money can't buy you happiness, doesn't know where to shop.

Anon

Basket weaver at the Industrial School for the Blind
(see page 176)

Arts and music

When one considers the average population of most of the Caribbean islands, the abundance of creative talent found surpasses the law of averages. Antigua and Barbuda is no exception. There is a wealth of fine craftspeople and artists who reflect the traditions and culture of these dual-islands' daily life. Arts, crafts, music and the performing arts are a significant part of the nation's heritage and the development of both tourism and local island tradition.

British and other European influences plus a strong celebration of African heritage are fused with West Indian customs and richly interwoven into a unique tapestry of culture: the arts, dance, theatre, poetry, music, costume and even cooking.

Creativity manifests itself in nearly every aspect of life, be it as simple as the wonderful clay pots used for cooking, dressing for church, the local dialect or major cultural events such as Carnival, Caribana, National Heritage Day, Wadadli Day or Christmas fairs and festivities.

Arts and crafts

Antigua's wild blazes of colour – from the tropical vibrant greens, the reds, oranges and yellows of its flowers, the fluorescent blue sea, the white sandy beaches and the multi-coloured sunsets form a very rich palate indeed and provide infinite inspiration.

Artists here are as diverse in their styles as they are in the materials they use. Often as not, Antigua's artists and craftspeople are to be found at their workshops scattered about the countryside. Albeit small, this twin-island nation offers the casual visitor or serious collector a wide variety of arts and crafts of the best quality and at affordable prices. The media vary enormously: water colour paintings, oil paintings, pen and ink, acrylics, hand-painted photography, collages, silk-screen work, batik, wrought iron and many others are offered in a wide spectrum of styles.

There is no national gallery for the nation's artists (Antigua Art Society, contact Jan Jackson tel: (268) 560 1364 e-mail: owenj@candw.ag), however, their works in various media can be seen and bought at many of the shops in St John's and around the island. Additionally, there are exhibitions which display all manner of arts and crafts at Island Arts (see Calendar of Events, page 70), Harmony Hall (see Calendar of Events, page 70) and the Museum of Antigua and Barbuda (see page 176).

On a more basic level, visit the public market on Friday or Saturday mornings, or take a stroll down Market Street, around Historic Redcliffe Quay, the Vendors Market and many other streets in St John's. Any day of the week you will see a wide array of excellent basketry, pottery, mini steel pans, paintings and many other forms of arts and crafts. Street vendors and beach hawkers also carry these items, as well as intricate and relatively inexpensive shellcrafts (bargaining is usual in most cases).

Wicker, woven grasses and bamboo are used to make decorative baskets and hats trimmed with bright, cotton bands that are more than just souvenirs; they are also very useful. Necessity, being the mother of invention, required the people of Antigua, from their first settlements to the present day, to practise the art of using natural materials and forming both utilitarian and decorative items. They are proficient in both, uniquely embellishing, embossing, carving, painting, and ornamenting the most functional item into a work of art.

Pottery

The art and craft of pottery making goes back millennia; pottery shards in the Antigua and Barbuda Museum date back to the Amerindians, so it is hardly surprising that it still flourishes here. Indeed, many present-day artists are beginning to incorporate the flowing, beautiful designs of the earliest Caribbean people in their work.

Whether you are interested in traditional Antiguan folk pottery, dating back to the early eighteenth century (see Coalpots, page 270) or the most modern, abstract designs, you will find Antigua has many collectable treasures, if you take the time to find them.

Different local clays, from various parts of the island have been lovingly hand formed and open-pit fired by many potters. Mainly such artisans, located in their studios, welcome visitors to see them at work, and either to buy a specific piece or to discuss a commission. Otherwise, of course, there are shops and outlets across the island where you can find various pottery items, albeit possibly of a more commercialised nature.

Sculpture

Nature is the source of much of the material used in local craft work and sculpture. Woods such as mahogany and lignum vitae are used by a number of excellent local carvers, who can invariably be found at their workshops scattered around the island. Shops in St John's, English Harbour and Jolly Harbour will also stock limited local sculptures.

Architecture

Whether influenced by the historical colonial style or the more modern American/European designs, architecture is very much based both on the necessity and the desire for an outdoor lifestyle. Daily social and functional activities often take place outside the main framework of the house, which itself is invariably of a very open nature. Even the smallest dwelling may have a gallery or verandah on which chores may be done, relaxing or entertaining enjoyed, whilst offering protection from sun and rain.

The original building method used by the early settlers was wattle and daub; a latticework of twigs and branches were covered with mud and allowed to dry, often topped with a thatched roof of palms. An example of this traditional structure can be seen on the road up to Shirley Heights and a model of a wattle and daub house is on display at the museum in St John's.

There are a few grand estate houses, built with the wealth of sugar cane income, which you may see either lovingly restored or awaiting restoration. However, a common form of dwelling which attracts much curiosity from visitors is the generations-old chattel house. These peaked wooden structures, often brightly painted, stand on blocks, above the ground. This

allows the owner to literally 'move' his or her house should he or she need to relocate from one area to another (a vital attribute, originating from the days when plantation workers did not own the land on which their houses stood). Another advantage of these lovely, small wooden dwellings is the ability to 'add on' another 'peaked' roofed room behind or at the side of the main structure. Some modern style chattel houses can be quite plain, whilst others boast wooden latticework, painted shutters, wooden railings and other decoration. Seen around the island, they all add delightfully to the quaintness, colour and atmosphere of the landscape.

As testimony to the wisdom and practicality of traditional styles, many eighteenth- and nineteenth-century two-storey buildings and small chattel houses are still firmly standing in St John's (see Walking Tour of St John's, page 181). A joy to the eye, they continue to maintain the integrity and character of Antiguan heritage and culture.

Dance

As with music and art, folklore and traditional dance owe much to the island's African heritage. Afro-Caribbean dance, rooted in African culture but with the dynamism, colour and expression unique to the West Indies, is a spectacle not to be missed. The major hotels will likely include such an event as part of their entertainment programme.

Captivating African dance and rituals with drummers and exotic costumes, sometimes in full national costume, are represented by such groups as the National Dance Theatre of Antigua and Barbuda (tel: (268) 461 9519), the Veron Stoute Dance Company, the Matumbi Dancers, and the Creative Arts Theatre Company Dancers. Local dancing groups have also formed the Antigua and Barbuda Dance Association with Veronica Yearwood as President.

The Nubian Centre for the Arts and Culture, on Airport Road, is where the Nubian Dance Theatre is based. It is also home to the Cotton Club, for the core of avid ballroom dancers on the island. Visitors are welcome to join these weekly ballroom dancing evenings, along with the distinctly more active weekly aerobic dance classes. The Nubian Centre is responsible for tirelessly endeavouring to keep the dance and performing arts aspects of local culture alive on the island. For further information on the Nubian Centre, call Nzinga Pelle tel: (268) 463 3950.

Check for announcements in newspapers, flyers and posters for new productions or shows, often staged at the Cathedral Cultural Centre or at the Multi Purpose Cultural Centre at Perry Bay. The government's Cultural Development department (tel: (268) 462 5644/3586) is often a good source of information as to what is taking place, when, and where.

Poetry and writing

Often with a rustic, quite local flavour, and sometimes in dialect, there is much insight to be gained by seeking out the work of local poets. It can open up a whole new dimension of understanding and appreciation of Antiguan and Barbudan culture, enabling one to see beneath the surface of its obvious attractions.

Inevitably, local poetry is very colourful and descriptive, concentrating on all aspects of daily life, history or religion. The Museum of Antigua and Barbuda's gift shop in St John's is an excellent source, as is the First Editions Bookshop in the Woods Centre, just outside St Johns.

A group of Antiguan writers and poets, Chrysallis, gives readings at the Hub restaurant in St John's every Thursday from 7pm, during most of the year. Poets and poetry lovers are welcome to hear both members of the group and guest artists as well as share some of their own work if desired.

There is also an Antigua Writers Guild, which embraces and welcomes all writers. For further information contact Mr Noval Lindsay tel/fax: (268) 461 5782.

Music

Music the fiercest grief can charm,
And fate's severest rage disarm.
Music can soften pain to ease,
And make despair a madness please.

Alexander Pope

Music used to be prohibited within hearing distance of the estate owners' houses during the centuries of the sugar plantocracy – for fear of provoking uprisings rather than fear of being woken by loud music. But undeterred, workers would meet a mile or so away to make their music, often using a landmark such as a tamarind tree as their meeting point.

It was during this time that the traditional fife band was conceived (see National Symbols, page 64), when spectators would dance the 'heel and toe' jig. Today, the Rio Band strives to keep these local and regional tunes alive with a charming repertoire, mainly heard as part of the larger hotels' entertainment circuits.

Following emancipation, people in the villages would organise 'singing meetings'. This was also the time when budding orators would use the Bible for refining their speeches and verses as well as recitals, poetry and hymns. Originally termed 'tea meetings' during the era of slavery (doubtless to conceal the real reason for such meetings from the estate owners), singing and speaking competitions consequently became very popular all over Antigua. Understandably, these were particularly popular with those who could neither read nor write and they became a main focal point for social interaction and participation.

Nowadays, music is in the air everywhere. It is heard from passing cars, emanating from houses, commercial buildings and shops, humming and singing by passers-by. Music is still perceived as a vital part of Antiguan and Barbudan life. Coupled with the inherent instinct for dancing, at any age, thus rhythm and music flow naturally through the West Indian body – an infectious energy which encourages even the most inhibited visitor to 'loosen up'.

The spectrum of sound to be heard is wide, from traditional music such as steel pan, calypso and gospel, moving through the more updated soca, reggae, dub and jazz to modern discotheque, hip-hop and dance-hall music. However, despite the pervasiveness of western music, you are constantly aware of the indigenous, pulsating West Indian rhythms.

There are frequent concerts throughout the year and one just has to read the newspapers and listen to the radio for announcements. These can range from the National Choir of Antigua and Barbuda, the St John's Youth Choir and Steel Orchestra, the Antigua Community Players, approaching their 50th anniversary, to the Expression Ensemble Singers, who perform cappellas, and on to the most popular bands on the island, such as the perennial kings of sound, the Burning Flames, Dread and the Baldhead and El A Kru (who regularly play at Lashing's Beach Café).

Calypso tunes, brought by West Africans to the islands at the beginning of the slave trade in the early 1600s, developed through the need to express the sentiments and stories of that era. This evolved into an often satirical form of music and was reviled by church and authority for centuries, but flourished 'underground' until these lyrical, tuneful sounds, unique to the Caribbean, became the art form they are today. Initially called 'bennas' in Antigua, which became one of the national symbols (see page 66), contemporary calypso lyrics are now more blatant and influential, and created in a witty, catchy way, ensuring a captive audience.

Extremely popular and entertaining to dance to, calypso also has a more serious side in drawing attention to highly sensitive or controversial topical subjects, becoming the unofficial voice of the people. Ascertaining the content of the latest calypso tunes will certainly apprise the visitor of the local gossip and feelings of the day regarding all manner of political and social issues.

The ambition of many a calypsonian is to woo his or her audience in the calypso 'tents', set up prior to Carnival (see page 79), sufficiently enough to secure the largest following and greatest impact on the night of the Calypso King and Queen contests, and at the same time increasing the sale of their recordings. Live calypso performances bring out the true Antiguan and Barbudan personality and are a fusion of music and theatre, as the calypsonians dance, prance and gesticulate wildly to make their point.

Steel pans (or drums) are universally recognised and respected, with homage paid to their creativity and originality by world famous artists (see page 251). From the mid-1900s, steel bands emerged in almost every village in Antigua. It was the aspiration of many a young boy to become a steel pan player and learn a tune or two on the 'ping-pong'. Pan yards sprang up all over the island and today there are many excellent steel bands playing at hotels, other venues, festivals, Carnival and, of course, at the legendary Shirley Heights 'jump-up' (see National Parks Authority, page 199). You are strongly recommended not to leave the island without hearing the skilful, lively playing of a steel band. Along with favourite modern tunes, hearing classical music on steel drums with the grace and depth of a symphony orchestra, is simply a breathtaking experience.

With its roots in Jamaica and heralded by the great, late Bob Marley, reggae has become internationally accepted and so, naturally, is on the menu of most musical presentations here. Reggae is performed by Antigua's leading groups and heard at major concerts as well as played by single performers in the corner of a restaurant. Its gentle, lilting sounds and lyrics which everyone can relate to, appeals to all.

A Fishy Business

by William Gore

Tommy was a young man of approximately 24 years. Of average height, powerfully built with pleasant features, he was a firm favourite with the ladies. He lived at Betty's Hope Garden where he worked as a head cart-man or an expert forker, who dug trenches out of the crop. He was the youngest, but he was worthy of the position. It was the duty of the head cartman, who had two helpers, to pack the cane into the cart. This may sound easy but it required skill and experience to catch the cane as handed up by his helpers and pack it expertly to fill the cart to its capacity with no possibility of its falling off on the way over the rough roads. Then again the head cartman was given a quota of oxen and they were his responsibility. He worked them as he saw fit and watched them as they drank and then fed them with linseed balls coated with black molasses. Cattle had to be overlooked as they drank their fill at the coppers because they had a tendency to over-drink.

When the cane reaping was finished, Tommy and his helpers dug trenches for drainage in the fields being planted. This was very hard work requiring a hard back [sic] to cope with clay soil; and endurance [sic] to keep this work up in the hot sun. These forkers were the aristocracy of the labourers. They worked as they saw fit, early or late, and were paid according to the amount of satisfactory work done.

Furthermore, Tommy possessed a horse and saddle when all the other labourers owned donkeys. This horse had been given to him by his uncle from Bethesda when it was only a foal, but now it was fully grown and well cared for by Tommy. He rode this horse two or three evenings a week to visit the nearby villages where he was regarded as a prime catch.

On one of his visits to the fishing village of Bethesda he became somewhat enamoured with a young lady who in due course returned his

interest. They, as was customary in those days, loved warmly but not very wisely and soon Elsie told her mother that she was pregnant.

Now it was rumoured that no one can fool around a Bethesda girl and get away with it and as Tommy did not seem anxious to pop the question, they decided to help him make up his mind. A concoction of rather esoteric ingredients including 'pond-moss' and 'brindle-dog hair', was developed and this Tommy would be persuaded to drink on his next visit.

The next Saturday night, Tommy purchased two pints of rum called by its purchasers 'mile and fall', as it was claimed that after two or three drinks, if you were walking you would fall in the first mile. In those days all rum shops bought their rum wholesale from the distillery, then coloured and mixed them to their own specifications.

When he arrived in Bethesda he was gladly welcomed as the men folk started on the rum while the meal of fish and dumplings was being prepared. The whole world is aware that the best fish for this purpose is the lady doctor as she is fatter than the male.

Now Tommy had a dog called Tiger who accompanied him on all his travels. Rolling stones, ghosts and other occult wanderers of the night are wary of dogs and don't interfere with people who are accompanied by dogs. This dog was never very far from Tommy.

The time came for the meal and a huge soup of local doctor fish and dumplings in gravy was placed in the place of honour for Tommy. The other men, like brothers, ate elsewhere at a different table. But now the 'mile and fall' was acting on Tommy and the sight of

that gravy made him shudder. Surreptitiously he managed to feed Tiger with the greater part of the fish.

When the meal was finished they started drinking again but it was obvious that Tommy was very nearly drunk. They surmised the liquor and the draught had him somewhat dizzy, but that did not matter, sooner or later he would come up with a proposal.

Soon Tommy was ready to leave but the dog could not be found. They searched all over but no Tiger. Tommy refused to leave without him. Eventually after hours of search Tiger was found in the church standing before the altar!

With thanks to the Museum of Antigua and Barbuda for permission to reprint.

Antiguan Sayings & Proverbs

Antigua's varied and rich culture has created a wonderful and colourful local patois describing everyday occurrences and life. Within these daily used sayings and proverbs are words of wisdom embodying folk values and common sense, typifying widely held opinions and morals. Here are a few you may hear:

A still tongue keep a wise head. If fish didn't open his mouth, he wouldn't get caught.
Don't talk too much.

A way you barn?
Where are you from/born?

An nah wanting a tongue, mek cattle can't talk.
You know something about a person but don't want to say.

Bush tee.
Fever grass, lime bush, soursop bush and various other bushes, making a delicious tea.

Chups.
A sound made by sucking the teeth to show displeasure or disappointment.

Cut eye.
To give a dirty look or a mother's look of 'don't touch'.

De worse o' livin' better than de bes' o' dead.
No matter how tough the going gets, it's good to be alive.

Dis sweet me bad.
I love it. It's funny.

Dress down to you teeth (or, you tack down, man).
Dressed nicely (or, you are well dressed).

Every dog is lion in he own backyard.
Even a coward is king on his own turf.

Every dog have dey day.
Your turn will come.

Every pepperpot ha'e fungee.
Every person will meet a companion.

Force make water go up hill.
Things will work out with a little effort.

Fu true, fu true.
It's the truth.

Gee Jack e' jacket.
Give credit where credit is due.

If you lie down wid dog you get up wid fleas.
If you keep bad company it will affect you.

Jumbie.
Ghost.

Jus cross dey.
Just over there (referring to giving direction).

Mash up.
Broken, break up.

Me a go a bayside today.
I am going to the beach.

Me garn.
I'm going, goodbye.

Me long fu see you.
I am longing to see you.

Me lub you bad bad.
I love you very much.

Me na know wey dat dey.
I don't know where it is.

Mek me show you.
Let me show you.

Moco jumbee.
A masquerade on stilts.

No push you head where you body can't pass.
Don't take on what you can't finish.

No tek me picture.
Do not take my photograph.

Obeah.
A form of black magic.

Old Year's night.
New Year's Eve.

One hand washes the other.
We help each other.

People like peas.
A vast crowd.

Plantain sucker follow de root.
Like father, like son.

Standpipe.
Waterpipe seen at street corners.

Wa eye no see heart no grieve.
What one does not see does not bother one.

Wah mek?
Why? What is the reason?

Wan ton ah people.
A large crowd.

When me done with sardines, me no meddle
with de tin.
Once you have hurt me, I won't trust you as a
friend again.

Whine up yourself.
Dance.

You drop something?
You have forgotten to give the usual greeting or
salutation.

The Museum of Antigua and Barbuda has
a comprehensive selection of reasonably
priced, locally written books and
booklets relating to Antigua
and Barbuda available
from their gift shop.
First Editions bookshop
at Woods Centre
sometimes also stocks
local poetry books.

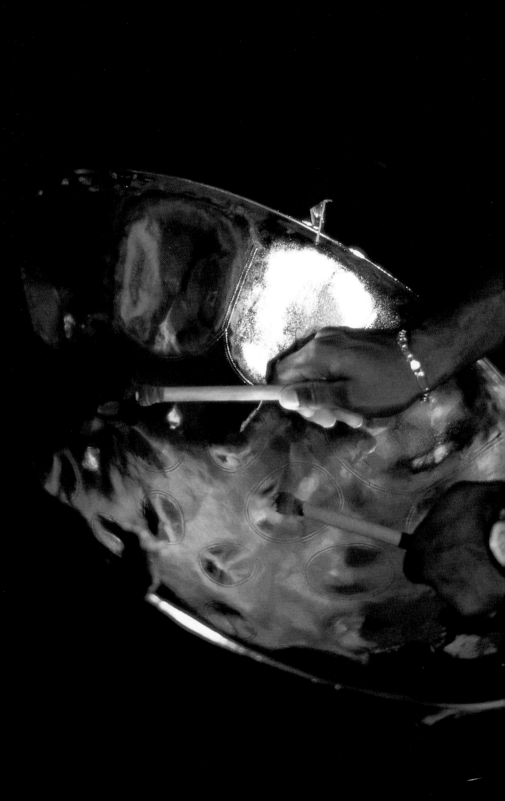

Rhythm in steel

So de man take de pan,
Wid de hammer in he han'
An' he say how he understand
Dat if de pan making one,
And de pan making two,
Den de pan can make quite a few.

So de man take de pan,
Wid de hammer in he han'
And he stoop down dere on de ground,
And he heat it,
And he beat it,
And he stretch it,
And he mark it,
And de pan start to make a new sound,
And de pan start to make a new sound.

From *Pan Rap*, about the creator and creation of steelpan, by the famous Grenadian/Trinidadian storyteller, Paul Keens-Douglas.

If people were asked the question, 'What was the last musical instrument to be developed?', it is likely there would be very few correct responses. The simple, but possibly surprising, answer is, the steel pan (the one before that was the saxophone).

Steel bands produce a distinctive and instantly recognisable sound known as pan. Such bands came into existence in the 1940s at the acknowledged birthplace of steel band music, Trinidad. They were the direct descendents of the pre-war Tamboo-Bamboo bands and gained respectability from 1950, when the first pan competition was held there.

Within another decade, and by then identified with the traditional calypso beat, pan was an established part of West Indian culture. Within a generation a steel band was playing Borodin and Offenbach at Carnegie Hall in a Liza Minnelli concert. Bands now may range in size from the conventional groups of 10 to 20 players to magnificent orchestras with 100 or more players.

Unbelievable to the average person, the basic material of the steel band is still actually an unromantic, ordinary 45- or 55-gallon oil drum.

This is an odd source of sound, but nevertheless, the science of sound applies as much to a steel drum as it does to a gleaming and expensive kettle drum. A steel pan has, in effect, a whole series of smoothed and shaped surfaces, each of which produces a different note.

The shallowest, the tenor pan, has 32 notes, while the bass pan, using the full length of the original oil drum, has only eight.

A steel band is made up of several types of pan, all corresponding to orchestral instruments. Tenor pans carry the melody; double tenor pans provide the harmony and guitar pans set the beat. Although bands have their own techniques for making their drums, all are chromatic and all the pitches are internationally accurate to play with violin, guitar, and so on.

Whilst these pannists still play entirely by ear, where rhythm seems to be a sixth sense, these surprisingly complex instruments can range over five octaves and virtually cover the full musical capacity of a symphony orchestra. Their repertoire extends from simple folk melodies, through reggae, jazz, Latin, melodic Strauss waltzes to the most complicated classical arrangements and professional musicianship.

With neither music scores nor a conductor, whilst impressive for even the simplest of melodies, this is a

phenomenal feat for such intricate, varied arrangements, which all have to be kept in the head! The most experienced bands can beat pan for five or six hours without repetition.

The fascination of this most stimulating and sophisticated music from a group of steel pans is no better epitomised than that emanating from the extremely proficient musicians of Antigua and Barbuda. Antigua may not be the founder of steelbands, but, having met with some resistance, it takes the credit for being the place where critics were first challenged in court to prove that the steel pan was a musical instrument.

Local transformation of the oil drum to a musical instrument, called a 'Ping Pong' (currently pan) was as early as 1945. In the earlier stages, the instruments used were bits of iron, empty metal bins and hollowed pipes, and so on, obtained from various blacksmiths and refuse dumps. When the steel band movement started and early band members had mastered the pan and its two rubber tipped sticks for playing, they went into St John's one Saturday, drawing vast crowds. This momentous event heralded the true advent of the steel band in Antigua and the second place on earth to have one.

However, for some time, people claimed the pan music sounded like a 'hell yard' when the gate was closing, and so evolved the band 'Hell's Gate'. From the early 1950s, this steel band was regularly invited to play at Government House for garden and cocktail parties and at Christmas. Brute Force was another major steel band at this time and, along with Hell's Gate, were the first in the world to record their music, released in 1952. It was also in 1952 when the first all-girl steel band was formed, breaking many social barriers as a result.

Antigua boasts many exciting steel bands and most play regularly at hotels island-wide. The following are the most famous and those you may see and hear whilst on the island are (and maybe in your home country, as they all travel frequently giving overseas concerts): the Hell's Gate Steel Orchestra, the Halcyon Steel Orchestra, the Harmonites International Steel Orchestra, the Gemonites, Le Chateau D'or, Supa Stars, Heartbeat, the Roots Steelband (the second steel orchestra in Antigua since the early 1950s to record their music on CD 'Moods of Pan I') and the National Pan Orchestra, amongst others. In the quest to keep this imperative Antiguan heritage alive, the Culture Department (tel: (268) 462 5644) conducts a junior school of pan and takes a keen interest in encouraging such classes. One such instructor, the universally acclaimed 'guru' of pan and steel band ambassador, is the Antiguan Victor 'Babu' Samuel. Members of the Antigua Steelband Association, with Leon 'Kuma' Rodney as president, keep island-wide pan programmes alive.

Be sure not to miss the romance of pan and to experience such noble ascendancy of Caribbean culture. These still present glory days of pan, as yet unaffected by the technology of the microchip world, thankfully continue to be honoured by the Caribbean people in what is their heritage and surely their second language.

The subtle resonances of this unique music is totally evocative of tropical, balmy nights and its sounds will astound and simply overwhelm you, guaranteeing you will hear the tree frogs and swaying of palms when heard once back home. Buy a tape and catch your breath as you relive the moments!

De whole music world talking 'bout de
steelband,
Experts cannot understand what dey hear,
Sweet, sweet music coming from out a
steelpan,
Music that could make angels shed a tear.

Tribute to the Panman, Pete Simon

BUILDING THE PANS

The curious and complicated tradition of creating music from oil drums continues and such innovative handicraft takes place at the band's panyard. This is also generally where a band practises to beat pan. Here the atmosphere of the workshop will be full of smoke from a fire of burning petrol and old tyres, hot enough to temper steel.

One such craftsman in Antigua, Eustace 'Gaytooks' Harris, has not only been perfecting his ability to make pans but also has his own steel band, the Gospanics. From his Grays Farm panyard, he has been supplying international clients as well as many of the local bands most of his life, with orders coming from Atlanta, USA, the Virgin Islands and Brazil.

After first tempering the oil drum over a simple fire, Gaytooks allows it to cool before cutting the drum to the required depth, depending on the type of pan required. Then comes the sensitive job of sinking the surface of the end of the drum with a special hammer so it becomes a smooth concave basin and forms the playing surface. Exact care has to be taken for the next stage of marking, the positions where the notes will be put, then separating them out by grooving. A nail-like tool is used for this purpose, creating grooves one-sixteenth to one-eighth of an inch

apart to isolate the notes from each other. The drum is now prepared for ponging up. That is, each note is very carefully hammered up from below the shallow dome, initially sending out unbalanced, flat notes.

Finally, after burning the pan to help it achieve a better tone, there is the delicate and most difficult task of tuning. Requiring infinite patience, Gaytooks taps each note with a hammer until it is in tune. This is quite a mysterious and precise art. Once each note has been done, he will have to start again, as most of the notes in the process will have gone out of tune again. Eventually, using his consummate skill, he coaxes, develops and settles these wild notes onto the curved metal and they resound, singing out into the warm Antigua air.

Whilst important not to mix up the builder and the master tuner, Gaytooks is, very unusually, both, and many consider it a privilege to sit and watch him at work. With the tremendous responsibility involved in creating such musical instruments, he takes his craft very seriously and intensely indeed.

Eating out

Eating out

– a mingling of traditional and international cuisines from diverse cultures

One cannot think well, love well, sleep well,
if one has not dined well
　　　　　Virginia Woolf *A Room of One's Own*

Visitors to Antigua will find a varied and interesting choice of dining spots on the island from first-class gourmet restaurants as fine as you would expect to find anywhere in the world, to colourful waterfront cafés, beach bars and fast food outlets. From hamburgers to haute cuisine to West Indian inspired and local dishes, Antigua has them all.

Whether you are seeking breakfast, lunch or dinner, you'll soon discover Antigua offers a range of delightful cuisine with an appealing mix of dining opportunities to suit all budgets and just about every taste.

Dishes and food you will be familiar with

from back home are readily available but it would seem such a shame not to experiment with all manner of exotic fruits, vegetables and spices (see also Antiguan Cuisine, page 261).

A notable number of French, Italian, English, North American, Mexican, Chinese, Indian and even Middle Eastern eateries exist reflecting the diverse population here. However, mainly prevalent are restaurants serving freshly prepared foods with African and western influences, as well as the French West Indian flavours of the spicy Creole cuisine. If staying in a hotel, you are likely to be offered a choice of both international and local dishes, as well as superb buffet dinners and succulent barbecues.

Breakfast, from your usual fare to local specialities, can be found in hotels, restaurants and cafés around the island. Favoured lunch spots for visitors tend to be casual or al fresco, at beach bars or cafés, inevitably serving excellent lobster, prawns and fish, with 'catch of the day' being a good value option, plus the ubiquitous hamburger and fries. The choice of meat ranges from first-class cuts imported from the US and Canada, to the growing and very good local trade, particularly in tasty pork, lamb and chicken.

BOTTLED HEAT!
HOT PEPPER SAUCE

Do not underestimate the fire-power of the reddish-orange coloured sauce often found on the tables of dining establishments. Be judicious with your initial tasting as this spicy sauce can have 50 times the heat of jalapeno peppers!

Containing a mixture of different types of peppers, it is blended with various spices and vinegar. Adored by West Indians it is used on all meats and fish and its excellent flavour becomes very popular with visitors. A reasonable and indigenous souvenir of the Caribbean, bottles of different pepper sauces can be found in supermarkets and gift shops – perfect to take home.

Drinks range from locally made fruit squashes and non-alcoholic drinks, including universally known soft-drink brands and bottled mineral water, to every type of alcoholic beverage, with a never-ending list of intriguing cocktails. Many bars feature discounted prices or 'two-fers' during their happy hour, which may vary from late afternoon to early evening, or even during mid- or late evening. There is an excellent range of beers available, whilst many of the locals' favourite tipple is either bottled Guinness or, naturally, rum.

Eating out is a popular and informal affair here, and many restaurants and cafés are open-air and well cooled or air-conditioned. Dress code here is very informal – casual during the day, but 'elegantly casual' in restaurants in the evening. Dinner reservations are normally recommended, especially in season and last orders in some restaurants can be as early as 9.30pm.

Check the menu and your bill to ascertain whether the prices and total amount are in EC or US dollars, to which government tax and invariably a service charge will be added. Major credit cards are accepted in most restaurants (check beforehand), although whilst fast food outlets and local cafés would only expect local EC dollar cash, US dollars and US dollar traveller's cheques are also often accepted.

The local newspapers and visitor publications will have some of the more popular dining spots, varying from snacks and quick, casual dining to sophisticated candlelit dinners. The dining out picture is an ever-evolving one. A new season can bring new faces, menus, hours of service and prices charged, so it is wise to call to confirm information in advance.

For a truly local, relaxed affair, try one of the 'rum shops' (see page 282) or a very economical and tasty local 'fish fry'. Traditionally, fish frys are available on Friday and Saturday from late afternoon until the early hours. Only found in local areas, villages usually have at least one household or premises where you can sample the freshest of fish cooked in all manner of ways, steamed, fried and so on, along with 'fish water' (a fish soup stew), conch, seafood, and sometimes goat water (goat soup stew). Have a memorable time!

He who does not mind his belly will hardly mind anything else

Dr Samuel Johnson

Antiguan cuisine

There's culture in the kitchen in Antigua. The island's history is deliciously reflected in its cookpots and traditional recipes. Aromatic, pungent, tangy dishes emerging from the simmering pots of Antiguan homes and restaurant kitchens give mouth-watering testimony to the diverse cultures and civilisations which have contributed to the island's way of life as we appreciate it today.

Distinctive Antiguan dishes are the result of centuries of tradition fused with Amerindian, English and African influences. It is said that, 'necessity is the mother of invention', and none was truer for the first settlers. Everyone was obliged to make 'a six a nine' and stretch available provisions with improvisation and creation. Antiguans enjoy fresh and hearty food – perfect sustenance, colourful and invariably with no waste.

Any visit here would not be complete unless you sample the exotic fruits, vegetables and local specialities while you are here. Don't just stick to those familiar items you see on the menus, dishes you can find back at home. Be adventurous and add to your experience of visiting Antigua by enjoying new tastes, learning about new foods you have probably never heard of, and may not find again when you return home. Be assured that they are nourishing and healthy, and, since they are locally grown (or plucked from the sea) they are likely to be fresher, sweeter and richer in colour than much of the fruit, vegetables and seafood you get back home.

Having gained much respect from visitors who increasingly seek out local dishes, Antiguan cuisine features a large variety of fresh fish and seafood, exotic vegetables and fruit, notably the succulently sweet 'black' pineapple, one of its national symbols (see page 65).

If you believe, as many do, that the pineapple is a relatively recent cultivation grown primarily in Hawaii, or in South Africa, you will be surprised to learn that a superbly sweet and delicious pineapple has been grown in Antigua for the past 2000 years. In England as far back as the seventeenth century King Charles II raved about the fruit as much as his wife, Catherine, raved about West Indian sugar which sweetened her tea. Sir Walter Raleigh brought not only tobacco back to England; he brought back the pineapple, which he found, ate and enjoyed during his expedition to what was to become Venezuela at the end of the sixteenth century. The fruit looked like a pine cone, and was thus given the name pineapple.

Historically, it appears that the Arawaks brought the pineapple plant to Antigua when they left South America in about 30 AD and paddled their way around the Caribbean islands looking for new lands. The volcanic soil in the south of Antigua suited the plants, turning the skin a dark yellow, giving the fruit the unique name of Antigua black.

When the first English settlers arrived in 1630, establishing themselves initially at Falmouth, they subsequently cultivated the Antigua black pineapple in and around the area. In 1789 John Luffman, wrote:

> The pines of the island are superior to all others, both in size and taste, there are two sorts, the yellow and the black, equally grateful, and in the proper seasons, as many may be bought for one or three shilling sterling as would fill a bushel.

A field of pineapples

Another and later devotee was Archie Bell who in his book, *The Spell of the Caribbean Islands*, wrote of his visit to Antigua in the mid-1920s and of the 'pineapples, from which, when the top is cut off, the distilled honey may be eaten with spoons'.

The black pineapple was cultivated in substantial quantities here until the nineteenth century, when sugar cane took over as the prime cash crop. Nevertheless, the popularity of this delectable Antiguan pineapple ensured a captive market for farmers, who still devote fields to its cultivation. The crops are easily seen, particularly when driving through Urlings and Old Road villages in the south. You can see these small gems for sale, lined up on the roadside stalls, right along to Fig Tree Drive or seek them out at some of the local supermarkets and at St John's market. Do not forego the opportunity to sample its nectar; it is truly a very special, sweet treat, unlike any other pineapple you will have tasted.

Of course the Antiguan black pineapple is not the only inheritence from the Arawaks – or for that matter the fierce Caribs, who probably combined some of their specialities with those of the Arawak they fought and usually conquered. One of these dishes, famous not only in Antigua but elsewhere in the West Indies, is pepperpot. Traditionally eaten here with fungee (a tasty ball of cornmeal and minced okra), the two form Antigua's national dish (see page 64).

Pepperpot is a nourishing, flavoursome, thick stew made with salted beef, pork, pigeon peas and an assortment of local vegetables. However, what gives pepperpot its 'kick' is its vital injection of local seasoning: a mixture of minced sweet peppers, onions, chives, thyme, marjoram, garlic, and a little hot pepper. The Arawaks made pepperpot in a big hole in the ground and kept it bubbling for weeks, constantly adding to the stew with fresh meat. It is not all that different, one might note, from traditional stews made in many parts of Europe

PINEAPPLE SYMBOLS

Whilst, in ancient times, the Middle East in particular regarded the pineapple as a symbol of fertility. Once it was introduced to Europe in the seventeenth century, it symbolised hospitality which explains the oft-sighted shapes of pineapples atop gate piers and entrance pillars.

This may also explain why, a century later, American sailors returning from West Indian travels would announce their arrival home by putting a pineapple on their gatepost. Such was the golden fruit's worthiness that its popularity spread in colonial America, adorning all forms of decorative arts from china to wallpaper. When Lord Dunmore, Governor of New York and then Virginia, returned home to his seat at Dunmore, Stirlingshire, Scotland, in 1777, he built the famed pineapple folly by way of announcing his arrival home.

Since then, the pineapple has continued to inspire artists, interior designers and potters and imaginative designs of this bountiful fruit can be seen in countless forms on china, fabrics and other decorative objects for the home.

and the United States. So, if you find it anywhere on any menu, or are invited to sample it at an Antiguan's home – do try it.

Invariably, there's always a pot of soup on the stove of Antiguan households, consisting of ground provisions and meat or fish. This could be oxtail soup, bullfoot soup, fish braff (broth) and 'man' soup, a particularly hearty concoction. Potato dumplings or bread would accompany these perennial local favourites.

Ducana, a great Antiguan speciality, is a tasty vegetable dish of grated sweet potato, pumpkin and carrot, mixed with butter, coconut, spices such as nutmeg and steamed in ducana, banana leaf or simply in foil. Another traditional old-time meal is salt fish, served as a hearty stew or served with fungee and dumplings. A popular salt fish, the ling fish, is also soaked and boiled, served on its own or with a seasoned sauce of onions and tomatoes. This may come with 'Johnny cakes', plantain, boiled dumplings or sweet potato.

'Goat water' is a favourite Antiguan dish and traditionally takes pride of place at wedding receptions, christenings, baptism, and so on. This is actually a stew; tender stewed goat is cooked with onions, butter, chives, thyme, cloves and browning and served alone or with bread to mop up the delicious gravy.

Then there are various types of West Indian curries, souse (boiled pork steeped in a salted water and lime juice marinade with onions, sweet peppers, a little hot pepper, garlic and spices, often served with bread to soak up the delicious juices) and a variety of meats which are prepared and cooked in different ways, often served with peas and rice. This savoury accompaniment uses pigeon or black-eyed peas, freshly available from November to March or dried.

When you order a dish of seasoned rice, you will get more than just a plate of rice. This is prepared with pigeon peas, onions, minced seasoning and different pieces of meat.

Popular in the Caribbean islands and widely available in Antigua, try the filling and tasty roti. Inspired by East Indian cuisine, this is ordered as a great, cheap snack or as a complete local 'fast food' meal in itself. Suitable for vegetarians, a tortilla-like wrapping is filled with lightly curried potato, vegetable and spices or with chicken and beef.

Apparently, the West Indians consume more chicken per head than anywhere else in the world. Hence, many diverse chicken dishes can be sampled, but the most 'local' way to enjoy one of them is from one of the many barbecue stands, in the early evening. It was the Carib Indians who first smoke-dried or cooked meat on a brabacot – a stand made up of sticks and animal bones which was placed over a fire. The Spanish adapted this art and called it barbacoa, hence the name barbecue. Particularly over the weekends, late afternoon and early evening you will see the simple wayside stalls of vendors where you can buy seasoned, freshly cooked chicken legs, wrapped in foil, served with barbecue sauce – and a paper napkin!

There will be many fruits, spices and vegetables which first time visitors may not be aware of. Take breadfruit, for example. For this strange, cannon ball like green vegetable which grows on trees in abundance around the island, that famous – or infamous – captain of HMS *Bounty*, Captain Bligh, has to be thanked. He brought it to the West Indies from the South Pacific. In its summer harvest season it is baked, boiled, deep fried, sautéed and stuffed.

Another popular vegetable is plantain, which looks like a banana but isn't, and it has to be cooked. The best way to eat it is fried or baked, like a yam – which you will find here and prepared exactly the same way.

Certainly there are also vegetables and fruits you will be served in Antigua which will be familiar: carrots, potatoes, courgettes, beans, pumpkin (frequently served here as an amazingly tasty and popular soup), marrows and corn-on-the-cob, oranges, bananas, grapes, apples, salad stuffs and a variety of tropical and subtropical fruits. But in addition you will see on the menus and be served such vegetable exotica as eddoe and cassava, and fruits such as mango, pawpaw, soursop and passion fruit. Tastes do differ, naturally, but do try everything.

That includes a wealth of fish. Red snapper is quite a delicacy here, a beautifully light, tasty fish prepared in a myriad of ways. Other popular fresh fish dishes will include: king fish, barracuda, grouper, swordfish, tuna, and many more served as simply pan-fried with some local lime juice or prepared with a Creole tang. You may see the famous West Indian flying fish on menus, so-called because it skims across the surface of the water for incredible distances as though on wings. This delicate fish will fly at your plate in several savoury forms. Dolphin is found frequently on menus all over the island. As mentioned previously, this is not the dolphin of the 'Flipper' type, who cavorts at sea aquariums to the delight of children of all ages, but the dolphin fish, mahi-mahi or dorado, no relation whatsoever. You can enjoy it with a clear conscience.

Seafood is enormously favoured with huge prawns and local lobster topping the bill, with less common ones such as the tempting, spicy crab backs and conch (you will recognise its familiar large, pink lined shell used for decoration in restaurants, on verandahs and lining gardens).

What gives Antiguan cuisine its special flavour is its generous use of many herbs and spices, locally referred to as 'seasoning', giving it a piquancy that wakes up the tongue and the palate in a delightful way.

Most of these herbs and spices are grown on the island or on nearby islands, and though you can find these at home too, they are combined in Antiguan dishes in the most unique and delightful ways. Pepper, chilli, thyme, marjoram, garlic, spring onions and cloves are mixed with a magical touch to bring the spice of life to Antiguan cuisine.

Many Antiguans have a sweet tooth and their desserts are a perfect ending to such appetising meals. Most restaurants and hotels serve wonderful locally made ice-cream in various flavours, including those made from the widely used coconut and local tropical fruit. Key lime pie, coconut pie, flambéed bananas with rum, stewed tropical fruit such as 'guava stew', sweet puddings, sugar cakes, guava cheese, carrot cake,

banana bread, bread pudding, chocolate cake and more are other favourites.

One of the best ways to familiarise yourself with Antiguan local fare is to visit the colourful, bustling marketplace in St John's. Market day is a time honoured custom, almost a social event. Early Friday and Saturday mornings are especially good times to pass by, when local farmers come to town to deliver their fresh country produce.

To create local dishes at home and to relive your holiday memories, take home the bottled seasoning, hot pepper sauce and spices found at many supermarkets. You could also look out for locally made preserves and chutneys, guava jam, marmalade and Antiguan acacia or logwood honey. And don't forget a bottle of Antiguan rum (see page 271)!

Coconut palm

Bush medicine

Virtually every culture has its share of foods, plants, herbs and spices considered prized for their healing properties. Such a culture still exists in Antigua. A rich heritage of 'bush medicine' is handed down through the local 'experts' of the family and much is still applied to today's illnesses and ailments. Over the generations, natural products were the settlers' only source of home remedies, to alleviate all manner of complaints. Many were also extensively utilised for seasoning, beverages, confectionery and general cooking. The list of centuries-old folk cures and health-giving 'medicines' which still exist in Antigua is extensive, and for interest, here are a few and their alleged curative properties.

Aloe (*Aloe vera*): already covered in the Flora and Fauna section (see page 97), this fleshy plant bursting with its strong smelling greenish jelly is widely used by locals and visitors to cool and soothe sun-exposed or itchy skin. It can be taken internally as a laxative, stimulating bile flow and digestion, or mixed with egg and molasses, as a popular, pleasant-tasting tonic. Its natural bitterness has been used to discourage nail biting in children.

Arrowroot (*Maranta arundinacea*): the root of this rhyzome is grated, boiled and allowed to settle to alleviate diarrhoea.

Big thyme (*Coleus amboinicus*): another ingredient of bush tea and infused alone as a tea believed to help flatulence.

Breadfruit (*Artocarpus altilis*): the leaves are infused in boiling water for hypertension (high blood pressure).

Cattle tongue (*Pluchea symphytifolia*): the leaves are regularly used as a tea for colds, in a warm bath to overcome fever, and dried as a poultice.

Chickweed (*Stellaria media*): the leaves are boiled for the treatment of bronchitis, pleurisy, coughs, colds, hoarseness, rheumatism, inflammation and as a poultice for skin disease, boils and burns.

Christmas bush (*Eupatorium odoratum*): a glossy leaved shrub which is one ingredient of the very pleasant bush tea, taken daily in most Antiguan households. Used for fighting off colds, it has a cinnamon-like fragrance and is often boiled with basil. Antiguans often eat porridge for breakfast, infusing a leaf of this bush in the boiling mix and taking it out when ready to eat. The leaves are also applied as a poultice for wounds.

Garlic (*Allium sativum*): locally used in cases of hypertension (high blood pressure) and for indigestion and flatulence.

Guava (*Psidium guajava*): the fruit is rich in vitamin C, iron and calcium and valued as a delicious jelly or jam. The bark, leaves and buds are infused in hot water in cases of diarrhoea and dysentery. Containing antibacterial properties, the juice from the leaves is reportedly good for stings, insect bites and infused for bathing wounds. Inhalation of the scent from the crushed leaves is said to help fainting spells. The boiled leaves mixed with cold water are used to soothe prickly heat externally and to ease swollen gums and mouth inflammation as a gargle or mouthwash.

Ginger (*Zingiber officinale*): as aloe is used for many external problems, so the ginger root is boiled for most internal ailments. Extensively used as a digestive stimulant and to alleviate flatulence, it is also added to bush tea as a remedy to relieve fever.

Lemon grass: locally called fever grass, is recommended as an infusion and taken as a tea for fevers.

Mint/Peppermint (*Mentha piperita*): the family of mint plant is utilised to stengthen the stomach and relieve indigestion, and peppermint tea for gastric upsets, nausea and for the relief of flatulence. Oil of peppermint is traditionally applied externally for toothache, headache, neuralgia, burns and rheumatism.

Parsley (*Petroselinum sativum*): rich in iron, vitamins C and A and folic acid, chewing the

Lemon grass

good for high blood pressure and its seeds and fruit for the relief of constipation. The boiled leaves and fruit help treat acute and chronic cystitis. Mashed ripe pawpaw mixed with orange juice is even used as a face pack for pimples or acne.

Pimento (*Pimenta officinalis*): oil from the green leaves is said to be good for indigestion and flatulence, whilst the fruit is also taken for upset stomach and diarrhoea.

Soursop leaves (*Annona muricata*): a native evergreen to the West Indies, the flesh of the prickly, kidney-shaped fruit is infused in water, strained, sweetened and drunk to help cool the blood in the event of heat rash. The crushed leaves produce a scent inhaled for dizziness and fainting spells and the infused leaves in hot water make a sedative tea in the case of insomnia.

Sugar apple (*Annona squamosa*): crushed leaves as an inhalant for fainting spells and a tea from the infused leaves for flatulence and diarrhoea.

Tamarind (*Tamarindus indica*): often seen sugared and eaten by children as tamarind balls, the brownish pod full of acid paste is consumed as a juice, jam or other sweetened forms as a natural purgative. Chopped and boiled bark of this tree is taken for the treatment of asthma.

Thyme (*Thymus vulgaris*): several varieties are used as a tea for spasmodic coughing, pains due to uterine disorders and kidney stones. The oil, called thymol, is said to be a strong antiseptic, and therefore used judicially, is taken in mouthwashes.

A less natural and most extraordinary remedy used throughout all the Caribbean islands is the use of the canned lubricant WD40! Some locals swear by it for rheumatism and spray it on their seized up, painful joints for purported real relief!

fresh leaves helps to rid the lingering after effects of garlic and onion. A tea from the infused leaves is believed to reduce the pain of arthritis and rheumatism, whilst this tea is also used to aid difficult urination, dropsy and jaundice (not recommended internally if kidney inflammation prevails).

Pawpaw (*Carica papaya*): with 45 species of this plant indigenous to the West Indies and Central America, it is extremely popular. Its digestive enzyme, papain, found both in the fruit and the leaves is universally acknowledged. Meat wrapped in the leaves and left to rest becomes tenderised; the crushed unripe, green fruit mixed with juice is said to also be

Folk pottery and the coalpot

Termed 'pepper pots', round bottomed, base-less pots were made on the sugar plantations by the African slaves. Placed on the fire, the pots were used for boiling the meat and vegetable stew, known as pepperpot (Antigua's national dish, see page 64). These Afro-Antiguans also made the 'yabba', a simple circular plate or frying pan, very similar to the earlier Arawak cassava pottery griddle, used for roasting and in the making of cassava bread and dumplings.

It was the people of Seaview Farm village who first learnt how to apply heat to clay and make their cooking pots more durable. The clay around that area was thought to be the only type on the island which could withstand and harden properly to heat; an art which was apparently taught to these villagers by the mill tower builders at the end of the seventeenth century.

However, it would appear that this took time to catch on around the island as some of the first coalpots seemed to have curiously been made of wood; at least it is said that when 260 houses caught fire in St John's in 1769, the devastation was caused by a wooden coalpot catching fire. Later, Mrs Lanaghan, in 1843 wrote in her invaluable record of the island, *Antigua and the Antiguans*,

the Antigua coalpot is nothing more than a deal box, clamped with iron or tin and lined with bricks plastered over ... no bellows are used except ... the owner's lungs ... or their large straw hat displaced from their heads ... with sundry ejaculations of 'Eh! Eh! war do de co-als today, me b'lieve dem no want to burney.'

Clearly, the popular cottage industry of pottery making subsequently changed and after emancipation when local villages were formed, with the gradual improvement of living conditions and a growing population, the demand for such folk pottery increased. With readily available natural resources, Seaview Farm village became the pottery making centre and 'king village'. Although sadly diminishing in production, locally fired and crafted household utensils and plant pots are still made here.

Driving around the island, you are bound to see the still widely used clay coalpot. A shape similar to the yabba sits atop a hollow base with an opening where charcoal is placed. The wide, dished plate above is studded with holes, so that when the fire is lit below, all manner of foods can be cooked or barbecued above. Wayside stalls use them for tasty chicken and fish snacks, and vendors on street corners set them up for the ever-popular roasted corn. It is indeed very tempting! The coalpot is now also a common sight in most Antiguan households. Typically on the back step, or in the garden, they offer a quick and tasty meal.

Women at Seaview Farm continue to collect the local clay to create their traditional pottery and it is still made in the time honoured way, without the wheel, moulds or coils and with their signature finger indentation as decoration. Either visit the village personally or more easily, visit the market, especially on a Saturday to view their wares and support these valuable artisans.

Rum revelry

– the spirit of Antigua

Rum conjures up the very essence of the Caribbean, home to all of the world's most famous brands and best loved spirits. It kindles images of romance, long sun-drenched days and heady music-filled nights.

Its history in this area originates from 1493 when Columbus brought sugar cane cuttings from the Canary Islands and first planted them in the West Indies. By the mid-1700s, sugar cane production was thriving and the discovery of this sweet liquor, known as rum, became the region's economic base. Many legends abound as to the origins of its name but it was accepted into the English language in 1651 as 'rumbullion', later shortened to 'rum' and still defined as a 'spirit distilled from sugar'.

Rum was initially produced here in the mid-seventeenth century on Antigua's first sugar plantation, Betty's Hope (see page 198), where later plans of the estate in 1710 and 1755 show separate buildings for the distillation of rum, and as witnessed by the many remaining sugar mills dotted around the island. As a by-product of refining sugar, molasses was used by many estate owners to create their own rum concoctions using crude 'pot stills'. Locally it was often referred to as 'mile and fall' (see A Fishy Business, page 246), as it was claimed that after two or three drinks, if you were walking, you would fall in the first mile. Due to the rare, favourable natural conditions prevailing on the island, Antigua's excellent light, mellow rum became well known for its uniquely elegant, fine characteristics.

When rum production finally ceased in the early 1900s, individual rum shop owners took over creating their own blends as tasty home brews, as an embrocation for fevers and with a high strength rum as an essential for the medicine chest. Realising the need to consolidate and maintain Antiguan rum, a group of nine enterprising Antiguan businessmen formed Antigua Distillery Ltd in 1932. The first continuous still was set up on the island and this was possibly the first local industry using only local capital.

The company bought nine estates and a small sugar factory in 1934, from English plantation owners who were retiring from the sugar industry. Producing its own molasses, Antigua Distillery sold two types of rum, an unaged rum and an

aged matured rum, called Caballero Rum. In the early 1950s, with a rum aged for a minimum of two years in oak casks, the first bottled product emerged named Cavalier Muscovado Rum.

However, as tastes and trends altered, by the 1960s the distillation had been changed to create the lighter bodied rum for which Antigua had first been honoured. As time progressed, several new brands of rum were introduced in the Cavalier range: a light, colourless aged rum, a 151-proof rum, and a special aged five-year-old rum, favoured by connoisseurs, in commemoration of Antigua and Barbuda's independence in 1981. These were all in addition to the normal Cavalier Antigua Rum blend.

Recognising the 25th anniversary of the famous Antigua Sailing Week, this privately owned company launched the English Harbour Antigua Rum brand in April 1992. With an exceptionally smooth mellow flavour, this rum benefits from a 'marrying' of older rums, with no articifial flavouring required. Such blending is carried out in aged oak vats for a minimum of six years, ensuring the true Antiguan characteristics – perfect consumed straight or 'on the rocks' with a twist of lime. Testifying to such ancestry of traditional skills and distinctive flavour, English Harbour Antigua Rum was honoured as winner of the Bronze award at the London-based International Wine and Spirits Competition in 1995.

All Antigua distillery rums are still produced and sold with the classic minimum two year-ageing process. Maintaining traditional practices, only copper pipes are used or a Coffey still for their five-column continuous patent. A master blender selects barrels, by both 'nosing' and tasting before they are blended. Matured in small 200-litre charred oak barrels, over 10,000 barrels are stored on their side in the company's warehouses, ensuring availability of aged spirits for premium rums. With two bottling lines packaging over 60 bottles a minute, the company exports to most of the Eastern Caribbean and due to its ever-growing popularity has entered the markets of the US, Canada, the UK and Belgium.

Sticks of sugar cane. Inset: chewing raw sugar cane

At the height of cane production at Betty's Hope, one acre of prime plantation land normally yielded 25–30 loads of cane, converting to one ton of sugar. One load of cane could produce up to 100 gallons of juice, depending on rainfall and age of the cane. One ton of sugar made 30 gallons of rum.

Taken only as an unmixed drink it was Mozart's favourite. Until around the early 1800s, it was the 'Rum Punch' (a mixture of rum, bitters, lime juice and crushed ice), which later became one of the most famous rum drinks. When Cuba gained independence from Spain in 1898, the well-known 'Cuba Libre' was unwittingly created and popularised by an American Army officer, mixing his favourite soft drink, Coca-Cola, with the golden spirit. The much ordered 'Daiquiri' was equally auspiciously named in 1896 by a mining engineer working near the town of Daiquiri, near the Sierra Maestra mountains in Cuba. He had combined light rum and lime juice, successfully impressing his friends – and more.

Savour such an illustrious, colourful history by imbibing Antigua's amber nectar. Even if a non-spirit drinker, do take the opportunity of appreciating the velvet taste of an Antiguan solitary aged rum or an exhilarating rum cocktail. All hotels, restaurants and bars can satisfy such a request, and then there's the 'rum shops', places where liquors are sold. However, they are often more than this, sometimes combining a village store and always acting as an informal community centre where local news and gossip is entertainingly discussed and lively board games played (see page 282).

Loved not just for its versatility as a soothing or exciting drink, rum is a wonderful addition to any cuisine and for adding that touch of gold to baking, desserts and sauces. Get out your shakers and blenders; treat your tastebuds and feel the warmth of the sun flow through you. Remember to take some Antiguan rum home!

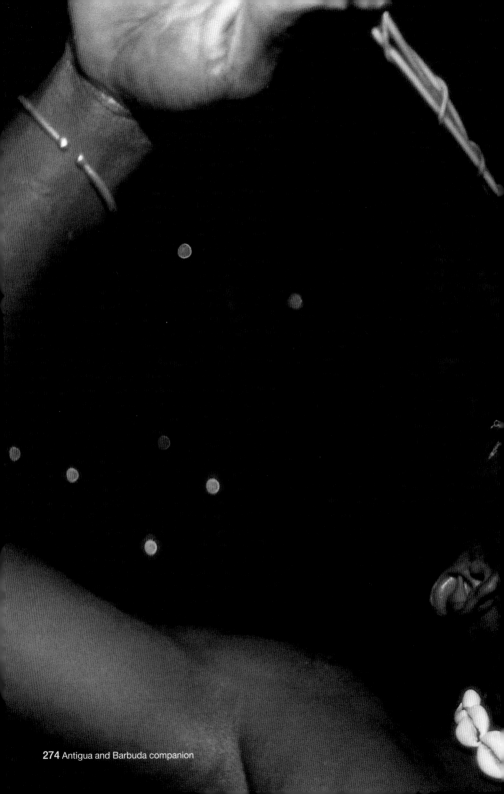

Nightlife

– the finishing touch

Nightlife

– the finishing touch

> On with the dance! Let joy be unconfined;
> No sleep 'till morn, when Youth and Pleasure meet
> To chase the glowing Hours with flying feet.
> Lord Byron

You may not quite feel like 'no sleep 'til morn' as Lord Byron suggests above, but if you do there is plenty of nightlife to keep you going until then. Alternatively, you may wish to start your evening by taking advantage of the many 'happy hour' (often longer than an hour) opportunities at various bars and restaurants, or simply sit and enjoy the many types of live entertainment available, or choose to play at the casinos (see page 281) until the early hours.

After a day of sunning, swimming, shopping or sightseeing, an evening's entertainment can be an outing in itself and the finishing touch to the day. Visitors here do not come for the bright lights and celebrity stage performers, but that is not to say Antigua doesn't have the nightlife, too. It's just that things are a little more relaxed. Most restaurants serve dinner between 6 and 10pm, so there's ample time to sample other aspects of Antigua's nightlife, whether before or afterwards.

The larger hotels provide a full entertainment programme throughout the week, featuring steel bands, reggae bands, limbo dancers, fire eaters, calypso singers, fashion shows, dance troupes or keyboard performers. But even the smaller hotels will have some form of evening entertainment a few nights a week, often with the opportunity of dancing during and after dinner. Such evenings are invariably open to non-residents and offer a good chance to investigate other hotels, their bars, restaurants and facilities.

There are a number of restaurants which offer entertainment in the evenings, particularly at the weekends. Whether simple or more sophisticated music, live or taped sounds, there is an ever-changing scene of local hangouts where locals and visitors 'lime'.

Strings of bars are mainly situated in three areas: on the waterfronts of English Harbour and Falmouth in the south, on the west coast in and around Jolly Harbour, and in the north at the popular Dickenson Bay and Runaway Bay. Too numerous to mention individually, you'll find a synopsis of the main haunts further on. There are bars and restaurants all over the island which feature live jazz, first-class bands, local cultural shows, some also with pool rooms, major sporting events on large television screens, films, bingo and backgammon nights.

Even karaoke has reached these shores. Its increasing popularity has resulted in karaoke nights being featured at many hotels and bars, creating new found talent and often a hilarious evening.

A must for every visitor is Sunday at Shirley Heights, where a quintessential Antiguan experience of six hours of non-stop entertainment begins at 4pm. It's a memorable experience. A local tradition which has established itself over the decades as the highlight of many a visitor's trip. From its famous, lofty vantage point overlooking English Harbour, standing on the terrace of the Lookout restaurant and bar, you can take in the stupendous views and watch the sun go down. There's the superb Halcyon Steel Orchestra, followed by a reggae band, an excellent barbecue, drinking and dancing. There is also a similar sundown party, if not arguably a quieter evening, on Thursdays, perfect for children.

Shirley Heights

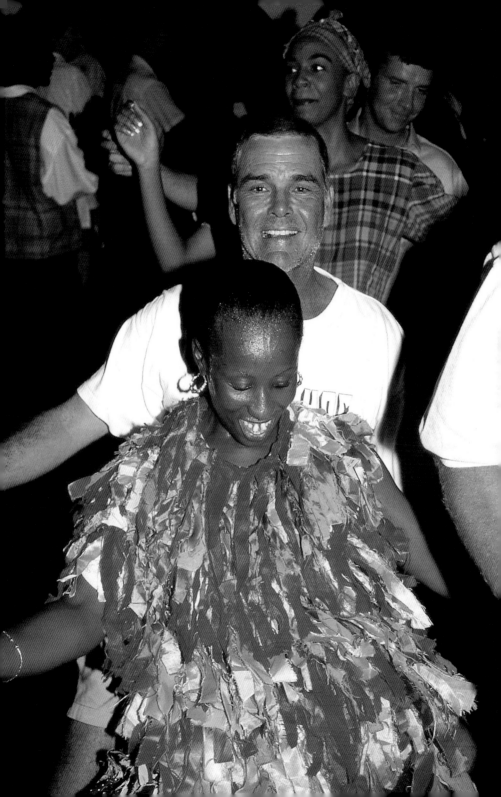

Discotheques and bars with live entertainment

If you are a discotheque or dancing fan, then you may want to wend your way to Ribbit, the biggest and most popular with visitors and locals alike. Located on the outskirts of St John's and open on Friday and Saturday nights (10.30pm–5am), its breezy, waterfront setting overlooking St John's Harbour suits many who are drawn to its multicultural, friendly and safe, yet pulsating, party environment. La Galleria in Deep Bay is the latest nightclub to open for 21-year olds and over and is open Friday and Saturday. For a more local Antiguan flavour, the Web Discotheque, just outside the centre of St John's, attracts many to its vibrant atmosphere. They all play the very latest international sounds, along with the favourite calypso, soca and reggae numbers. Lashings Sports Café and Bar is an extremely well-frequented nightspot. Owned by Antiguan ex-test cricketer and West Indies captain, Richie Richardson, its popular bar, restaurant and deck are situated on the beautiful stretch of Runaway beach. Top live bands can be heard on Friday and Saturday evenings and there is a twice daily happy hour, bar open 24 hours, restaurant open until 2am and pizzas served until 4am.

Antigua has a terrific choice of great bars island-wide (almost all with happy hours), whether on the beach, in town, or a 'rum shop' (see page 282). Some of the most well-known would include: the long established Miller's Beach Bar and Restaurant, at Fort James, north of St John's, which stands out for assuring a different live band or entertainment every lunchtime and evening of the week, including karaoke. Not much further on will bring you to Runaway and Dickenson Bays where you will always find a good 'lime' and lots of action. Regarded very much as a local hangout (open until the last person leaves!) is Putters Bar and Grill. This is endowed with an expansive deck with pool table and long bar, serving food until late, and it has good music plus its popular 18-hole miniature golf which is played

well into the late night hours. You will also find the air-conditioned Outback Nightclub here at Putters, open Wednesday, Friday and Saturday. The romantic Coconut Grove has a congenial bar and top local bands playing at the weekends. Casino Riviera has live music nightly in its excellent restaurant and bar, adjacent to the gaming tables (see page 281). Further round the north coast and to Cedar Grove, just before Hodges Bay, will bring you to Bambu Strip Sports Bar, open daily with happy hour, pool tables, satellite TV, Internet room and live entertainment.

In St John's there's Big Banana in Historic Redcliffe Quay which has live music every Thursday at 10pm, satellite television and 'the largest selection of CDs on the island'. Still in this attractive part of St John's, every Thursday afternoon (2–5pm) on the boardwalk at Historic Redcliffe Quay, you'll find a Wadadli beer festival with Wadadli and the Roots steel band. At the same venue, on Friday nights (5–10pm) join the many who congregate at this evening beer festival with music provided by the Harmony 6 (for further entertainment dates and times at the quay, call Key Properties (268) 562 1960). O'Grady's Pub is situated on the upper floor, airy premises in Redcliffe Street and, as it sounds, offers good bar food and snacks with live entertainment and karaoke.

On the west coast, at Jolly Harbour, Dogwatch Tavern has a good atmosphere with music, bar, pool tables and restaurant. At the other end of this marina complex, is the large, open air Steely Bar BBR Sportive. This is a good meeting spot with all major sports and films screened on satellite television, live entertainment, karaoke, bar and restaurant.

In the south, at English Harbour, Abracadabra is always a perfect spot and much frequented venue for dancing in the open air on the deck or amongst the gardens to the latest sounds and top live bands, jazz and piano bar. It has a disco-

Abracadabra

bar with DJs, large outdoor video screens for films, documentaries, sport, and so on, plus fashion shows and special events situated next to their renowned restaurant. At the Antigua Yacht Club in Falmouth, the Last Lemming often has live bands on a raised outdoor deck overlooking the marina, plus a great bar and a good restaurant. Playbach, located on the left-hand side approaching Falmouth Marina, has three popular pool tables and live music in season, when it is open seven nights a week. Colombo's, in the grounds of the Galleon Beach Hotel at English Harbour, has long been a regular stop particularly on Wednesday nights when there is a live band.

Holidaymakers tend to opt for outdoor evening entertainment, but should you wish to take in the latest film, there is a very good, large and air-conditioned cinema, the Deluxe, in St John's. It shows various films to suit both the local and international filmgoer. Hotels, especially the larger ones, may provide cable television and can often rent videos.

If you haven't had a chance to be afloat during the day, then how about indulging in the fun and romance of a cruise under the stars (see Day Sailing, page 162)? Popular with locals as well, so whether for a sunset cocktail or party cruise, it's a great chance to get to know Antiguans and party with them, as only they know how!

Needless to say, the main events on the Antiguan calendar always ensure an almost carnival-like feeling when the atmosphere can become quite electric. These extra busy periods become a melting pot of faces, culture, music and dance. High on this list would be test cricket (see page 75), the Classic Yacht Regatta (see page 123), Antigua Sailing Week (see page 119) and, of course, Antigua Carnival, itself (see page 79).

The local entertainment scene can change, especially between the 'high' season and the summer months. Check with the hotel reception, your local tour representative, the daily papers, posters and flyers, or just ask around to find out what's happening during your stay. Have fun and enjoy yourself to the fullest!

A very merry, dancing, drinking,
laughing, quaffing, and unthinking time!

John Dryden

Casinos

If you fancy a flutter on the tables, there are several first-rate casinos on the island, which offer a range of gaming tables including roulette, 21 blackjack, American craps, Baccarat, Caribbean stud poker and the usual 'one-armed bandit' slot machines. Your game of chance is not restricted to the evening either; the main ones open from 10am. Notably the largest establishment, King's Casino, at Heritage Quay, is air-conditioned and frequented by locals, cruise ship passengers and tourists. This enormous casino, with complimentary drinks for players, also has a sophisticated sports lounge and bar with television and a 10-foot screen, covering major sporting events all day via satellite television, plus live entertainment, happy hour and 'state of the art' slot machines, including the largest in the world.

The elegant air-conditioned Casino Riviera near Runaway Bay, also offers the discretion of private gaming rooms with complimentary bar and snacks. As well as a good restaurant, bar and regular live entertainment, its main gaming tables attract many overseas visitors, as well as the local public, to gamble the hours away, whilst served complimentary drinks.

On the west coast, at the Jolly Harbour Marina, is Coral Reef Casino. Located next to the Dogwatch Tavern, they have a progressive jackpot, roulette, blackjack and Caribbean stud poker. Open seven days a week from 10am (in season), their table games operate nightly from Monday to Saturday in air-conditioned surroundings. At the other end of the island is the sumptuous decor and European ambience of the completely refitted St James's Club Casino at the hotel of the same name in Willoughby Bay. This 'Las Vegas-style' casino offers state-of-the-art gaming in glittering surroundings.

There are also smaller casinos in town: Joe Mike's Downtown Hotel Plaza, on the corner of Nevis Street, has a variety of table games and a wide assortment of slot machines with progressive jackpot, cocktail bar and restaurant. On St Mary's Street is Keno Palace Casino with 21 blackjack, Caribbean stud poker and slot machines, and one street away in High Street is the Jackpot Casino. There are no table games here but both slot machines and poker machines are available with progressive jackpots and bar in an air-conditioned, local atmosphere.

The Royal Antiguan at Deep Bay has completely refitted its casino area to suit all the family. This now encompasses an entertainment lounge, slot machines, pool tables and a children's video gaming arcade.

Casino Riviera

Rum shops

You may have noticed colourful little bars and restaurants around Antigua and, if you have driven past any, taking in the tantalising smells of fish and chicken, some of these are likely to be Antigua's local 'rum shops'.

Many visitors are curious to visit these lovely local haunts and the trip is certainly recommended (see list below). Where meals are served they are exceptionally tasty and reasonable, but many go just for the sights and sounds of the voracious domino playing which is a daily competition for many Antiguans.

Rum shops are places for people to 'chill out', who like to have a few drinks, relax, play dominoes, argue, or all four. But such arguments are not to be taken in the wrong vein (although by the shouting it is quite easy to be misled into thinking there is a major row going on). They are normally about politics or sport and deviate quickly and unpredictably between anger and laughter, with no harm meant or done.

In the eighteenth and nineteenth centuries, rum shops were referred to as 'dram shops' (there were many merchants of Scottish descent in Antigua at that time). The laws previously forbidding slaves to leave their sugar estates became more relaxed around 1720–30 and they were given passes to visit the Sunday market where slaves bartered foodstuffs and goods.

When the masters visited their townhouses on a Sunday, they would then take their slaves, who would visit the market and subsequently visit the 'dram shops'. Such trade ultimately increased and is noted in Gaspar's book, written in 1885, that in 1740, there were 'now 10 dram shops for every punch house opposite Ottos and 'Negro Market'.

Rums were produced in pot stills by individual estate owners and in the back yards of dram shop proprietors, who distilled their own brews (see Rum Revelry, page 271). This was a time when rum was often referred to as the 'mile and fall' drink (see A Fishy Business, page 246). Now, however, rum is not the only drink available at such bars and you can get most popular soft or alcoholic drinks.

The ancient African Warri board game (see page 283) can also be seen played by groups of friends sitting chilling out or limin'. The accompanying noise of the clicking of 'nickars' (the Warri seeds) or the 'slapping of bones' as the dominoes are hammered down on the table, together with the accompanying loud and enthusiastic spectators, is something you can't ignore.

Sample a 100 per cent Antiguan welcome, hospitality and some of the best evening's local entertainment to be found anywhere. Perhaps after calling ahead for opening hours, directions and to be sure they are not closed for holidays, try to visit the highly recommended rum shops below:

Ethlyn and Grantley,
Bloody Mary Bar and Restaurant
Urlings Village tel: 462 8042
Clammon Cherry Bar and Restaurant
Bethesda Main Road, Christian Hill
tel: 463 2788
Gervey, Gervey's Rum Shop
Nut Grove, Golden Grove tel: 463 8070
Harry, Smiley Harry's Place Beach Bar
Half Moon Bay tel: 460 4402

Warri

– the game of houses

As mentioned in Rum Shops, you may witness the highly skilled, ancient game of warri being played around the island. Originating from Africa, this most interesting strategy game was brought to the West Indies by African slaves during the sugar-cane era.

Adopted as one of Antigua's national games, warri has been elevated to world championship level, ranking alongside chess, bridge, backgammon, draughts and all other classic 'thinking' games requiring intellectual agility. The World Mind Olympiad held at the Royal Festival Hall, London represents more than 30 different games of this kind requiring considerable mental skills.

Adept players from all over the world compete in the Warri event, including Antigua. Of great note, Antiguans, Sakile Richards and Trevor Simon, were crowned Adult World Individual Champions by winning gold medals respectively in the 1997 and 1998 events, with Trevor Simon also taking the gold medal in 1999 and 2000. Antigua also won a gold medal in the World Championship Team competition in 1998.

The word 'warri' means 'house' from the African Ijo dialect and is played by two opponents, who each start with 24 counters. These counters are small bare nuts from the Antiguan Guillandria bush, called 'nickars', and represent houses. The aim is to win with the capture of 25 or more nickars by the judicious and skilful movement of the counters around the board.

The often beautifully carved and ornate rectangular wooden boards played upon are traditionally two and a half inches deep, nine inches wide and 27 inches long with twelve

hollows (or houses) three inches in diameter, arranged as six on each side. In the hollowed holes, four seeds or nickars are placed, making a total of 48 nickars on the board. A vast range of techniques, encompassing considerable mathematical wizardry, can be applied to win, but verbal intimidation is also pretty high on the list when watching players in combat.

The players enjoy an audience and welcome overseas players, so take the opportunity of learning about reputedly the 'world's oldest game' here, in Antigua.

Everton Jacobs, President National Warri Association (and the Antigua and Barbuda Domino Association), tel: (268) 460 4290 or Trevor Simon tel: (268) 480 5770

Property

A home in the sun? **286**

A home in the sun?

– the property market

Arriving in Antigua you may well aspire to acquiring an apartment or villa for annual holidays, retirement or investment. Driving or sailing around the beautiful island you will see a wide variety of homes and properties of various styles from Georgian to contemporary, the typical West Indian chattel house to large mansions and plantation houses. The following article will help direct you to find your dream property.

THE TIME IS RIGHT

Antigua has a stable growing economy, driven by tourism and by an attractive Offshore International Business Corporations legislation. This growth has increased the demand for tourist accommodation and for rental and investment properties. This has continued to drive a consistent building boom of quality housing, tourist accommodation and commercial buildings.

HOLIDAY, RESIDENTIAL AND RETIREMENT HOMES

By far the highest demand for property is for single family residences including apartments, condominiums, and detached or semi-detached houses. The highest demand is in the popular north end residential areas of Hodges Bay, Crosbies, Paradise View, Cedar Valley and Galley Bay. Other popular areas include English Harbour, Falmouth and Jolly Harbour, with such areas as St James's Club, Emerald Cove, Half Moon and Brown's Bay, developing at an encouraging rate.

Project developments offering swimming pools, golf, tennis, squash, shopping, bars and restaurants, community services and security attract discriminating buyers and renters who are prepared to pay extra for value added services and amenities. Developments which are representative of the projects in Antigua are the Van Gogh Club, the St James's Club, The Peninsula, Cedar Valley

Springs, Friar's Hill Development and Jolly Harbour.

The Van Gogh Club is Antigua's newest and most exclusive residential development of prestige homes priced in excess of US $1.5 million. Located adjacent to the Galley Bay resort, the project features 33 parcels of fully serviced building plots on which four homes are already built. The parcels sell from US$ 400,000, with purchasers contracting with the developer for architect's plans and building contracts.

The St James's Club has been revitalised through innovative management by Antigua Resorts. Remodelled and updated two and three bedroom villas in the Village are offered for sale from US$250,000, while building plots on the hillside are also available.

The Peninsula, on the northeast side of the island, is protected by a chain of uninhabited islands and coral reefs, offering a small number of waterfront homes for those desirous of peace and tranquillity, just 20 minutes from the airport. With breathtaking views, plots are generally of approximately one acre and slope towards inlets within Spencer Bay. Utilities including electricity and water are underground. A choice of house designs is available reflecting West Indian architecture and can be tailored to the buyer's needs.

Jolly Harbour is Antigua's most complete residential community. There are 501 pre-built two-bedroom attached townhouses, most with their own boat slip, some fronting onto the 18-hole golf course. Building plots on the beaches, harbour side, golf course and hillside allow for custom designed residences. Many new designs have already been built complementing the Mediterranean style of the main building theme. The Marina is one of the best in the Caribbean with full services in the dockyard and marina. The shopping centre has 30 retail outlets, restaurants, bars, and banking and other community services. Prices for the build-

ACQUISITION CONSIDERATIONS

1 A licence is required by any non-citizen to purchase property. The cost is 5% of the value of the property.
2 Government transfer fees or stamp duties to the buyer is 2.5% and to the seller is 7.5%.
3 On several projects, such as Jolly Harbour, the transfer fees and non-citizen's licence is waived and a 3% fee is applied.
4 Property taxes/rates are very low and based on rental value. Legal costs are 1% to 2% depending on the value of the transaction.
5 Most property is fee simple or freehold.
6 No title insurance. Properties are registered at the Land Office.
7 Estate agent commissions are from 5% to 7%.
8 Property management fees are usually 10%. Rental commissions 8.33% of the value of the lease.
9 Withholding taxes are 25% of net rental income for non-residents.
10 Insurance coverage is approximately 1%, deductible of 2%.
11 Owner takes back or bank financing is available.
12 Most houses are serviced by septic tank. Water cisterns are required.

ing lots start at US $35,000 and the two-bedroom villas start at US $131,500.

The Friar's Hill Development offers various designs in a classical Caribbean style, as well as various lot sizes to choose from, where the client's needs and wishes are taken into keen consideration. After completion of the home, the Friar's Hill Development offers a wide range of after sales service.

Villa rentals and property management services are offered by most of the developments as well as some estate agents who look after your investment while you are absent. There is much demand for villas, for one or two weeks, especially for those which offer amenities or are close to beaches, have pools or other features. There is currently a shortage of upmarket villas for long and short term accommodation.

BUSINESS AND COMMERCIAL PROPERTIES

There are many opportunities in a growing economy; some reserved for locals such as day charter operations. In a tourist and service economy, the government welcomes investments which provide jobs or stimulate the economy. New business start-ups, especially those associated with the Internet, offshore financial services and the hospitality industry, are welcome. There are attractive fiscal incentives available to developers.

AFFORDABLE HOMES AND HOLIDAYS

The Caribbean style chattel house varying in size, style and utilising wood, cement or other materials can be attractive and is in demand by locals and visitors alike. Properties which provide this affordable living experience for long and short term stays include, Marsh Village in English Harbour and Peter Murphy's villas overlooking Galley Bay.

Several local builders offer affordable homes at low prices. These houses can be built quickly on site or delivered as a complete unit to your freehold plot. House and land can be acquired from US $35,000 to US $100,000.

TIME SHARE AND INTERVAL OWNERSHIP

Interval ownership or time share is offered at Antigua Village, St. James's Club and Jolly Harbour. The concept divides the ownership, costs and utilisation over 52 weeks. It also allows for the exchange with over 3,000 resorts worldwide.

PROFESSIONAL SERVICES

There are several estate agencies offering a full range of professional services on the island. Some specialise by area and others by property type. The lawyers, builders, engineers and architects are well trained and knowledgeable of both European and North American requirements. The services of professionals are strongly recommended.

ment

An overview of tax benefits
– meeting international standards

Antigua and Barbuda is one of the countries which paid serious attention to G7 reviews through the OECD programme on 'harmful tax' and the FATF.

Over the past two years, Antigua and Barbuda's financial centre has transformed its laws, strengthened its regulatory and supervisory machinery and improved its capacity for law enforcement with regard to financial crimes.

Indeed, it is true to say that today Antigua and Barbuda stands far ahead of many jurisdictions worldwide, in terms of its laws and practices with respect to combating money laundering and other financial crime.

BACKGROUND
Offshore financial institutions are governed by the International Business Corporation (1982) Act [IBCA], and the Money Laundering (Prevention) Act (MLPA) of 1998, as amended in 1999 and again in early 2000, which have created a regulatory and compliance environment equal to, or stronger, than most international financial centres.

In 1983, the first offshore bank, Swiss American Bank, opened in Antigua. The bank welcomed the steps taken by the jurisdiction to meet all the standards set by the international community. This major bank, and the others which followed in its steps, support the view that a strong legal and regulatory infrastructure is a requirement to identify and repel illicit funds, whilst providing a safe haven for the management of legitimate wealth. The reality is that the abuse of secrecy and tax evasion are no longer competitive advantages for offshore centres. Indeed, it is the fact that Antigua is not attractive to fraudulent or criminal behaviour that makes it favoured by the more discriminating investor.

REGULATORY CONTROL
To focus supervision more closely on its financial institutions the government established a new statutory authority known as the International Financial Sector Regulatory Authority (IFSRA) and charged it with responsibilities to supervise and regulate the sector. The current board comprises senior public servants drawn from the Solicitor General's office, Law enforcement and Foreign Affairs.

KNOW YOUR CUSTOMER
Entrenched in the amended IBC Act, are strong 'know your customer' requirements to govern the conduct of banks and their clients. No anonymous accounts can be established. Each account application must provide evidence of identity, place of residence and other current banking relations. Also, customers cannot hide behind corporate veils. Banks require disclosure of true beneficial ownership and the true identity of directors and shareholders. It is the responsibility of banks to know their customers, so that in the event the supervisory authority requires information under the law, it can be made available. There are also provisions for maintaining adequate records, reporting suspicious transactions and ensuring appropriate training for employees.

BANKING SECRECY
The confidentiality afforded to clients by banks will not provide a safe harbour to criminals. The provisions of the MLPA will stand as the governing Act, notwithstanding any obligation to secrecy or other restriction regarding the disclosure of information by any law or otherwise. In general, bank clients need not be concerned with this issue. It is only relevant to those who are the subject of a criminal investigation involving the offence of money laundering and when the court in Antigua has, on application by the competent Antiguan authority, ordered the disclosure of information. In

other words, the privacy of customers' banking information remains fully confidential unless it can be established in a court of competent jurisdiction that a crime has been committed.

NO CASH DEPOSIT

In April 1999, Antigua and Barbuda became the first, and possibly only, jurisdiction to ban the acceptance of cash or bearer negotiable instruments in any amounts. Antigua demonstrated its commitment to be proactive against money laundering. Given that money laundering begins with the conversion of currency, and one of the concerns expressed has been that anonymous and illicit funds can be returned to their financial systems via correspondents for offshore banks, the Antigua prohibition is a positive and innovative action. And, while it does not prevent money laundering by other means of fund transfers, such other means allow for full identification of the transaction details.

INTERNATIONAL COOPERATION

In 1995, Antigua was amongst the first countries in the Caribbean region to sign a maritime law enforcement counter drug agreement and an updated extradition treaty with the US. Mutual legal assistance treaties in criminal matters were signed with both the US and the UK in 1996. The jurisdiction is a member of the Caribbean Financial Action Task Force (CFATF) and, as recently as March 2000, showed that it is in full compliance with all its requirements. Also in March 2000, Antigua became the first country to sign a commitment letter to the principals of the UN Offshore Forum (UNOF), which confirmed the government's agreement to adhere to the UN's minimum performance standards relating to banking practices, transparency rules and international cooperation. At the FATF Plenary in Paris, June 2000, Antigua was recognised as a cooperating country to combat money laundering, having successfully passed an in-depth review.

INTERNATIONAL BUSINESS CENTRE

The remarkable growth of the Internet is having a great impact on economies around the world, and Antigua is no exception. As an independent nation, with a history of political and economic stability, it is well positioned to attract international business for electronic commerce. The combination of a well regulated financial services sector, an excellent communications infrastructure, an English-speaking and skilled workforce, and strong professional resources provide a positive environment for electronic business.

Investment incentives

Money is better than poverty, if only for financial reasons

Woody Allen

PERMANENT RESIDENCE SCHEME

The following outlines the benefits of Antigua as a centre for international tax planning and also describes incentives available to encourage domestic investment. In June 1995, Parliament passed amendments to the Immigration and Passport Act and Income Tax Act. The purpose of these two amendments was to accommodate a permanent residence scheme aimed at high net-worth individuals, specifically to encourage wealthy individuals to settle in Antigua and establish it as their permanent place of residence.

Antigua is one of the very few countries in the world which has:
– no personal income tax
– no capital gains tax
– no inheritance tax
– no wealth tax

There are taxes on the profits of corporations and proprietorships doing business in Antigua, but personal income tax for resident individuals was abolished in 1977.

Included under the revised definitions of a resident individual is an individual who main-

PricewaterhouseCoopers

tains his or her permanent place of abode in Antigua and is physically present in Antigua for not less than 30 days in the year. In addition, he or she must be the holder of a permanent residence certificate. This certificate will be issued once an application has been approved by the Cabinet and a levy of at least US$ 20,000 has been paid. The certificate is issued for one year and is renewable annually upon payment of the levy.

Due to a number of infrastructural developments in recent years, the country is carrying a large national debt and the government has been under pressure to re-introduce personal tax. It has resisted doing so and has introduced the permanent residence scheme as a way of turning personal tax-free status for individuals into a positive economic factor. The country is hard pressed to balance its budget and at the same time exempt its resident individuals from income tax. However, with a population of about 70,000, the influx of say 1000 permanent residents under this scheme would have a dramatic effect on the balance of payments. Permanent residents will not have to pay Antiguan income tax on their worldwide income, whether earned or unearned, and whether remitted or not. All their income will be tax free in Antigua.

Before being approved by the Cabinet, each application will require recommendation from independent professionals who will have verified that the source of the individual's wealth is legal. However, it will not be necessary for the individual to file any details of his or her wealth or income.

In order to establish a permanent place of abode here, the person will need to purchase or lease a property. It is expected that most applicants will build homes on land which is available at developments in a number of very pleasant, secure locations. As the law presently stands, persons who have been resident in Antigua for seven years are eligible to apply for citizenship. However, this scheme is not intended as an economic citizenship programme.

Antigua has never had any capital gains tax and it is expected that persons wishing to realise capital gains in their present countries of residence will take advantage of this scheme. Although this act requires the individual to be resident in Antigua for a minimum period of 30 days in a year, there is no maximum period. With proper planning, a person can avoid being 'ordinary resident' in the country in which the capital gain arises.

The absence of inheritance tax makes Antigua an attractive place to establish domicile and those with long-term plans in mind will consider setting up trusts, which can easily be done.

For retired people there are special provisions in the legislation for pensions. In certain circumstances, it may be possible to substantially reduce taxation on overseas pensions.

Since its introduction, the scheme has been successful. The favourable economic impact of the new permanent residents from the levies and their spending power, will ensure that their presence will continue to be welcomed.

INTERNATIONAL BUSINESS CORPORATIONS

The International Business Corporations Act contains provisions for international business companies, banks, insurance and trust companies. The benefits provided under this act are:
– complete tax exemption
– complete exchange control exemption
– automatic 50-year guarantee of tax free status
– bearer shares (except for banks, trusts, insurance)
– inward and outward redomiciliation provisions

For international business companies engaged in international trade and investment, there is no minimum capital requirement and no statutory audit requirement.

International banks, trusts and insurance companies are required to file annual audited accounts and the minimum capitalisation requirements are as follows:

Banks	US$ 5,000,000 (of which US$ 1,500,000 must be maintained in a licenced financial centre in Antigua)
Trust companies	US$ 500,000
Insurance companies	US$ 250,000

The government has identified the provision of offshore financial services as an area of huge potential growth and importance to the economy. Accordingly, the Attorney-General is working on legislative changes that will further enhance Antigua's attractiveness as a financial centre.

DOMESTIC INVESTMENT INCENTIVES

Under the Fiscal Incentives Act, manufacturers receive corporate tax holidays of between 10–15 years. Certain export-oriented industries qualify for a maximum 20-year tax holiday. Equipment, machinery, spare parts and raw materials used in production are able to be imported duty free.

In order to promote tourism, hotel operations are granted a five-year tax holiday, together with duty-free concessions on importation of all materials required to build and equip the hotel. Basically, the government is committed to encouraging foreign investment and offers a package of generous incentives.

For further information and a free copy of 'Doing Business in Antigua and Barbuda', contact:
PricewaterhouseCoopers,
11 Old Parham Road, St John's, Antigua WI
tel: (268) 462 3000 fax: (268) 462 1902
e-mail: donald.ward@ag.pwcglobal.com

The Antigua and Barbuda Red Cross

The sterling humanitarian and relief services carried out by the worldwide organisation of the priceless Red Cross are ably represented here in Antigua.

Initially established as a branch of the British Red Cross on 20 October 1941, Antigua and Barbuda was recognised by the International Committee of the Red Cross on 4 November 1992, making it the 153rd member of the National Societies of the International Red Cross Movement and Red Crescent Movement.

Subsequently recognised by the government of Antigua and Barbuda as a voluntary aid society auxiliary to the public authorities, it acts for the benefit of the civilian population under the fundamental principles of the Red Cross: humanity, impartiality, neutrality, independence, voluntary services, unity and universality. It is a voluntary relief movement, not motivated in any manner by desire for gain.

Gerald R. Price, the Director General, a Red Cross member for nearly 30 years, constantly strives to attain the society's main objects: promoting membership of the Red Cross to all citizens; the participation of children and young people in the work of the Red Cross; propagating the fundamental principles of the Red Cross and of international humanitarian law in order to develop the ideals of peace, mutual respect and understanding among all men and women and all peoples; to act in case of armed conflict according to the scheduled conventions on behalf of war victims, civilian and military; to contribute to the improvement of health by presenting programmes of training and services for the benefit of the community and to organising, within the scope of the national plan, emergency relief services for victims of disasters.

Of the latter objective, Gerald Price and his unstinting crew have had rather too much recent experience: with the earthquake of 1974, Hurricane Hugo in 1989, the devastating Hurricane Luis in 1995 and, of course, in the same year, the volcanic eruption on Montserrat.

In becoming a true disaster response area for this very close neighbouring island, Antigua pioneered an extremely successful project, funded by a European Community Humanitarian Office (ECHO) donation. Based at the Antigua and Barbuda Red Cross head office, they and the British Red Cross carried out a six-month displaced Montserratian relief programme, involving a unique food voucher system for exchange at various supermarkets. With happy recipients and total accountability, this policy will now be adopted by other Red Cross societies around the world.

Red Cross societies everywhere all respond to each other's needs, hence, whilst looking after the great concerns during the aftermath of Hurricane Luis in 1995, the Antigua and Barbuda Red Cross also sent urgent supplies to St Lucia, which suffered serious flooding.

Vital stocks and donated supplies are kept in various store rooms and in the society's two huge containers in preparation for any disaster, or to assist any person or family during a smaller scale or personal tragedy, such as a house fire. During 1997, 450 families lost their homes to fire and had to be rehabilitated to lead a normal life.

To further improve the emergency–disaster-response capability of the island and to establish Antigua as the Red Cross sub-regional disaster preparedness centre, ECHO has also funded a project to include the construction of a 24,000 cubic-foot emergency response centre which will house enough non-food items to provide immediate assistance to 3,000 persons.

Immensely cost-effective fundraising has to be achieved in order to maintain such stocks of goods and materials. Once the domain of dinners and tea parties, these avenues are now too competitive and alternative means have had to be sought to raise the necessary funds.

Red Cross week is usually held in Antigua during the first week in June, when fêtes, bingo sessions and dinners take place, and volunteers with their familiar Red Cross tins collect donations. To make their accessible, large building, located by the cricket ground in St John's, pay its way, the Red Cross rooms are rented out in the evenings for various organisations to hold meetings. There is an adjoining charity shop, The Depot (open Monday to Friday, 8am–3pm), which accepts anything that is saleable. So, at the end of your trip, if you have any clothes, shoes, books, bags, and so on, you could leave here (or any unused currency), you couldn't donate to a much better cause. Major donors appreciate the Red Cross track record for audited funds, clearly detailing how every dollar is spent, aspects which open many doors otherwise closed for lack of accountability elsewhere.

Whilst Gerald Price is paid to see that the society's work goes through in the most efficient way possible (in 1997, he was awarded the Golden Venezuelan Cross by the President of the International Red Cross based in Geneva, for 'his unconditional dedication to humanitarian work in the region'), it is the many devoted volunteers who put most of it into effect. In the quest to continually give quality service to the community, ongoing training takes place with weekly workshops on subjects like mental health and stress management.

The Red Cross has evolved from its initial concept in the 1850s of basic first-aid care and education to disaster relief and welfare. Apart from the latter two, the activities of the Antigua and Barbuda Red Cross encompass audiology services, first-aid courses, home nursing, community disaster training, HIV/AIDS education, refugee management, medical equipment loans, swimming and water safety, help in tracing missing persons, and search and rescue.

For donations and further information contact the Antigua and Barbuda Red Cross, Old Parham Road, PO Box 727, St John's, Antigua, tel: (268) 462 9599/462 0800/461 1655 fax: (268) 460 9595 e-mail: redcross@candw.ag

Barbuda

History of Barbuda

During Pleistocene times, sea levels were about 200 feet lower than they are now and Antigua and Barbuda were connected by land until about 9600 BC, when sea levels rose sufficiently to separate the islands. Barbuda is therefore still connected underwater to Antigua by the Barbuda Bank, but leaving the island a mere 10 feet above sea level, except at the highlands, near the north end, where it attains a height of 125 feet. Surrounded by reefs, with a large lagoon on the northwest side, Barbuda's limestone and sand surfaces are barely covered by soil.

It would appear that around 500 years BC, Amerindians first lived at a locality called **Sufferers**, near **Spanish Point**, where there are abundant marine food resources. Situated on a rare deposit of soil, the settlement was able to grow its main staple, the cassava tuber. Approximately 19 Amerindian sites are known in Barbuda, some found in the caves of the **Highlands area**, including one with a petroglyph or rock drawing (see page 305), the only example found in Antigua and Barbuda. The Caribs who followed to forage in Barbuda, called the island Wa'omoni.

The latter-day unique history of Barbuda began on 13 September 1625, when, by patent under the Great Seal of England, Barbuda, along with Antigua, Nevis and St Christopher (later called St Kitts) was taken under royal protection. As with Antigua, several attempts were made to colonise the island by the British and the French, both of whom found conditions unsuitable for settlement – not least of which were attacks by the fierce Caribs. According to 'Travels and Observation' in a diary kept by Captain John Smith (of Pocahontas fame), in 1628,

> Master Littleton (a planter from St Kitts) with some others, got a patent from the Earl of Carlisle to plant the isle called Barbuda 30 leagues northward of St Kitts, which by report of the informers and undertakers for the exellences and pleasantness, the reef is called Dulcina, but when they came there they found it such a barren rock, they left it.

In 1632, when the first English from St Kitts settled with determination on Antigua, they tried once again to colonise Barbuda, but were again driven off by the Caribs. Some accounts of the time stated that the Caribs were raiders from Dominica. Others claimed that the Caribs lived on the island. In any case, several further colonising attempts failed, with the people according to an early diarist 'frequently forced to leave their plantations, for there hardly passed a year in which they [the Indians] did not make one or two incursions'.

Not until 1666 were settlers able to establish a foothold on the island strong enough to fight off the Caribs and build a permanent settlement. Precisely where that first settlement was has never been confirmed, but the oldest buildings of any kind on record were on the site of the present village of Codrington.

The Codrington family entered the picture in 1680, when King Charles II of England granted a 50-year lease to Christopher and John Codrington. Christopher lived in Antigua (see also Betty's Hope, page 198) and John in Barbuda. But a year later six war canoes carrying about 240 Caribs attacked the small settlement, comprising just 20 white settlers. According to one historian. 'some of these Englishmen managed to escape while the Indians were drinking rum.'

Four years later a new lease was granted to the Codringtons for 50 years, at the rate of 'one horse annually, to be paid to the Governor of Antigua by the grantees.' A clause in the lease granted the Codringtons 'all wreckage' with which they could do little at the time. But the potential was there; surrounding Barbuda are reefs on which there have been to date over 150 known shipwrecks.

It was from this bounty that the Codringtons derived much income. Trained crews would race to the stricken ship, removing its cargo which would later be sold in Antigua.

John built **Highland House** at the northwestern edge of what is described as the 'highlands' (see page 304), one of the highest points on this flat island. When he died in 1688 Christopher became sole lease-holder of the island.

By now Christopher had vast sugar plantations in Antigua and many slaves. He began to use Barbuda as a stock farm for the provisioning of Antigua, since in addition to the richness of its marine life, the island then had a plentiful supply of deer, boar and guinea fowl.

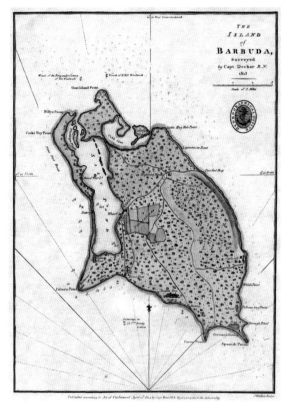

Many Barbudan men today are particularly tall and it is alleged that their height and strength originates from the men Codrington originally placed on the island. As well as pursuing any farming tasks and their own trades, it is apparent that these men were specifically chosen for the purpose of producing the finest, fittest offspring for work as future slaves. However, historians more prosaically suggest that the early Barbudan physical attributes were due to the fact that the slaves were able to eat more meat and fresh vegetables.

Early the next century (1705), Queen Anne granted Codrington a 99-year lease, at the rent of 'one fat sheep (upon demand)' annually. However, disaster struck five years later when French privateers attacked the island, blew up the castle at Codrington, carried off all the slaves and vandalised everything of value. Apparently the French didn't think it worthwhile to remain on the island, knowing in any event there would be a strong British counter attack. Thus eventually another Codrington, William, a cousin who lived in Barbados, rebuilt the castle, and petitioned the English crown for a free grant of Barbuda in perpetuity, since the lease had only 22 years to run, too short a time for him to bother with improvements.

Sir William did not have an easy time. Smallpox plagued the island. A brother, Christopher Bethel, tried to stir up a slave rebellion and take over the island as governor, and, some 10 years later, having overcome those problems, he was challenged over the legality of his leasehold by the actual governor, George Thomas. The governor failed in his action but for more than 50 years arguments raged over the leasehold until 1820, when King George IV renewed it for Sir William's son, also a Christopher – and still at the rate of one fat sheep a year.

Unfortunately, the island then was hit economically – as was Antigua – by a serious downturn in the sugar market. Codrington complained that he was labouring under the 'hardness of the times.' West Indian sugar was taxed on entry into England while sugar from other sources was allowed in duty free. Furthermore, while the profitable slave trade had been outlawed for Britons since 1807, other countries continued to take advantage of it. And because of the animosity between Britain and the United States following the War of Independence and the War of 1812, trade between the British West Indies and the United States was prohibited.

All in all, Codrington was suffering. A revolt by the slaves in 1832 was resolved without bloodshed but continuing agitation in Britain by such groups as the Anti-Slavery Society kept the freedom pot boiling. Shortly afterwards, in 1834, slavery was abolished completely.

Initially, abolition did not do the freed slaves much good. There were some 500 on the island, with no work except on the sugar plantations – but Codrington now was in financial trouble. He employed them for a time, but eventually couldn't afford to pay them, and suggested they find work in Antigua.

For decades these freed slaves lived in dismal poverty in Barbuda. Back in Britain, too, they presented a problem. While the leasehold of the island belonged to Codrington, Barbuda nevertheless was owned by the crown, which, therefore, was responsible for the welfare of all who lived there. For several years the British government tried to give the island to any country that would have it, but in the circumstances, nobody wanted to take on its problems.

Finally, in 1860, by government edict, Antigua was given responsibility for Barbuda, and in July 1870 the Codringtons relinquished their lease. This of course did nothing to resolve the economic problems. Happily, over the ensuing years, in tandem with Antigua, these problems were resolved and the economy improved. Conditions were modernised – and today the two islands are one nation, thriving, moving ahead with the times, building an economic infrastructure with tourism, agriculture, light industry and banking all playing important parts.

The island was declared a crown estate in 1903, and Antigua established an official warden there. Following this form of administration, in 1976, the warden was replaced by the Barbuda Council, enabling the island to be virtually self-governing.

Today, it is sparsely populated with only 1500 people, most of whom live in the town of **Codrington** and nearly all of whom are direct descendents of slaves brought to the island by the Codrington family. Today, Barbudans live traditionally by fishing and farming.

The Historical and Archaeological Society, Museum of Antigua and Barbuda, St John's tel: (268) 462 4930 tel/fax: (268) 462 1469 e-mail: museum@candw.ag web site: www.antiguanice.com

Christopher Codrington has created a web site entitled, 'Historic Antigua and Barbuda'. It is a meeting place for all those interested in the history, archaeology and genealogy of Antigua and Barbuda. e-mail: coopcod@village.ios.com web site: idt.net/~coopcod

---

Possibly the most accurate account of Barbuda between 1680 to 1870 was made by the Codrington family whilst they resided there, dominating economic and social life. These carefully preserved documents were being kept in the UK until Antigua could provide the necessary specially prepared environment in which to store them. Happily, the unique Codrington Papers were shipped to the island at the end of 1999. Acquired by a friendly benefactor prior to the country's independence in 1981, as a gift to the government and the people, this complete history of the Codrington family and their operations in Barbuda are now safely installed at the specially constructed National Archives storage facilities (see Island Exploration, St John's, page 177).

Barbuda

– the irresistible lure

The quintessential Caribbean vision of translucent blue water and miles of powdery sand beaches beckon. Visitors yearning for a peaceful, relaxing escape come to this quaint, unspoilt island with its pristine breathtaking beaches, miles upon miles of uninhabited, pinky coral sand (the longest being an unbroken 17 miles), caressed softly by crystal clear waters of iridescent turquoise. It is often referred to as one of the Caribbean's best kept secrets as so few people seem aware of this small isle's many attributes.

A large coral atoll lying just 27 miles away to the north of Antigua, Barbuda is rich in natural wilderness and has rather an interesting history (see page 298). Most visit this fascinating island for its marine life, to see the few sights and then claim their refuge on a typically stunning deserted beach for swimming and relaxing, but many also come for its superb diving, snorkelling, fishing, walking, birdwatching, caving, beachcombing and photography.

It is hard to believe when flying into this single-village island over its unremarkable, flat landscape that such treasures could await. Indeed, only a few hundred visitors make the trip from Antigua, but those who do not are truly missing out on the island's surprising number of natural attributes.

Go for just a day trip, or longer, by taking a mere 15-minute air flip from Antigua. One of the least frequented islands in the region, though its land area (62 square miles) is close to two thirds of the land mass of Antigua (108 square miles), it is sparsely populated. Most of its 1500 inhabitants live in the sleepy town of **Codrington** (named after Christopher Codrington, once the governor of the Leeward Islands, see page 53), and are proud of having a heritage and historical aspects which in part are quite different from that of their sister-island, Antigua, enabling Barbudans to establish their own identity.

The whole island, 14 by 8 miles, is surrounded by protective reefs, many now home to several centuries' worth of over 200 shipwrecks – much to the delight of divers. These spectacular reefs are forested with corals and teem with marine life, also due to the presence of many ideal breeding and spawning grounds, such as large submarine banks and mangrove areas around the coasts.

Barbuda is virtually a wildlife and nature reserve. **Palaster Reef**, in the southeast, is the national marine park, where fishing is not permitted. However, Barbuda is well populated with fishermen and women and fishing trips can easily be arranged for barracuda, shark, tuna and various other local fish, including lobster. Increasingly sought after, Barbuda specialises in bone fishing, a type of fishing sport which is in great demand.

Wild donkeys graze everywhere; wild pigs roam and lizards dart here and there. The island's high spot for nature lovers and ornithologists is the **nature reserve of the frigate bird** (see page 108). Not far from the airstrip, in the lime-

Frigate birds

green waters of **Codrington Lagoon**, this is also home to approximately 400 bird species, including the rare West Indian whistling duck, tropical mockingbirds, warblers and pelicans. Many species of waterfowl flourish in the large lagoons, creeks, swamps and mud flats, attracting many migratory North American species.

A local boatperson/guide will take you from the wharf on the 40-minute ride over to the

Martello tower

lagoon, through the mangrove narrows to within feet of the nests. Most of these boatpeople are a source of interesting local knowledge and are excellent guides. This is the largest nesting colony of the glossy black magnificent frigate bird (*Fregata magnificens*) in the world. The mangroves spread for seven miles by about two miles, still perfectly intact and completely unpolluted, supporting this fantastic avian and marine life (see page 108).

The eighteenth-century **Martello tower** and fort, locally known as **River Fort**, once defended the southwestern approach to Barbuda, and was used as a lookout and signal station. This landmark site, about three miles south of Codrington, is the most impressive building of historical interest in Barbuda. The still complete round Martello tower is 56 feet high and, once graced with nine guns in position, affords splendid views which demonstrate its strategic position.

Located at the island's principal trading port, the fort's main function was to defend this reef-free anchorage, from any attacking force, whilst also able to function as a lookout and last place of refuge. Be careful if the more adventurous of you try to climb down the rickety ladder into the first floor – swarms of bees sometimes make their homes inside here!

It is at the untouched southeast end of **Spanish Point** where you will find miles of totally unpopulated land and the remains of the **Spanish Point Tower**, built to defend the island from marauding Caribs (shown as 'the castle' on some maps). This lookout offers terrific views. Apart from superb snorkelling at the lovely beach here, a walk around the point to the windswept eastern coast is recommended for treasure hunting and exploring. **Sufferers**, is an extensive Amerindian site, where worked shells, flint, painted pieces of pottery, hand tools made from conch shells (adzes) still attest to the Amerindian settlement nearly 2000 years ago.

The walks are great, especially beachcombing on the quieter but spectacular Atlantic, eastern windward side. Here, the **Highlands** region has the highest point on the island at 125 feet and is where the remains of the Codrington **Highland House** can still be seen, albeit somewhat overgrown with evergreen woodland. Perhaps, as William Codrington built the house around 1720, Barbudans call the locality **Willybob**.

A long, rocky trail to the north of this area leads to the narrow entrance of **Dark Cave**, in the Pleistocene limestone terrace of Barbuda, about four miles east of Codrington. This is a rock-lined, collapsed sinkhole, 180-feet deep with a pool of fresh water at the bottom. A short crawl through a narrow slit leads to the bottom of a large cavern, about 400 feet long and about 60 feet wide, which in turn leads to a passageway. If anyone wishes to proceed along this, the descent is about 400 feet obliquely downward (a 45-degree angle) and for the hardy only, as it is overhung by huge boulders requiring frequent stooping. Fruit-eating bats inhabit these passages, where the rare millipede of the genus *Epinannolene* lives amongst their droppings.

The end of these passages takes you to broad chambers with alcoves either side and the first of a series of five freshwater pools. In the darkest of these lives the rare blind shrimp and certain species of crustacea found nowhere else in the world.

At the south end of the highlands is probably the most extraordinary natural feature of Barbuda. **Darby's Cave**, about six miles from the west coast, located in the north central highlands, is one of hundreds of sink holes. This is the largest, about 350 feet in diameter and 70 feet deep. Within its vertical walls lies a lush rain forest, with tree frogs, birds and bats, in the otherwise desiccated surrounding land above.

One of the commonest trees is the palmetto palm growing to over 50 feet among the fascinatingly hidden, sun-dappled forest of vegetation deep within this circular sink hole! Clearly, such luxuriant growth testifies that Barbuda has a wealth of underground water. There is even a perfectly smooth and solid, translucent flat-topped stalagmite, a startling eight feet high and not less than two feet in diameter, formed from intermittent drops of water from the 30-foot overhang of the cliff face.

Situated in the windswept part of the northeast coast is probably the most fascinating Barbudan prehistoric site. The small and compact **Indian Cave**, at **Two Foot Bay**, is reached by a winding path leading to the vegetated covered entrance. Next to a roofless stone ruin, a series of caverns goes directly into a round chamber of a lower level called the **Drop Cavern**. This in turn connects to the **Bat Chambers**, conical caverns about 35-feet high with, not surprisingly, many hanging bats.

It is from the main entrance corridor that two Amerindian rock carvings (petroglyphs) can be seen, aided by the daylight which floods into a nearby cave. Associated with Amerindian religion, they are the only ones within Antigua and Barbuda known to date.

The island is famed for its striking pinky coral beaches and visitors savour these havens of isolation and privacy. The only time any action is evident is on holiday weekends, when locals arrive by the car and jeep load well-equipped with picnics, barbecues and music. With the few hotels on Barbuda, most will have no facilities, so travel prepared and whilst most beaches boast calm, shallow waters, some can have strong currents at certain times of the year.

Shopping is limited but there are a few general shops selling gifts and t-shirts as well as essentials. You can watch locals producing various arts and crafts such as baskets, decorative brooms, hats, shellwork and items incorporating the famous Barbudan pink sand at the **Arts and Crafts Handicrafts Centre**. This government run outlet is situated opposite the post office in Codrington.

You will find restaurants and bars in Codrington (not elsewhere, unless at one of the hotels) which, whilst catering mainly to the local trade, offer excellent fare. Bars may have television and pool tables – and always a friendly atmosphere. Meeting locals is easy. Barbuda has such a strong community spirit that inevitably there are at least a couple of food fayres every month, often held in the middle of the village locally referred to as **Madison Square**. Consisting of around five or six local vendors, you can feast on barbecued chicken, fried dumplings, fish and other local favourites.

Fish frys are traditionally popular with varieties of freshly fried, seasoned fish, plus sometimes serving the speciality dish, goat water (goat meat soup, see Antiguan Cuisine, page 261). These particular gatherings are located outside the **Green Door Tavern**. This local haunt has all the atmosphere of a pub with the coldest beer in town and is always a central meeting and chatting spot. Say hello to Byron Askie, the congenial owner who will make you very comfortable when visiting this local haunt.

Events in Barbuda include cricket matches, which are played Sundays during the season (January to July) at the **Holy Trinity School grounds** and the colourful, entertaining **Barbuda Caribana** – the island's carnival starting on the last Thursday in May for about five days and full of pageantry, dance, calypso and fun.

The villagers are most obliging and full of character, probably due to inheriting the spirit of their ancestors who, as a result of years of virtual non-supervision by plantation owners, were far more free and independent than the average local of that era. Hence, today, Barbudans understandably also cling to their traditional livelihoods of fishing and farming.

Noted for their hospitality and willingness, there are quite a few on-island companies and guides able to arrange exactly the kind of day trip, or longer you want. These are especially popular as there is not an abundance of taxi services on the island and, whilst it is possible to rent a jeep (see page 315), there is only a single petrol station!

All Barbudans are extremely welcoming and can organise pretty much anything you wish

from vehicle hire, sightseeing trips, fishing, snorkelling, diving, hiking to the caves, lunch, beach barbecues, school visits, even a village walking tour to experience local life.

Abundant and varied in its marine and bird life, this is an outstanding experience for those seeking some unhurried hours of peace and space, surrounded by nature in all its glory. It is unquestionably well worth a visit to this quiet and charming neighbouring sister isle, devoid of the usual commercial trappings, souvenir shops, vendors, beach bars and the like – the perfect retreat. It is here that you will find fewer footprints per square acre than you are likely to have experienced before, whether on the beach or inland.

Either simply book a flight direct from Antigua (there are no flights from anywhere else in the world), or book an organised day trip, or longer, through your hotel or with any of the reputable travel agencies in St John's (see page 320).

If you wish to stay in Barbuda, there is a good choice from small guesthouses to luxury resorts (see Appendix, page 318). It would be wise to engage the services of a local guide if travelling independently and with the lack of shops and facilities on Barbuda, be prepared for all that you wish to do, taking snorkelling gear, provisions or specialist equipment. And, don't forget your sunhat, sunscreen, camera or camcorder!

Barbuda Tourist Council, Codrington tel: (268) 460 0077 fax: (268) 460 0410 opening hours: Monday to Thursday 8am–4.30pm, Friday 8am–3pm.

Tourist Information, Codrington tel: (268) 460 0604 opening hours: 8am–4.30pm.

Redonda

Redonda

Many people dream of having their own tropical island and during the last century an Irishman named Matthew Phipps Shiel made this come true by being crowned King of Redonda, albeit on this windswept hunk of rock he had only seagulls and various other creatures as subjects. On his death, Shiel's literary executor, a London poet, declared himself King Juan I of Redonda. However, this John Gawsworth would offer knighthoods and other titles to those who showed him any worthwhile favours in lieu of money. In his quest to produce a literary and intellectual aristocracy for the realm, he bestowed titles on such friends as Arthur Ransome, Alfred Knopf, Victor Gollancz, J. B. Priestley, Ellery Queen, Stephen Potter, Dorothy Sayers, Lawrence Durrell, Dylan Thomas, and Rebecca West.

This light-hearted legend continues with the somewhat nebulous status maintained. A present successor, living in Antigua, has titled himself King Robert the Bald. With 65 friends as 'loyal subjects', he sailed to Redonda on 31 May 1998 to secure the kingdom. Sailing on the suitably majestic 130-foot square-rigged topsail schooner, *Sir Robert Baden-Powell*, he planted the newly designed flag and performed other such 'royal' tasks.

As with previous reigns, the new king will ensure that the island is spared the 'depredations of man. It will remain a home for the existing wildlife', he said.

Called 'Ocanamanru' by the seafaring Caribs, who used the island as a way station, when Columbus passed by on 11 November 1493, he named it after a chapel in Cadiz cathedral called Santa Maria la Redonda, meaning St Mary the Round, and reported it as an inaccessible rock.

The remnant of a volcanic cone and rising to about 1000 feet, it is characterised by sheer cliff sides which fall into the deep ocean about 35 miles southwest of Antigua. Only a mile long and about a third of a mile at its widest, Redonda had been a dependency of Montserrat up to 1872, when it became part of the state of Antigua and Barbuda.

The worldwide demand for calcium phosphate in the 1860s generated a lucrative industry for Redonda which was covered in chemically rich bird guano and little else. A later discovery of aluminium phosphate on the cone beneath this guano resulted in large mining operations by the American owned Redonda Phosphate Company. This reached its zenith in 1895, when 5778 metric tons were produced using the labour of 130 Montserratians who had to be hauled up in a mining bucket on a cable way to reach the works.

Following the outbreak of World War I, consequent shipping problems and the fact that Germany was one of the company's biggest clients suspended mining, but a skeleton crew was kept to maintain the equipment. However, technical advances made during the war rendered further mining uneconomical and the staff finally left in 1929 when a hurricane blew most of the buildings away. The lease was relinquished in 1930.

The revival of the phosphate industry was attempted by the government in 1978. In order to raise a modest additional revenue from philatelists, a caretaker was appointed and a small post office built at the foot of the cliffs. A year later, after hurricane David washed away the post office, the stamps became a rare collector's item and Redonda was once again left to its uninhabited isolation.

Today, the odd yacht anchors there and at times various trips are arranged, although climbing the steep cliffs of the island can be hazardous. Basically undisturbed, there is very little to see save for the remains of the Company buildings, rusty machinery, goats, large hermit crabs, lizards, rats, the burrowing owl (*Speotyto cunicularia* – which became extinct in Antigua after the introduction of the mongoose) and thousands of nesting seabirds.

Royal Redondan Navy

H.M. King Robert the Bald Admiral of the Fleet, and H.M. Queen Elizabeth, as well as the entire Court of the Kingdom of Redonda wish you a very Happy New Millennium

Appendix

Everything should be made as simple
as possible, but not simpler.

Albert Einstein

AIRLINES

INTERNATIONAL SCHEDULED

Air Canada tel: (268) 462 1147
fax: (268) 462 2679
American Airlines
tel: (268) 462 0952
fax: (268) 462 2067
British Airways tel: (268) 462 0876
fax: (268) 462 3218
BWIA International
tel: (268) 480 2900
fax: (268) 480 2941
Condor tel: (268) 462 0528
fax: (268) 462 8999[1]
Continental Airlines
tel: (268) 462 1147
fax: (268) 462 2679[3]
Virgin Atlantic tel: (268) 560 2079
fax: (268) 562 1629[1]

INTERNATIONAL CHARTERED

Air 2000 tel: (268) 462 0528
fax: (268) 462 8999[1]
Air Guadeloupe tel: (268) 462 2523
fax: (268) 462 5185
Allegro Airlines tel: (268) 462 0528
fax: (268) 462 8999[1]
Britannia tel: (268) 480 5700
fax: (268) 480 5625[2]
JMC tel: (268) 462 0528
fax: (268) 462 8999[1]
Miami Air tel: (268) 462 0528
fax: (268) 462 8999[1]
Royal Air tel: (268) 480 5625[2]
fax: (268) 480 5700
Ryan Air[2] tel: (268) 480 5700
fax: (268) 480 5625
Skyservice tel: (268) 462 0528
fax: (268) 462 8999[1]

[1] Agent – Airport Services (Antigua) Ltd
[2] Agent – LIAT (1974) Ltd
[3] Agent – Air Canada

REGIONAL INTER-ISLAND TRAVEL

Scheduled
BWIA International
tel: (268) 480 2900
fax: (268) 480 2941
Carib Aviation
tel: (268) 462 3147/3452
fax: (268) 462 3125
e-mail: caribav@candw.ag
Caribbean Star Airlines
tel: (268) 480 2590
fax: (268) 480 5905
e-mail: croberts@flycaribbeanstar.com
LIAT (1974) Ltd tel: (268) 480 5601
fax: (268) 480 5625

Charter
Carib Aviation
tel: (268) 462 3147/3452
fax: (268) 462 3125
e-mail: caribav@candw.ag
Caribbean Helicopters
tel: (268) 460 5900
fax: (268) 460 5901
e-mail: helicopters@candw.ag
Inter-Island Aviation
tel/fax: (268) 460 2611
mobile: (268) 464 6553
e-mail: harveyj@candw.ag
Norman Aviation
tel: (268) 464 8522
tel/fax: (268) 462 2445
e-mail: aviation@candw.ag
Port Services Ltd
FBO 2000 tel: (268) 462 2522
fax: (268) 462 5185
e-mail: psltapa@candw.ag

BANKING HOURS AND SERVICES

ANTIGUA BARBUDA INVESTMENT BANK

St John's tel: (268) 480 2700
Monday to Thursday 8am–2pm
Friday 8am–4pm
Woods Centre tel: (268) 480 2860
Monday to Thursday 9am–3pm
Friday 9am–4pm Saturday 9am–1pm
Falmouth Harbour
Wednesday to Friday 9am–1pm
tel: (268) 480 2775
Jolly Harbour tel: (268) 480 2281
Monday to Thursday 8am–2pm
Friday 9am–1pm
ATM locations Heritage Quay
(King's Casino), Woods Centre
Credit card cash withdrawals
Mastercard, Visa

ANTIGUA COMMERCIAL BANK

St John's tel: (268) 462 1217
Monday to Thursday 8am–2pm
Friday 8am–5pm
Airport tel: (268) 462 3052
Monday to Friday 8am–3pm
Bureau de Change (Airport)
Monday to Friday 3pm–9:30pm
Saturday and Sunday 12 noon–7pm
Barbuda tel: (268) 480 0066
Tuesday, Wednesday, Thursday
9am–3pm
Credit card cash withdrawals
Diner's, Visa

BARCLAYS BANK

St John's tel: (268) 480 5000

Monday to Thursday 8am–2pm
Friday 8am–4pm
Credit card cash withdrawals
Discovery, Mastercard, Visa

BANK OF ANTIGUA

St John's and Airport
Monday–Thursday 8am–3pm
Friday 8am–4pm Saturday 8am–1pm
tel: (268) 480 5300
Nelson's Dockyard
Monday to Thursday 8am–3pm
Friday 8am–4pm
Saturday 8am–1pm
tel: (268) 480 5300
Bank on Wheels (mobile bank)
Monday to Friday
tel: (268) 480 5300
Credit card cash withdrawals
Mastercard, Visa

BANK OF NOVA SCOTIA

St John's tel: (268) 480 1500
Monday to Thursday 8am–2pm
Friday 8am–4pm

CANADIAN IMPERIAL BANK OF COMMERCE

St John's tel: (268) 480 8500
Monday to Wednesday 8am–2pm
Thursday 8am–1pm
Friday 8am–5pm
ATM locations St John's
Credit card cash withdrawals
Novus, Mastercard, Visa

CARIBBEAN BANKING CORPORATION

St John's tel: (268) 462 4217
Monday to Thursday 8am–2pm
Friday 8am–4pm
Credit card cash withdrawals
Mastercard, Visa

ROYAL BANK OF CANADA

St John's and Airport
tel: (268) 480 1150
Monday to Thursday 8am–3pm
Friday 8am–5pm
ATM locations Airport, St John's
Credit card cash withdrawals
Cirrus, Mastercard, Visa, cards with
the PLUS symbol

SWISS AMERICAN BANK/ ANTIGUA INTERNATIONAL TRUST

Woods Centre tel: (268) 480 2240
Monday to Friday 8am–1pm
Credit card cash withdrawals
Mastercard, Visa

WESTERN UNION MONEY TRANSFER
St John's tel: (268) 463 0102
Monday to Thursday
8.30am–4.30pm
Monday to Sunday 8am–10pm
Friday 8.30am–4pm
Saturday 8.30am–2pm
c/o M and M's Gas Service Station
Old Parham Road
tel: (268) 452 4444

BUSINESS TRIPS
BOARDS, INSTITUTES, ASSOCIATIONS AND ORGANISATIONS
Alliance Française
tel: (268) 462 3625
e-mail: hansen@candw.ag
Antigua and Barbuda Bar Association
tel: (268) 462 4468/9
fax: (268) 462 0327
e-mail: chancellor@candw.ag
Antigua and Barbuda Chamber of Commerce and Industry
tel: (268) 462 0743
fax: (268) 462 4575
e-mail: chamcom@candw.ag
Antigua and Barbuda Department of Tourism
tel: (268) 462 0480
fax: (268) 462 2483/6093
e-mail: info@antigua-barbuda.org
www.antigua-barbuda.org
Antigua Hotels and Tourist Association
tel: (268) 462 0374
fax: (268) 462 3702
e-mail: ahta@candw.ag
Antigua and Barbuda Humane Society
tel: (268) 461 4957
e-mail: abhumane@candw.ag
Antigua Trades and Labour Union
tel: (268) 462 0090
fax: (268) 462 4056
e-mail: atandlu@candw.ag
Barbuda Tourism Council
tel: (268) 460 0077
fax: (268) 460 0410
Caribbean Agricultural Research and Development Institutes (CARDI)
tel: (268) 462 0661
fax: (268) 462 1666
e-mail: cardi@candw.ag
Caribbean Council for the Blind
tel: (268) 462 4111
fax: (268) 462 6371
e-mail: ccb@candw.ag

Employers Federation
tel/fax: (268) 462 0449
e-mail: aempfed@candw.ag
Environmental Awareness Group
tel: (268) 462 6236
fax: (268) 460 1740
e-mail: eag@candw.ag
Red Cross Society
tel: (268) 462 0800
fax: (268) 460 9595
e-mail: redcross@candw.ag
West Indies Cricket Board
tel: (268) 460 5462
fax: (268) 460 5452
e-mail: wicb@candw.ag

CONFERENCE FACILITIES
Jolly Beach Hotel
tel: (268) 462 0068
fax: (268) 462 1827
Heritage Hotel
tel: (268) 462 1247
fax: (268) 462 1179
e-mail: heritagehotel@candw.ag
Rex Halcyon Cove Hotel Conference Room
tel: (268) 462 0256
fax: (268) 462 0271
e-mail: rexhalcyon@candw.ag
web site: www.rexcaribbean.com
Sandals Antigua
tel: (268) 462 0267
fax: (268) 462 4135
e-mail: sandals@candw.ag
web site: www.sandals.com
St James's Club
tel: (268) 460 5000
fax: (268) 460 3015
web site: www.antigua_resorts.com

CONVENTION FACILITIES
Multi Purpose Cultural Centre
tel/fax: (268) 460 7388
Royal Antiguan Hotel
tel: (268) 462 3733
fax: (268) 462 3732

INCENTIVE DESTINATION MANAGEMENT
Alexander Parrish (Antigua) Ltd
tel: (268) 462 4458
fax: (268) 462 4457
e-mail: apal@candw.ag
web site: www.mstarr.com
Antigua Vacations
tel: (268) 460 6919
fax: (268) 463 8959
e-mail: antvacation@candw.ag
Bo-Tours Antigua Ltd
tel: (268) 462 6632
fax: (268) 463 5336

e-mail: botours@candw.ag
web site: www.botours.com
Destination Antigua Ltd
tel: (268) 463 1944
fax: (268) 463 3344
e-mail: labarrielc@candw.ag
www.destinationantigua.com
Kiskidee Travel and Tours
tel: (268) 462 4801
fax: (268) 462 4802
e-mail: kiskidee@candw.ag

SOCIAL CLUBS
Jaycees/Antigua Junior Chambers
tel: (268) 462 4979
fax: (268) 462 5985
General meeting 7pm last Tuesday every month at the Red Cross Building, St John's

Kiwanis
tel: (268) 462 0134
fax: (268) 462 9166
The club meets every week on Thursday at 7.30pm at the Heritage Hotel, Heritage Quay, St John's; contact the President, Mr Everett Lake, on the above numbers.

Lions/Leo
tel: (268) 462 0665
fax: (268) 560 1796
General meeting at 8pm first and third Tuesday every month at Cross Street, St John's

Optimists Club of St John's
tel: (268) 480 5616
Meets 6.30pm every second and fourth Wednesday of each month at the Heritage Hotel, Heritage Quay

St John's Rotary
tel: (268) 480 3250
fax: (268) 480 3270
Meets 12.30pm every Wednesday at the Royal Antiguan Resort, Deep Bay

DIPLOMATIC AND CONSULAR REPRESENTATION

RESIDENT DIPLOMATIC REPRESENTATIVES
Resident Acting British High Commissioner
PricewaterhouseCoopers,
Old Parham Road, St John's
tel: (268) 462 0008/9
fax: (268) 462 2806
Embassy of the People's Republic of China
Crosbies tel: (268) 462 6414
fax: (268) 462 0986
Resident adviser, European Union
St George's Street, St John's
tel: (268) 462 2970
fax: (268) 462 2670
Director OAS
Factory Road, St John's
tel: (268) 462 1284
fax: (268) 462 3543
Venezuelan Ambassador
Embassy of Venezuela
Redcliffe Street, St John's
tel: (268) 462 1574
fax: (268) 462 1570

NON-RESIDENT DIPLOMATIC REPRESENTATION (DIPLOMATIC CORPS)
Antigua and Barbuda Ambassador at large
HE Ms Yvonne Maginley, MBE
tel: (268) 481 1650
fax: (268) 481 1676
Antigua and Barbuda Ambassador for People's Republic of China, CARICOM, Venezuela and ACS countries
HE James A.E. Thomas, CMG
tel: (268) 462 1052
fax: (268) 462 2482
Antigua and Barbuda Ambassador to Cuba
HE Colin Murdoch
tel: (268) 462 1052
fax: (268) 462 2482
Non-resident Ambassador to the Republic of Haiti
HE Dr Patrick Lewis
tel: (212) 541 4117
fax: (212) 757 1607
Ambassador to (some) Middle East States, Antigua and Barbuda Envoy to Syria
HE Mr Ramez Hadeed
tel: (268) 462 3303/0713
fax: (268) 462 2110

CONSULAR REPRESENTATIVES
Barbados
Mr Pedro Corbin
c/o Antigua Catering
tel: (268) 462 3121/2
fax: (268) 462 3479
Canadian warden
Mr John Warren
c/o Brysons
tel: (268) 462 1210/1332
fax: (268) 462 0320
Denmark
Mr Michael Hall, OBE
c/o Anjo Insurance
tel: (268) 462 0183
fax: (268) 480 3076
France
Mrs Florence Suttie
c/o Historic Redcliffe Quay
tel: (268) 460 6428
fax: (268) 460 6172
Germany
Mr Carston Biel
Hodges Bay tel: (268) 462 3174
fax: (268) 462 3496
Guyana
Mr Joseph Al Gouveia
Crosbies tel: (268) 461 2240
fax: (268) 462 2975
Italy
Mr Carlo Falcone
c/o Antigua Yacht Club Marina
tel: (268) 460 1543
fax: (268) 460 1444
Jamaica
Mrs Myra Walwyn
Stapleton Lane, St John's
tel: (268) 462 0031
fax: (268) 462 0031
Netherlands
Mr Donald Gomez
St John's tel: (268) 462 0308
fax: (268) 462 2472
Norway
Mr Eustace B. Francis
c/o Francis Trading, St John's
tel: (268) 462 4555/0954
fax: (268) 462 0849
Spain
Mr Noel Walling
7 St George's Street, St John's
tel: (268) 462 0889
fax: (268) 462 1651
Syria
Mr Joseph Hadeed
tel: (268) 462 2664
fax: (268) 462 2661
Switzerland
Mrs Ilse Cooper
tel: (268) 462 8975
fax: (268) 462 1262

United States consular agent
Mrs Juliet G. Ryder
tel: (268) 463 6531
fax: (268) 460 1569

OVERSEAS ANTIGUA AND BARBUDA DIPLOMATIC REPRESENTATION
Canada
Consulate General of Antigua and Barbuda
Miss Madelaine Blackman
60 St Clair Avenue East, Suite 205
Toronto, Ontario M4T 1N5, Canada
tel: (416) 961 3085
fax: (416) 961 7218
Joint Mission
HE George Bullen
O.E.C.S.,112 Kent Street Suite 1610 Ottawa, K1P 5P2, Canada
tel: (613) 236 8952
fax: (613) 236 3042

UK
High Commissioner
(and non-resident Ambassador to France and Russia)
HE Mr R. Sanders, CMG
High Commission of Antigua and Barbuda, 15 Thayer Street, London W1M 5LD, UK
tel: (0207) 486 7073
fax: (0207) 486 9970

USA
Ambassador, Permanent Mission of Antigua and Barbuda to the United Nations
HE Dr Patrick Lewis
610 5th Avenue Suite 311,
New York 10020, USA
tel: (212) 541 4117
fax: (212) 757 1607

Ambassador, Embassy of Antigua and Barbuda
HE Mr Lionel Hurst
O.E.C.S. Building,
3216 New Mexico Avenue NW,
Washington DC 20016, USA
tel: (202) 362 5122/5166
fax: (202) 362 5225

Consulate-General of Antigua and Barbuda
Dr Norman Athill
25 SE Second Avenue, Suite 300
Miami, Florida 33131, USA
tel: (305) 381 6762
fax: (305) 381 7908

GETTING AROUND AND PUBLIC TRANSPORT

CAR AND JEEP HIRE
Archibald Rent-A-Car
tel/fax: (268) 562 1709
Avis Rent-A-Car tel: (268) 462 2847
fax: (268) 462 2848
Budget Rent-A-Car
tel: (268) 462 3009
fax: (268) 460 9177
Dollar Rent-A-Car
tel: (268) 462 0362
fax: (268) 462 5907
Hertz Rent-A-Car
tel: (268) 462 4114
fax: (268) 462 1048
Holiday Car Rentals
tel: (local only) 462 9780
Hyatt Rent-A-Car
tel: (268) 463 2012
Jonas Rent-A-Car
tel: (268) 462 3760
fax: (268) 463 7625
Lion Car Rental tel: (268) 460 1400
fax: (268) 460 2708
Matthew's Car Rental
tel: (268) 462 9532
fax: (268) 463 9030
National Rent-A-Car
tel/fax: (268) 462 2113
Oakland Car Rental
tel: (268) 462 3021
Slane's Car Rental
tel: (268) 462 8789
Thrifty Car Rental
tel: (268) 463 5188
fax: (268) 463 9030
Titi Rent-A-Car tel: (268) 460 1452
fax: (268) 460 1450

Barbuda
Beachbums Rentals
tel: (268) 560 2680
Junie Walker Rentals
tel: (268) 460 0150

SCOOTERS AND MOTORBIKES
JT's Rent-A-Scoot
tel: (268) 463 3578
Paradise Yacht Sales
tel: (268) 460 7125
fax: (268) 460 9651

BICYCLES
Bike Plus tel: (268) 462 2453
fax: (268) 460 7587
Cycle Krazy tel/fax: (268) 462 9253
Paradise Yacht Sales
tel: (268) 460 7125
fax: (268) 460 9651

Shipwreck Rent-A-Scooter
tel: (268) 464 7771/460 6087

Barbuda
Beachbums Rentals
tel: (268) 560 2680

TAXI SERVICES
Antigua Reliable 24 Hr Taxi Service
tel: (268) 460 5353
Antigua Taxi Stand
tel: (268) 462 5190
ATS Taxi and Limousine Service
tel: (268) 562 1709
Beachcomber Taxi Stand
tel: (268) 462 3366
Brother's Taxi Service
tel: (268) 462 6464
Daylight Taxi Stand
tel: (268) 462 3015
Heritage Quay Taxi Stand
tel: (268) 460 8213
Ivor's Taxi Stand tel: (268) 460 1241
King's Casino Taxi Stand
tel: (268) 462 1729
Reliable Taxi Service
tel: (268) 462 1510
Sandals Antigua Taxi Stand
tel: (268) 462 2504
West Bus Station (24 Hour)
Taxi Service tel: (268) 460 5353

Barbuda
Beachbums tel: (268) 560 2680
Burton's Enterprises
tel: (268) 460 0465
George 'Prophet' Burton Taxi
tel: (268) 460 0103
The Earl's Tours
tel/fax: (268) 462 5647
Paradise Tours tel: (268) 460 0081
Red Fox Taxis tel: (268) 460 0065

CONDUCTED SIGHTSEEING TOURS
Bo Tours tel: (268) 462 6632
fax: (268) 462 5336
Estate Safari Historical Tours
tel: (268) 463 4713
fax: (268) 460 1468
International Travel Consultants
Ltd tel: (268) 462 0811/2053
fax: (268) 462 4156
Rendezvous Tour Company
tel: (268) 463 5550
fax: (268) 461 9750
Tropikelly Trails tel: (268) 461 0383
fax: (268) 462 9253
XO Tours Ltd tel: (268) 460 8687
fax: (268) 460 8686
Coral Isle tel: (268) 460 5625
fax: (268) 460 5626

Barbuda
Barbuda Island Tours
tel: (268) 460 0103/464 8241
Beachbums tel: (268) 560 2680
fax: (268) 480 7480
Burton's Enterprises
tel: (268) 460 0465
The Earl's Tours
tel/fax: (268) 462 5647
Paradise Tours tel: (268) 460 0081
Red Fox Day Trips
tel: (268) 460 0065
fax: (268) 460 0434

HOTELS AND VILLA RENTALS

Admiral's Inn D4
Nelson's Dockyard, English Harbour
PO Box 713, St John's
Antigua WI
tel: (268) 460 1027/1153
fax: (268) 460 1534
e-mail: admirals@candw.ag
www.gray.com/people/admiralsinn
Rooms: 16

Allegro Resort Pineapple Beach E2
Long Bay
PO Box 2000
St John's, Antigua WI
tel: (268) 463 2006
fax: (268) 562 1158
e-mail: a.m.pineapple@candw.ag
Rooms: 135

Amaryllis Hotel B2
Airport Road
PO Box 2624
St John's, Antigua WI
tel: (268) 462 8690
fax: (268) 462 8691
Rooms: 22

Antigua Village Condo Beach Resort B1
Dickenson Bay
PO Box 649
St John's, Antigua WI
tel: (268) 462 2930
fax: (268) 462 0375
e-mail: antiguavillage@candw.ag
www.antiguavillage.net
Rooms: 77
Villas: 23

Antigua Beachcomber Hotel C1
Winthrope Bay
PO Box 1512
St John's, Antigua WI
tel: (268) 462 3100/2756

fax: (268) 462 4012
e-mail: beachcom@candw.ag
Rooms: 28

Barrymore Beach Club
PO Box 1774
Runaway Bay
St John's, Antigua WI
tel: (268) 462 4101
fax: (268) 462 4140
e-mail: barrymorep@candw.ag
Rooms: 32

Blue Waters Hotel B1
Soldier Bay
PO Box 256
St John's, Antigua WI
tel: (268) 462 0290
fax: (268) 462 0293
e-mail: bluewaters@candw.ag
www.bluewaters.net
Rooms: 77

Bougainvillea Hotel B2
All Saints Road
PO Box 1236
St John's, Antigua WI
tel: (268) 462 0939
fax: (268) 462 1743
e-mail: sandpiper@candw.ag
www.sandpiperreef.com
Rooms: 24

Caribbean Inn B2
Radio Range
PO Box W368
Woods Centre, Antigua WI
tel: (268) 562 0210
fax: (268) 562 0209
Rooms: 14

Carlisle Bay Club B4
Old Road Village
PO Box 1515
St John's, Antigua WI
tel: (268) 462 1377
Rooms: 42

Catamaran Hotel and Marina D4
Falmouth Harbour
PO Box 958
St John's, Antigua WI
tel: (268) 460 1036
fax: (268) 460 1339
Rooms: 16

Chez Pascal Deluxe Rooms
Five Islands
PO Box 2356
St John's, Antigua WI
tel: (268) 462 3232
fax: (268) 460 5730

e-mail: chez@candw.ag
www.antiguanice.com
Rooms: 4

City View Hotel B2
Newgate Street
PO Box 2692
St John's, Antigua WI
tel: (268) 562 0256
fax: (268) 562 0242
e-mail: cityview@candw.ag
Rooms: 37

Cocobay
Valley Church
PO Box 431
St John's, Antigua WI
tel: (268) 562 2400
fax: (268) 562 2424
e-mail: cocobay@candw.ag
www.cocobayresort.com
Rooms: 50

Coco's Antigua B2
Valley Road
PO Box 2204
St John's, Antigua WI
tel: (268) 460 2626
fax: (268) 462 9423
e-mail: cocos@candw.ag
Rooms: 12

The Copper and Lumber Store Hotel D4
English Harbour
PO Box 184
St John's, Antigua WI
tel: (268) 460 1058
fax: (268) 460 1529
e-mail: clhotel@candw.ag
Rooms: 14

Cortsland Hotel B2
Upper Gambles
PO Box 403
St John's, Antigua WI
tel: (268) 462 1395
fax: (268) 462 1699
Rooms: 42

Curtain Bluff Hotel B4
Old Road
PO Box 288
St John's, Antigua WI
tel: (268) 462 8400
fax: (268) 462 8409
www.curtainbluff.com
Rooms: 63

Dickenson Bay Cottages B1
Dickenson Bay

PO Box 1379
St John's, Antigua WI
tel: (268) 462 4940
fax: (268) 462 4941
Rooms: 12

Dove Cove Hotel
Dry Hill
PO Box 2694
St John's, Antigua WI
tel: (268) 463 8600
fax: (268) 462 3601
Rooms: 12

Falmouth Harbour Beach Apartments D4
English Harbour Village
PO Box 713
St John's, Antigua WI
tel: (268) 460 1094
fax: (268) 460 1534
e-mail: admirals@candw.ag
www.gray.maine.com/people/admiralsinn
Rooms: 26

Galleon Beach Club D4
English Harbour
PO Box 1003
St John's, Antigua WI
tel: (268) 460 1024
fax: (268) 460 1450
e-mail: galleonbeach@candw.ag
Rooms: 26

Galley Bay A2
Five Islands
PO Box 305
St John's, Antigua WI
tel: (268) 462 5600
fax: (268) 462 4551
Rooms: 69

Halcyon Heights
Trade Winds
PO Box 1345
St John's, Antigua WI
tel: (268) 462 5012
fax: (268) 462 7760
e-mail: halcyonheights@candw.ag
Rooms: 24

Harmony Hall
Nonsuch Bay
PO Box 1558
St John's, Antigua WI
tel: (268) 460 4120
fax: (268) 460 4406
e-mail: harmony@candw.ag
www.harmonyhall.com
Rooms: 6

Hawksbill Beach Resort A2
Five Islands
PO Box 108
St John's, Antigua WI
tel: (268) 462 0301
fax: (268) 462 1515
e-mail: hawksbill@candw.ag
www.hawksbill.com
Rooms: 111

Heritage Hotel B2
Heritage Quay
PO Box 1532
St John's, Antigua WI
tel: (268) 462 1247
fax: (268) 462 1179
e-mail: heritagehotel@candw.ag
Rooms: 20

Hodges Bay Club
Hodges Bay
PO Box 1237
St John's, Antigua WI
tel: (268) 462 2300
fax: (268) 462 1962
Rooms: 26

The Inn at English Harbour D4
English Harbour
PO Box 187
St John's, Antigua WI
tel: (268) 460 1014
fax: (268) 460 1603
e-mail: theinn@candw.ag
www.theinn.ag
Rooms: 28

The Island Inn
McKinnons
PO Box 1218
St John's, Antigua WI
tel: (268) 462 4065
fax: (268) 462 4066
e-mail: barnardd@candw.ag
Rooms: 10

Joe Mike's Hotel Plaza B2
Nevis Street
PO Box 136
St John's, Antigua WI
tel: (268) 462 1142/3244
fax: (268) 462 6056
e-mail: joemikes@candw.ag
Rooms: 12

Jolly Beach Hotel A3
Jolly Harbour
PO Box 1793
St John's, Antigua WI
tel: (268) 462 0061
fax: (268) 462 7686

e-mail: jollyhbradv@candw.ag
www.jollyharbour-marina.com
Rooms: 476 (+ 130 villas)

Jolly Castle Hotel A3
Jolly Harbour
PO Box 1136
St John's, Antigua WI
tel/fax: (268) 463 9001
e-mail: jollycastle@candw.ag
Rooms: 27

Jolly Harbour Beach Resort A3
Jolly Harbour
PO Box 1793
St John's, Antigua WI
tel: (268) 462 6166
tel: (268) 462 6167
e-mail: jollyharbour@candw.ag
Rooms: 44

Jumby Bay Resort D1
Long Island
PO Box 243
St John's, Antigua WI
tel: (268) 462 6000
fax: (268) 462 6020
e-mail: jumbyb@candw.ag
Rooms: 39

Lashing's Sports Café Bar and Inn
Sandhaven
PO Box 2456
St John's, Antigua WI
tel: (268) 462 4438
fax: (268) 462 4491
e-mail: lashings@candw.ag
Rooms: 15

Long Bay Hotel F2
Long Bay
PO Box 442
St John's, Antigua WI
tel: (268) 463 2005
fax: (268) 463 2439
e-mail: hotel@longbay.antigua.com
Rooms: 20

Mango Bay Hotel and Beach Club F2
Dian Bay
PO Box W1400
St John's, Antigua WI
tel: (268) 460 6646
fax: (268) 460 8400
e-mail: mangobay@candw.ag
www.mangobayantigua.com
Rooms: 52

The Marina Bay Resort B1
Dickenson Bay

PO Box 1187
St John's, Antigua WI
tel: (268) 462 3254
fax: (268) 462 2151
e-mail: marinabay@candw.ag
www.s/caribbean.commarinabay
Rooms: 27

Ocean Inn D4
English Harbour
PO Box 838
St John's, Antigua WI
tel: (268) 460 1263
fax: (268) 463 7950
Rooms: 12

Pelican Isle E2
Johnson's Point
St John's, Antigua WI
tel: (268) 462 8385
fax: (268) 462 4361
e-mail: pelican@candw.ag
www.caribvillas.com/pelican
Rooms: 6

Pigottsville Hotel
Wireless Road
PO Box 521
St John's, Antigua WI
tel: (268) 462 0592
e-mail: marcellec@candw.ag
Rooms: 16

Rex Blue Heron Hotel A4
Johnson's Point Beach
IPO Box 1715
St John's
Antigua WI
tel: (268) 462 8564
fax: (268) 462 8005
e-mail: bheron@candw.ag
www.rexcaribbean.com
Rooms: 64

Rex Halcyon Cove B1
Dickenson Bay
PO Box 251
St John's
Antigua WI
tel: (268) 462 0256
fax: (268) 462 0271
e-mail: rexhalcyon@candw.ag
www.rexcaribbean.com
Rooms: 210

Roslyn's Guest House B2
Upper Gambles
PO Box 161
St John's, Antigua WI
tel: (268) 462 0762
Rooms: 2

Royal Antiguan Resort A2
Deep Bay
PO Box 1322
St John's, Antigua WI
tel: (268) 462 3733
fax: (268) 462 3732
Rooms: 282

Runaway Beach Club B1
Runaway Bay
PO Box 874
St John's, Antigua WI
tel: (268) 462 1318
fax: (268) 462 4172
e-mail: sayert@candw.ag
Rooms: 7

Sandals Antigua Resort
and Spa B1
Dickenson Bay
PO Box 147
St John's, Antigua WI
tel: (268) 462 0267
fax: (268) 462 4135
e-mail: sandals@candw.ag
www.sandals.com
Rooms: 193

Sandpiper Reef Resort C1
Crosbies
PO Box 569
St John's, Antigua WI
tel: (268) 462 0939
fax: (268) 462 1743
e-mail: sandpiper@candw.ag
www.sandpiperreef.com
Rooms: 25

Siboney Beach Club B1
Dickenson Bay
PO Box 222
St John's, Antigua WI
tel: (268) 462 0806
fax: (268) 462 3356
c mail: siboney@candw.ag
www.turk.com/siboney/
Rooms: 12

St James's Club E4
Mamora Bay
PO Box 63
St John's, Antigua WI
tel: (268) 460 5000
fax: (268) 460 3015
www.antigua_resorts.com
Rooms: 185

Sunsail Club Colonna C1
Hodges Bay
PO Box W1892
Woods Centre, Antigua WI

tel: (268) 462 6263
fax: (268) 462 6430
e-mail: colonna@candw.ag
www.sunsail.com
Rooms: 117

The New Barrymore Hotel B2
Fort Road
PO Box 10
St John's, Antigua WI
tel: (268) 462 1055
fax: (268) 462 4062
e-mail: barrymorehotel@candw.ag
Rooms: 30

Time-A-Way Beach Apartments B1
Runaway Bay
PO Box 189
St John's, Antigua WI
tel: (268) 462 0775
fax: (268) 462 2587
e-mail: tyronek@hotmail.com
Rooms: 6

Tradewinds Hotel B1
Dickenson Bay
PO Box 1390
St John's, Antigua WI
tel: (268) 462 1223
fax: (268) 462 5007
e-mail: twhotel@candw.ag
Rooms: 45

Trafalgar Beach Villas A2
Deep Bay
PO Box 1585
St John's, Antigua WI
tel: (268) 462 2548
fax: (268) 462 2531
Rooms: 26

Yepton Beach Resort A2
Deep Bay
PO Box 1427
St John's, Antigua WI
tel: (268) 462 2520
fax: (268) 462 3240
e-mail: yepton@candw.ag
www.yepton.com
Rooms: 38

Barbuda

Coco Point Lodge
Barbuda
PO Box 90
St John's, Antigua WI
tel: (268) 462 3816
fax: (268) 462 5340
Rooms: 12

The Earl's Villa and Efficiencies
Newgate Lane
PO Box 3180
St John's, Antigua WI
tel/fax: (268) 462 5647
e-mail: visitbarbuda@hotmail.com
www.antiguanice.com
Rooms: 3

KClub F2
Barbuda
PO Box 2288
St John's, Antigua WI
tel: (268) 460 0300
fax: (268) 460 0305
e-mail: kclub@candw.ag
Rooms: 33

Palmetto Beach Hotel F1
Codrington,Barbuda
Antigua, WI
tel/fax: (268) 460 0440
www.palmettohotel.com
Rooms: 22

VILLA RENTAL COMPANIES

Antigua Villas
English Harbour
St John's, Antigua WI
tel: (268) 463 7101
fax: (268) 463 8744
e-mail: marlowl@candw.ag
www.antiguavillas.com

Caribrep
39 Heritage Quay
PO Box W212
Woods Centre
St John's, Antigua WI
tel: (268) 463 2070
fax: (268) 560 1824
e-mail: caribrep@caribrepvillas.com
web site: www.caribrepvillas.com

Island Rentals
Antigua Yacht Club Marina
English Harbour
St John's, Antigua WI
tel: (268) 463 2662
fax: (268) 463 0825
e-mail: islandrentals@candw.ag

MARINAS
Antigua Slipway
English Harbour
tel: (268) 460 1056
fax: (268) 460 1566
e-mail: antslipway@candw.ag
web site: www.antiguaslipway.com

Antigua Yacht Club Marina
Falmouth Harbour
tel: (268) 460 1544
fax: (268) 460 1444
e-mail: falconec@candw.ag
web site: www.aycmarina.com

Catamaran Marina
Falmouth
tel: (268) 460 1503
fax: (268) 460 1506
e-mail: colslartigue@hotmail.com

Falmouth Harbour Marina
Falmouth Harbour
tel: (268) 460 6054
fax: (268) 460 6055
e-mail: falmar@candw.ag
web site:
www.antiguamarineguide.com

Jolly Harbour Marina
Jolly Harbour
tel: (268) 462 6042
fax: (268) 462 7703
e-mail: jollymarina@candw.ag
web site:
www.jollyharbour-marina.com

Nelson's Dockyard
English Harbour
tel: (268) 460 1053
fax: (268)
e-mail: npa@candw.ag
web site:
www.paterson.com/nelsondockyard

St James's Club
Mamora Bay
tel: (268) 460 5000
fax: (268) 460 3015
web site: www.antigua_resorts.com

MEDICAL CARE AND HEALTH

DENTISTS
Dr Bernard Evan-Wong, BDS
Gambles Medical Centre, St John's
tel: (268) 462 3050
fax: (268) 463 9601
Dr SenGupta, BDS and Associates
Woods Centre, St John's
tel: (268) 462 9312
fax: (268) 462 9314

DOCTORS
Dr Kelvin P. Charles
Long Street, St John's
tel/fax: (268) 462 4973
Dr Nicholas Fuller

Long Street, St John's
tel/fax: (268) 462 0931
Dr Marlene Joseph
Charlesworth Ross Street and
Independence Drive, St John's
tel: (268) 462 0542
Dr Frances Kelsick
Women's Clinic: Deanery Lane
St John's
tel: (268) 462 4133
Dr Prince Ramsey
Camacho's Avenue, St John's
tel: (268) 462 0522
fax: (268) 462 1614

HEALTH FOOD STORES
Discount Health Food Store
Nevis Street, St John's
tel: (268) 462 2207
The House of Vitamins
Redcliffe Street, St John's
tel: (268) 462 1370
fax: (268) 461 1049
Nature's Family Store
Lower Market Street, St John's
tel: (268) 462 1167
fax: (268) 462 1153
**The Sunflower Naturopathic
Centre**
tel: (268) 562 1200

HOSPITALS AND EMERGENCIES
The Adelin Clinic
Fort Road, St John's
tel: (268) 462 0866
Patients: (268) 462 9198
fax: (268) 462 2386
The Holberton Hospital
St John's
tel: (268) 462 0251/0252/1809/4634
fax: (268) 462 2461
Spring View Hospital, Barbuda
tel: (268) 460 0076
fax: (268) 460 0585
Medical Air Services
(Air Ambulance)
tel: (268) 462 6256/462 6239
Nevis Street fax: (268) 463 9250/
463 9225

OPTICIANS
Antigua Optical Company Ltd
Stapleton Lane Clinic
Stapleton Lane, St John's
tel/fax: (268) 462 0031
Dr Jillia Bird
Milburn House, Old Parham Road
St John's
tel: (268) 462 1513
fax: (268) 462 5622
Eyeland Optical

Woods Centre, St John's
tel: (268) 462 2020
fax: (268) 460 5905
Pearle Vision
General Insurance Building
Upper Redcliffe Street, St John's
tel: (268) 562 3937
fax: (268) 462 1976

PHARMACIES
Alpha Pharmacy
Redcliffe Street, St John's
tel: (268) 462 1112
fax: (268) 462 5258
Mon–Thurs 8am–8pm
Fri 8am–6pm; Sat 7pm–9pm
Sun 9am–1pm
Benjie's Department Store
Redcliffe Street, St John's
tel: (268) 462 0733
fax: (268) 462 0985
Mon to Thurs 8:30–5pm
Fri 8:30–6pm; Sat 8.30am–5pm
Ceco Pharmacy
High Street, St John's
tel: (268) 462 4706
fax: (268) 462 0225
Sun–Sat 8.30am–12 midnight
City Pharmacy
St Mary's Street, St John's
tel: (268) 462 1363
Mon–Fri 8am–5pm
Sat 8.30am–4.30pm
Food City Pharmacy
Deepwater Harbour Road, St John's
tel: (268) 480 8720
fax: (268) 480 8729
Mon–Sun 7am–11pm
J.F.K. Pharmacy
Long Street, St John's
tel: (268) 562 1620
fax: (268) 562 1621
Mon–Sun 8:30am–12:30pm
and 5:30pm–8:30pm
Sysco Pharmacy
Jolly Harbour, St John's
tel: (268) 462 5917
Mon–Sat 9am–5.30pm
Sun 11am–4pm
Woods Pharmacy
Woods Centre, St John's
tel: (268) 462 9287/8
fax: (268) 462 9289
Mon–Sat 9am–10pm
Sun 11am–6pm

SPORTS, BACK AND JOINT INJURIES
Dr Ward M. Allred
Upper Redcliffe Street, St John's
tel: (268) 462 3266

Denis Gobinet, Physiotherapist
Crosbies
tel: (268) 462 2231
fax: (268) 461 0761
Dr Patrick Matthews
All Saints Road, St John's
tel: (268) 462 0631
fax: (268) 562 0911
Dr K.K. Singh
Woods Centre, St John's
tel: (268) 462 1932
fax: (268) 461 8065
Tree House Body Shop
English Harbour tel: (268) 460 3434
fax: (268) 460 3200

POLICE

Royal Police Force of Antigua
and Barbuda Headquarters
American Road, St John's
tel: (268) 462 0125
fax: (268) 462 0954
Commissioner of Police
Mr Truehard Smith, QPM, CPM
tel: (268) 462 0360
fax: (268) 462 0954
Codrington, Barbuda
tel: (268) 460 0074/0354

PROPERTY PURCHASE AND RENTAL

AGENTS
ABI Realtors
tel: (268) 461 6162 fax: 562 0093
e-mail: abi@candw.ag
www.abirealtor.com
Empire Realty
tel: (268) 562 0023 fax: 461 1335
e-mail: camachod@candw.ag
John Hall Real Estate
tel: (268) 480 3060
fax: (268) 480 3064
e-mail: anjo_ins@candw.ag
Jolly Harbour Villa Sales
tel: (268) 462 1873
fax: (268) 462 2180
e-mail: pidduckg@candw.ag
Real Estate Antigua Ltd
tel: (268) 462 4525
fax: (268) 462 4527
Re/Max Antigua Ltd
tel: (268) 462 1873
fax: (268) 462 2180
e-mail: pidduckg@candw.ag
Tradewind Realty Ltd
tel: (268) 460 1082
fax: (268) 460 1081
TIME SHARE
Antigua Village Resort Sharing Ltd
tel: (268) 461 1569

fax: (268) 462 0375
e-mail: avbc@candw.ag
www.best-caribbean.com
O.P.B.M. Ltd
tel: (268) 460 6726
fax: (268) 462 8752
e-mail: opbm@candw.ag
www.timeshareantigua.com
St James's Club
tel: (268) 460 5000
fax: (268) 460 3015
e-mail: sjcexec@candw.ag
www.antigua-resort.com

TRAVEL AGENCIES AND TOUR COMPANIES

Alexander Parrish (Antigua) Ltd
tel: (268) 462 4458
fax: (268) 462 4457
e-mail: apal@candw.ag
www.mstarr.com
Antours
tel: (268) 462 4788
fax: (268) 462 4799
e-mail: antours@candw.ag
Bo Tours
tel: (268) 462 6632
fax: (268) 463 5336
e-mail: botours@candw.ag
www.botours.com
Bryson's Travel
tel: (268) 480 1230
fax: (268) 462 5324
Carib World Travel
tel: (268) 480 2990
fax: (268) 480 2995
arthurtonp@candw.ag
www.carib-world.com
Chez Blanche–Carib World Tours
tel: (268) 480 2990
fax: (268) 480 2995
e-mail: arthurtonp@candw.ag
Global Travel and Tours
tel: (268) 480 1000
fax: (268) 480 1006
International Travel Consultants Ltd
tel: (268) 462 0811
fax: (268) 462 4156
e-mail: itc@candw.ag
Jenny's Tours
tel/fax: (268) 461 9361
e-mail: burke@candw.ag
Kiskidee Travel and Tours
tel: (268) 462 0582
fax: (268) 462 4802
e-mail: kiskidee@candw.ag
Nicholson's Travel Agency
tel: (268) 463 7391
fax: (268) 480 8661
e-mail: kiskidee@candw.ag
Regal Travel and Tours

tel: (268) 460 7433
fax: (268) 463 7433
e-mail: regal@candw.ag
Travel Creations
tel: (268) 462 3963
fax: (268) 462 4780
Tri Star Travel
tel: (268) 481 1702
fax: (268) 481 1701
Wadadli Travel and Tours Ltd
tel: (268) 462 2227
fax: (268) 462 4489

Index

324 Index